scott 106
office

jean.whaley@pcc.edu

P9-DWP-965

Sahar.

English in Action

3

Homework
① workbook
Page 57-58

② Grammar
future tense
with will

Second Edition

Barbara H. Foley

Elizabeth R. Neblett

User sahar.vazirizadeh

Pa Saharsasan 2014

my Pcc

— How was your weekend?
— what did you do?
— where did you go?
— who were you with?
— what was the best part of your weekend? why?

— the best part of my weekend was ....

Homework

grammer   uses of will and I

workbook - Pages   59-60

HEINLE
CENGAGE Learning

Australia · Brazil · Japan · Korea · Mexico · Singapore · Spain · United Kingdom · United States

English in Action 3
Second Edition
by Barbara H. Foley and Elizabeth R. Neblett

Publisher: Sherrise Roehr

Acquisitions Editor: Tom Jefferies

Managing Development Editor: Jill Korey
O'Sullivan

Assistant Editor: Lauren Stephenson

Director of Content and Media Production:
Michael Burggren

Marketing Director, U.S: Jim McDonough

Sr. Product Marketing Manager: Katie Kelley

Sr. Content Project Manager: Maryellen E.
Killeen

Sr. Print Buyer: Susan Spencer

Cover / Text Designer: Muse Group, Inc.

Compositor: PreMediaGlobal

© 2010, 2003 Heinle, Cengage Learning

For product information and technology assistance, contact us at
Cengage Learning Customer & Sales Support, 1-800-354-9706.
For permission to use material from this text or product, submit
all requests online at **cengage.com/permissions**
Further permissions requests can be emailed to
permissionrequest@cengage.com

Library of Congress Control Number: 2010926622

ISBN-13: 978-1-4240-4992-9
ISBN-10: 1-4240-4992-X

Heinle
20 Channel Center Street
Boston, MA 02210

Cengage Learning is a leading provider of customized learning solutions with
office locations around the globe, including Singapore, the United Kingdom,
Australia, Mexico, Brazil, and Japan. Locate your office at
international.cengage.com/region

Cengage Learning products are represented in Canada
by Nelson Education, Ltd.

For your course and learning solutions, visit **www.cengage.com**
Purchase any of our products at your local college store or at our preferred
online store **www.cengagebrain.com**

Printed in the United States
1 2 3 4 5 6 7 13 12 11 10

Acknowledgments

The authors and publisher would like to thank the following reviewers and consultants:

Karin Abell
Durham Technical Community College, Durham, NC

Sandra Anderson
El Monte-Rosemead Adult School, El Monte, CA

Sandra Andreessen
Merced Adult School, Merced, CA

Julie Barrett
Madison Area Technical College, Madison, WI

Bea Berretini
Fresno Adult School, Fresno, CA

Mark Brik
College of Mount Saint Vincent, The Institute for Immigrant Concerns, New York, NY

Debra Brooks
BEGIN Managed Programs, Brooklyn, NY

Rocio Castiblanco
Seminole Community College / Orange County Public Schools, Sanford, FL

Sandy Cropper
Fresno Adult School, Fresno, CA

Carol Culver
Central New Mexico Community College, Albuquerque, NM

Luciana Diniz
Portland Community College, Portland, OR

Gail Ellsworth
Milwaukee Area Technical College, Oak Creek, WI

Sally Gearhart
Santa Rosa Junior College, Santa Rosa, CA

Jeane Hetland
Merced Adult School, Merced, CA

Laura Horani
Portland Community College, Portland, OR

Bill Hrycyna
Franklin Community Adult School, Los Angeles, CA

Callie Hutchinson
Sunrise Tech Center, Citrus Heights, CA

Mary Jenison
Merced Adult School, Merced, CA

Mark Labinski
Fox Valley Technical College, Appleton, WI

Rhonda Labor
Northside Learning Center, San Antonio, TX

Lisa Lor
Merced Adult School, Merced, CA

Eileen McKee
Westchester Community College, Valhalla, NY

Jennifer Newman-Cornell
College of Southern Nevada, Las Vegas, NV

Sonja Pantry
Robert Morgan Educational Center, Miami, FL

Eric Rosenbaum
BEGIN Managed Programs, Brooklyn, NY

Jodi Ruback
College of Southern Nevada, Las Vegas, NV

Linda Salem
Northside Learning Center, San Antonio, TX

Evelyn Trottier
Seattle Central Community College, Lynnwood, WA

Maliheh Vafai
Overfelt Adult Center, San Jose, CA

Nancy Williams
Bakersfield Adult School, Bakersfield, CA

Anne Bertin
Union County College, Elizabeth, NJ

Marinna Kolaitis
Union County College, Elizabeth, NJ

John McDermott
Union County College, Elizabeth, NJ

The students at the Institute for Intensive English
Union County College, Elizabeth, NJ
For your smiles and your stories

Contents

Contents

Contents

Reading	Writing Our Stories	English in Action	CASAS
• Discipline • Understanding an author's opinion	• A Note to the Teacher • Writing a school note	• Reading a Report Card • Understanding a Teacher's Comments	0.1.2; 0.1.3; 0.1.5; 0.1.8; 0.2.3; 0.2.4; 2.2.4; 2.3.3; 2.8.1; 2.8.4; 2.8.5; 2.8.6; 2.8.8; 3.6.5; 5.1.6; 7.2.4; 7.4.2; 7.5.4; 7.5.5; 7.5.6; 7.6.3; 8.1.1; 8.1.2; 8.1.3; 8.1.4; 8.2.1; 8.2.3
• Shoplifting • Reading online forums and discussions	• A Moving Van • Writing quotes	• Understanding the Arrest Process • Looking at a Jury Trial	0.1.2; 0.1.5; 0.1.6; 0.2.1; 0.2.4; 2.1.2; 2.3.1; 2.5.1; 5.3.1; 5.3.2; 5.3.3; 5.3.7; 5.3.8; 5.5.3; 5.5.6; 7.2.1; 7.2.3; 7.2.5; 7.4.4; 7.4.8; 7.5.6; 7.7.1; 7.7.3
• Automotive Service Technicians and Mechanics • Using the *Occupational Outlook Handbook* • Scanning for information	• Writing a Resume • Understanding resume format • Editing a resume	• Researching a Career • Thinking about Your Skills and Interests • Researching a Career Online	0.1.2; 0.1.5; 0.2.1; 0.2.2; 0.2.4; 2.3.4; 2.8.1; 2.8.2; 4.1.2; 4.1.3; 4.1.4; 4.1.5; 4.1.7; 4.1.8; 4.1.9; 4.4.5; 7.1.1; 7.1.2; 7.1.3; 7.2.5; 7.2.6; 7.2.7; 7.4.1; 7.4.2; 7.4.4; 7.5.1; 7.5.5; 7.5.6: 7.7.2; 7.7.3
• Smart Growth Communities • Visualizing the story	• The Pros and the Cons • Using *first*, *next*, and *finally* • Stating an opinion	• Getting to Know My Community • Learning about Community Activities • Going Online to Find Information about a Community	0.1.2; 0.1.4; 0.1.5; 0.2.1; 0.2.4; 1.4.1; 2.3.1; 2.2.3; 2.3.2; 2.6.1; 2.7.3; 2.7.6; 3.4.2; 4.1.8; 5.1.6; 7.2.3; 7.2.5; 7.2.6; 7.2.7; 7.3.4; 7.4.4; 7.5.6; 7.7.3

To the Teacher

In our many years of teaching, we have found that most textbooks progress too quickly. There is a presentation of a new structure and a few exercises to practice it, and then another grammar point is introduced. We discovered that our students needed more time with grammar — time to practice it, see it in context, use it to talk about a theme, and apply it to themselves. We could not find a series that provided sufficient practice and recycling, so we decided to write our own series — and *English in Action* was born.

English in Action is a four-level core language series for English language learners. Each level provides extensive practice and review of basic structures as it gradually adds more advanced structures to challenge students. It teaches language through thematic units that are clear, engaging, and interactive.

English in Action, 2nd edition is a comprehensive revision and expansion of the first edition. Content has been added, deleted, and changed based on our experiences teaching with the text and feedback from our students and colleagues. In addition, one of the major goals of the revision was to provide a more explicit focus on language competencies.

Book 3 is designed for students who have been introduced to the basic tenses and can apply them in everyday situations. The text presents structures in more challenging contexts and encourages students to expand their use of English while discussing topics such as geography, health, crime, and careers. By the end of Book 3 students will feel comfortable talking, reading, and writing about their lives and the world around them.

Each unit will take between five and seven hours of classroom time. In classes with less time, the teacher may need to choose the exercises that are most appropriate for the students. Some of the activities can be assigned for homework. For example, after previewing **Writing Our Stories,** students can write their own stories at home instead of working on them in class.

Features

- **Unit Opener:** Each unit opens with an illustration or photo and discussion questions to introduce the topic and draw the students into the unit.
- **Active Grammar:** The first half of the unit integrates the context and the new grammar. Users of the second edition will notice that there is enhanced grammar support, with full-color grammar charts and sample sentences. There are many whole-class, teacher-directed activities.
- **Pronunciation:** The pronunciation points, such as verb endings, contractions, question intonation, and syllable stress, complement the grammar or vocabulary of the lesson.
- **The Big Picture:** This is our favorite section. It integrates listening, vocabulary, and structure. A large, engaging picture shows a familiar setting, such as a restaurant, a doctor's office, or an office supply store. Students listen to a short story or conversation and then answer questions, fill in information, review structures, or write conversations.
- **Reading:** A short reading expands the context of the lesson. We did not manipulate reading selections so that every sentence fits into the grammatical structures presented in the unit! The readings include new vocabulary and structures. Teachers can help students learn that understanding the main idea is their primary goal. If students can find the information they need, it isn't necessary to understand every word.
- **Writing Our Stories:** In the writing section, students first read a paragraph written by an English language learner or teacher. Then they brainstorm and organize their ideas using graphic organizers. Next, students write about their experiences, ideas, or their research on a topic.

New to This Edition

The second edition includes two new units. Unit 3, Spending and Saving, focuses on present tense questions. We merged the two adjective units from the first edition into one (Unit 7: Around the World). This allowed for the inclusion of a second new unit, Unit 11: At Work, that focuses on modals.

The new features in the second edition include the following:

- The expanded and improved grammar feature presents easy-to-read charts and grammar notes throughout the units. In addition, grammar charts in the appendix provide students with a valuable reference of all the grammar points covered in the book. A new exercise, Teacher Dictations, is located in the Active Grammar section.
- **Word Partnerships Boxes** This feature presents high-frequency word collocations that relate to the theme of the unit.
- **Working Together** These partner and group activities are spread throughout the units. They encourage students to work together in active ways. There are pictures to discuss, interviews to conduct, conversations to develop, and discussion questions to answer. Several units also include a **Student-to-Student** activity in which each student in a pair looks at a different page containing a different set of information. Students exchange information in order to answer questions about a picture or to complete maps or charts with missing information.
- **Sharing Our Stories** These activities encourage students to read and talk about each other's writing.
- **Reading and Writing Notes** The notes give students additional support in developing reading and writing skills in English.
- **English in Action** This two-page section provides practice in the everyday skills students need to interact as community members, citizens, students, and workers. Activities include role plays, presentations, and problem-solving exercises to help students become more comfortable in real-life situations.

Ancillary Components

- **Student Book Audio CDs** These include all of the audio in the student book: dialogs, descriptions, pronunciation exercises, and The Big Picture.
- **Workbook and Workbook Audio CD** These components include additional vocabulary, grammar, reading, and writing activities related to key topics in the student book. Each unit also includes listening activities related to the grammar and theme of the unit. The new edition of the workbook includes new material to reflect content changes made to the new edition of *English in Action 3*.
- **Teachers Guide** The guide provides student book pages with embedded answer keys, audio scripts, and a grammar summary designed to give teachers more information about the grammatical structures and points taught in each student book unit. It includes new material to reflect content changes made to the new edition of *English in Action 3*. Each unit includes two new features, **More Action!** and **Teaching Tips.** These sections provide teachers with supplemental activities, explanations of difficult concepts, and a variety of classroom management topics.
- **Interactive CD-ROM** The CD gives students the opportunity for practice and self-study at their own convenience. It provides interactive practice activities of the grammar, vocabulary, listening, and speaking skills taught in the student book.
- **Presentation Tool** These pre-loaded interactive worksheets for each unit can be used on any IWB or dataprojector. There is also an asset bank with all Student Book 3 art files, grammar charts, audio files, and audio scripts.
- **Assessment CD-ROM with *ExamView®*** A bank of test items allows teachers to create and customize tests and quizzes quickly and easily.
- **Website** Teachers can access an **English in Action** website that provides additional practice activities, games, and the answer key to the workbook.

The complete *English in Action* package includes everything necessary for students and teachers to facilitate learning. Visit elt.heinle.com to learn more about available resources.

Fun, engaging, and action-packed!

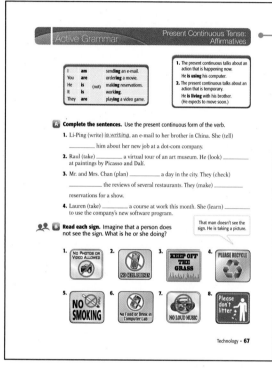

"Active Grammar" sections present clear, contextualized grammar explanations along with a rich variety of practice activities.

"The Big Picture" sections include engaging integrated skills practice around a story or conversation, motivating students to listen and use new grammar and vocabulary.

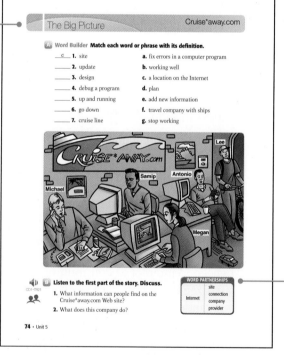

NEW TO THIS EDITION!

"Word Partnerships" provide students with common collocations to promote fluency.

Fun, engaging, and action-packed!

"Reading" sections provide before-you-read discussion questions, encouraging students to think about the reading topic.

UPDATED FOR THIS EDITION!

Interesting readings based on the unit theme recycle the vocabulary and grammar presented earlier in the chapter.

Reading   Computer Addiction

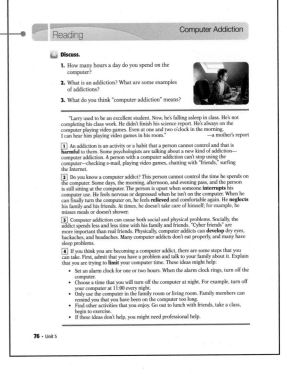

A Discuss.

1. How many hours a day do you spend on the computer?
2. What is an addiction? What are some examples of addictions?
3. What do you think "computer addiction" means?

"Larry used to be an excellent student. Now, he's falling asleep in class. He's not completing his class work. He didn't finish his science report. He's always on the computer playing video games. Even at one and two o'clock in the morning, I can hear him playing video games in his room." —a mother's report

1 An addiction is an activity or a habit that a person cannot control and that is **harmful** to them. Some psychologists are talking about a new kind of addiction—computer addiction. A person with a computer addiction can't stop using the computer—checking e-mail, playing video games, chatting with "friends," surfing the Internet.

2 Do you know a computer addict? This person cannot control the time he spends on the computer. Some days, the morning, afternoon, and evening pass, and the person is still sitting at the computer. The person is upset when someone **interrupts** his computer use. He feels nervous or depressed when he isn't on the computer. When he can finally turn the computer on, he feels **relieved** and comfortable again. He **neglects** his family and his friends. At times, he doesn't take care of himself; for example, he misses meals or doesn't shower.

3 Computer addiction can cause both social and physical problems. Socially, the addict spends less and less time with his family and friends. "Cyber friends" are more important than real friends. Physically, computer addicts can **develop** dry eyes, backaches, and headaches. Many computer addicts don't eat properly, and many have sleep problems.

4 If you think you are becoming a computer addict, there are some steps that you can take. First, admit that you have a problem and talk to your family about it. Explain that you are trying to **limit** your computer time. These ideas might help:

- Set an alarm clock for one or two hours. When the alarm clock rings, turn off the computer.
- Choose a time that you will turn off the computer at night. For example, turn off your computer at 11:00 every night.
- Only use the computer in the family room or living room. Family members can remind you that you have been on the computer too long.
- Find other activities that you enjoy. Go out to lunch with friends, take a class, begin to exercise.
- If these ideas don't help, you might need professional help.

76 · Unit 5

B Word Builder (Circle) the letter of each correct answer.

1. Eating too much _____ is **harmful** to your health.
   - **a.** fruit   **b.** junk food
2. You **interrupt** someone who is reading when you _____.
   - **a.** walk by quietly   **b.** start to talk to her
3. You feel **relieved** when your teacher tells you that _____.
   - **a.** you passed the test   **b.** you failed the test
4. If you **neglect** your health, you _____.
   - **a.** will get sick   **b.** will feel better
5. If you read without your glasses, you will **develop** a _____.
   - **a.** good story   **b.** headache
6. If you **limit** the time you watch TV, you watch _____.
   - **a.** more TV   **b.** less TV

C Write the number of the correct paragraph next to the topic of the paragraph.

___2___ The signs of computer addiction

_____ Ways to control computer addiction

_____ Problems that computer addiction can cause

_____ The definition of computer addiction

> **READING NOTE**
> **Identifying the topic of a paragraph**
> The topic of a paragraph tells what the paragraph is about.

D Answer the questions.

1. What is one sign of computer addiction?
   _____
2. What is one problem that computer addiction can cause?
   _____
3. What is one way to help a person limit the use of the computer?
   _____

Technology · **77**

"Word Builder" activities provide additional vocabulary practice, encouraging students to develop a deeper understanding of the target words.

Fun, engaging, and action-packed!

"Writing Our Stories" sections expand students' literacy by giving a closer look at real people in real communities and providing students with guided practice activities.

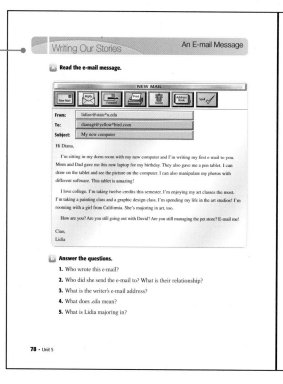

Writing Our Stories — An E-mail Message

A Read the e-mail message.

NEW MAIL

From: lidiav@state*u.edu
To: dianagt@yellow*bird.com
Subject: My new computer

Hi Diana,

I'm sitting in my dorm room with my new computer and I'm writing my first e-mail to you. Mom and Dad gave me this new laptop for my birthday. They also gave me a pen tablet. I can draw on the tablet and see the picture on the computer. I can also manipulate my photos with different software. This tablet is amazing!

I love college. I'm taking twelve credits this semester. I'm enjoying my art classes the most. I'm taking a painting class and a graphic design class. I'm spending my life in the art studios! I'm rooming with a girl from California. She's majoring in art, too.

How are you? Are you still going out with David? Are you still managing the pet store? E-mail me!

Ciao,
Lidia

B Answer the questions.

1. Who wrote this e-mail?
2. Who did she send the e-mail to? What is their relationship?
3. What is the writer's e-mail address?
4. What does *.edu* mean?
5. What is Lidia majoring in?

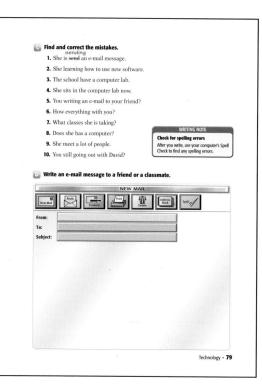

C Find and correct the mistakes.

1. She is ~~send~~ *sending* an e-mail message.
2. She learning how to use new software.
3. The school have a computer lab.
4. She sits in the computer lab now.
5. You writing an e-mail to your friend?
6. How everything with you?
7. What classes she is taking?
8. Does she has a computer?
9. She meet a lot of people.
10. You still going out with David?

> **WRITING NOTE**
> **Check for spelling errors**
> After you write, use your computer's Spell Check to find any spelling errors.

D Write an e-mail message to a friend or a classmate.

NEW MAIL

From:
To:
Subject:

NEW TO THIS EDITION!

"English in Action" sections practice the everyday skills students need to interact and solve problems in the real world.

UPDATED FOR THIS EDITION!

"Working Together" activities build learner persistence through cooperative tasks, enhancing the classroom community.

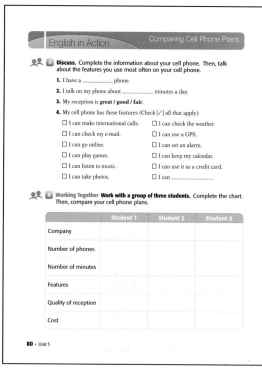

English in Action — Comparing Cell Phone Plans

A Discuss. Complete the information about your cell phone. Then, talk about the features you use most often on your cell phone.

1. I have a _____ phone.
2. I talk on my phone about _____ minutes a day.
3. My reception is **great / good / fair**.
4. My cell phone has these features (Check [✓] all that apply):

☐ I can make international calls.   ☐ I can check the weather.
☐ I can check my e-mail.   ☐ I can use a GPS.
☐ I can go online.   ☐ I can set an alarm.
☐ I can play games.   ☐ I can keep my calendar.
☐ I can listen to music.   ☐ I can use it as a credit card.
☐ I can take photos.   ☐ I can _____.

B Working Together Work with a group of three students. Complete the chart. Then, compare your cell phone plans.

	Student 1	Student 2	Student 3
Company			
Number of phones			
Number of minutes			
Features			
Quality of reception			
Cost			

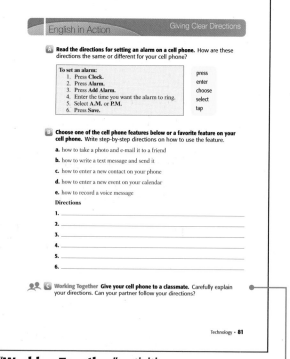

English in Action — Giving Clear Directions

A Read the directions for setting an alarm on a cell phone. How are these directions the same or different for your cell phone?

To set an alarm:
1. Press **Clock.**
2. Press **Alarm.**
3. Press **Add Alarm.**
4. Enter the time you want the alarm to ring.
5. Select **A.M.** or **P.M.**
6. Press **Save.**

press
enter
choose
select
tap

B Choose one of the cell phone features below or a favorite feature on your cell phone. Write step-by-step directions on how to use the feature.

a. how to take a photo and e-mail it to a friend
b. how to write a text message and send it
c. how to enter a new contact on your phone
d. how to enter a new event on your calendar
e. how to record a voice message

Directions
1. _____
2. _____
3. _____
4. _____
5. _____
6. _____

C Working Together Give your cell phone to a classmate. Carefully explain your directions. Can your partner follow your directions?

"Working Together" activities build workplace skills with teamwork tasks such as clearly communicating information and presenting and following instructions.

About the Authors

Liz and I work at Union County College in Elizabeth, New Jersey. We teach at the Institute for Intensive English, a large English as a Second Language program. Students from over 80 different countries study in our classes. Between us, Liz and I have been teaching at the college for over 40 years! When Liz isn't writing, she spends her time traveling, taking pictures, and worrying about her favorite baseball team, the New York Mets. I love the outdoors. I can't start my day without a 15- or 20-mile bicycle ride. My idea of a good time always involves being active: hiking, swimming, or simply working in my garden. I also enjoy watching my favorite baseball team, the New York Yankees.

Barbara H. Foley
Elizabeth R. Neblett

The First Week

A Read.

Hi. My name is Kenji, and I'm a student at the University of California, San Diego. I'm taking Listening and Pronunciation in Room 142. There are ten students in my class, four men and six women. We are from five different countries. Our class meets on Mondays, Wednesdays, and Fridays from 10:30 to 12:30. My teacher is Ms. Burak. Her office is in Room 12.

B Complete the sentences about yourself.

1. My name is _____ Sahar _____.

2. I'm a student at _____ P.C.C. _____.

3. I'm taking _____ English class _____ in Room _____ 125 _____.

4. There are _____ 25 _____ students in my class, _____ 12 _____ men and _____ 13 _____ women.

5. I have class on _____ monday , wednesday and friday _____.
                                                days

6. My teacher is _____ mrs jean _____. His / Her office is in Room _____ 123 _____.

Listen. Gloria is interviewing Kenji about his life in the United States. Take notes. Then, compare your notes with a partner.

CD1·TR1

Kenji:

Japan

six months

 Look at your notes. Answer the questions about Kenji.

1. What country is Kenji from?

2. How long has he been in the United States?

3. Why is he in the United States?

4. How many people are in his family?

5. Where does he live?

6. Is he a new student?

7. Does he work?

8. Is he married?

9. How old is he?

10. How often does he swim?

11. What other interests does he have?

12. What kind of music does he like?

13. What kind of computer does he have?

14. How will he meet other students at college? What do you think?

Positive ↑

Simple Present Tense: Affirmatives

> I **am** a student.
> I **live** in New York.
> I **work** part time.
> I **have** a computer.

> She **is** a student.
> She **lives** in New York.
> She **works** part time.
> She **has** a computer.

> They **are** students.
> They **live** in New York.
> They **work** part time.
> They **have** computers.

A **Complete the sentences.**

1. Eva and Mariola (be) _____ are _____ sisters.

2. They (study) _____ study _____ English at Summit Adult School.
   Peak - Top

3. Eva (work) _____ works _____ full time.

4. Mariola (have) _____ has _____ two small children.

5. They (go) _____ go _____ to school two nights a week.

Eva and Mariola

6. Eva (drive) _____ drives _____ to school.

7. She (pick up) _____ picks up _____ Mariola on the way to school.

8. On the way to school, they (talk) _____ Talk _____ about their families.

B **In your notebook, write ten sentences about Pierre.**

Name: Pierre Dorval   his name is ,

Age: 29   He's 29 years old

Country: Haiti   He's From Haiti.

Years in U.S.: Four   He has been in US, for
Four years.

School: Bay Adult School; Intermediate
red ✓ level; Mondays and Wednesdays,
9:00 A.M. to 12:00 P.M.
average
Marital Status: Married, one son   medium

Occupation: Waiter; West Hotel; six nights
a week

Interests: Soccer and guitar

Computer: Yes

Music: Jazz and rock

C **Working Together** **Interview a classmate.** Take notes.

1. What's your name? _____

2. What country are you from? _____

3. Is your family here in the United States? _____

4. How many people are in your family? _____

5. How long have you been in the United States? _____

6. Where do you live? _____I live here in Portland._____

7. Are you a new student in this school? _____

8. How do you get to school? _____

9. Do you have a driver's license? _____

10. Are you married? Do you have any children? If yes, how many?

    _____

11. Do you work? Where do you work? What do you do?

    _____

12. What are your interests? _____

13. What kind of music do you like? _____

14. Do you have a computer? _____

  D **Working Together** **Introduce your partner to the class.**

I'd like you to meet my classmate, Oscar. He's from Colombia. Oscar lives here in Los Angeles. He's . . .

CULTURE NOTE

To introduce a person, say:
I'd like to introduce (*name*).
I'd like you to meet (*name*).
This is my friend, (*name*).

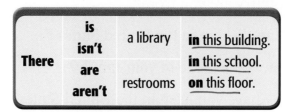

	is isn't	a library	**in** this building. **in** this school.
There	are aren't	restrooms	**on** this floor.

A **Complete the sentences about the school map.** Use the prepositions in the box.

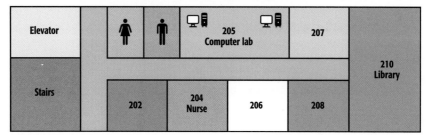

1. The library is ___at the end of___ the hall.

2. The nurse's office is ___in___ Room 204.

3. There is an elevator ___next to___ the stairs.

4. The women's restroom is ___across from___ Room 202.

5. The library is ___on___ the second floor.

6. The stairs are ___at the end of___ the hall.

7. The men's restroom is ___next to___ the women's restroom.

8. There are a few computers ___in___ the library.

9. There is a computer lab ___on___ the second floor.

10. There are many computers ___in___ the computer lab.

> **at the end of** the hall
> **in** Room 201
> **on** the second floor
> **next to** the stairs
> **across from** Room 202

B **Take a tour of your school.** Circle the rooms and facilities in your school.

ATM	copy machine	library	swimming pool
bookstore	counselor's office	nurse's office	theater
cafeteria	day care center	restrooms	tutoring center
computer lab	gym	student center	water fountains

 C **Working Together** **Talk about the facilities at your school.**

D **Answer the questions about your school.**

1. Is this school in a city?

2. Is this school large?

3. Is this school open in the evening?

4. Are there many students in this school?

5. Are there many computers in this classroom?

6. Is there a library in this building?

7. Is the library open today?

8. Is there a water fountain on this floor?

9. Are there any restrooms on this floor?

10. Is there a cafeteria in this building?

11. Is the cafeteria's food good?

12. Is there a bookstore in this building?

13. Are the books expensive?

14. Are the students friendly?

15. Are the students from many different countries?

> Is there a library in this building?
> Yes, there is.
> No, there isn't.

> Is this school small?
> Yes, it is.
> No, it isn't.

> Are there any restrooms on this floor?
> Yes, there are.
> No, there aren't.

> Are the students friendly?
> Yes, they are.
> No, they aren't.

CD1·TR2

E **Pronunciation: Sentence Stress Listen and repeat.** Then, listen again and underline the stressed words.

1. The cafeteria is on the first floor.

2. The nurse's office is across from the elevator.

3. The bookstore is in the student center.

4. The computer lab is on the third floor.

5. There is a copy machine in the library.

6. The restrooms are next to the stairs.

> The important words in a sentence receive stress. We say these words a little more clearly and give them a little more emphasis.

How much
How many

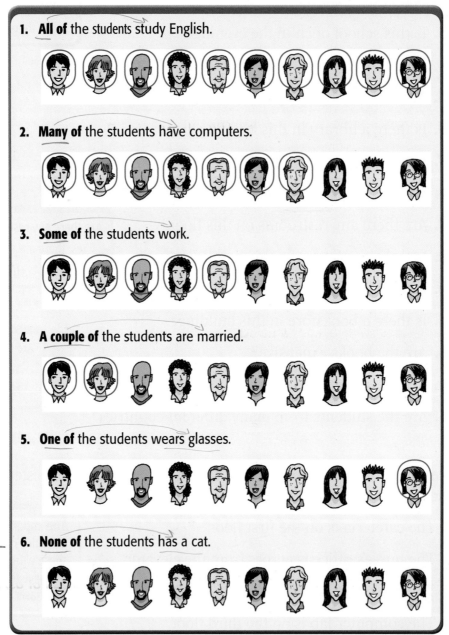

1. **All of** the students study English.

2. **Many of** the students have computers.

3. **Some of** the students work.

4. **A couple of** the students are married.

5. **One of** the students wears glasses.

6. **None of** the students has a cat.

p: 242 ろ←
explain

A (Circle) **the correct verb.**

1. Many of us **is / are** from Spanish-speaking countries.

2. Ten of the students **work / works** part time.

3. Most of the students **have / has** computers.

4. One of the students **take / takes** the train to school.

5. None of us **live / lives** in a dormitory.

WORD PARTNERSHIPS	
none	
one	
a couple	
some	of us
a few	of them
ten	of the students
most	
all	

B **The chart shows how students in Mr. Clark's class get to school.** Look at the chart and answer the questions.

1. How many students are in the class? *all of the students are in the class.*

2. How do most students get to school? *most of the students Drive to school.*

3. How many students take the bus? *Six students Take the bus.*

4. How many students walk? *some of the students walk to school.*

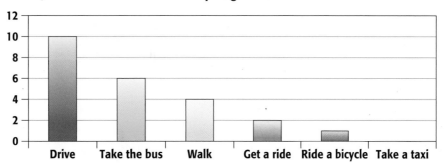

How do you get to school?

C **Complete the sentences about the chart in Exercise B.**

1. <u>Ten of the students drive</u> to school.

2. <u>Six of the students take the bus</u> to school.

3. <u>some of the students walk</u> to school.

4. <u>a couple of the students get a ride to school.</u>

5. <u>one of the students ride a bicycle to school.</u>

6. <u>none of the students Takes a Taxi to school.</u>
   or→ Take a taxi

D **Working Together** **Survey your classmates.** Then, complete the chart. In your notebook, write five sentences about the information. Use *all of us, many of us, some of us,* and so on.

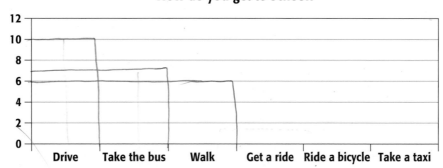

How do you get to school?

In my country, we can come to school a few minutes late.

Only the teacher can talk. We can speak if the teacher calls our name.

We call the teacher "Teacher," not his or her name.

We don't buy our books. The school gives us our books, notebooks, and pencils.

CD1·TR3

A **Listen to the statements about school in other countries.** Then, make statements about school in your native country and in the United States.

B **Check (✓) the statements that are true for your class.**

☐ **1.** All the students come to class on time.

☑ **2.** We bring our books, paper, and a pencil.

☐ **3.** It is OK to speak to your classmates when the teacher is explaining something.

☑ **4.** We have homework every night.

☐ **5.** It is fine to copy someone else's paper.

☑ **6.** I can bring a cup of coffee to class.

☐ **7.** I can text message during class.

☑ **8.** If I want to ask a question, I raise my hand.

☑ **9.** We speak English in class.

☐ **10.** I can leave school early every day.

C **Write three more expectations in your class.**

1. _____

2. _____

3. _____

In my country, we cannot bring food to class. But, it's OK to bring a cup of coffee into the classroom.

We work quietly by ourselves or listen to the teacher.

We have to turn off our cell phones before class.

We have many hours of homework every night.

D **Ask your teacher the questions about your school and your class.**

1. Where is your office?

2. Can I e-mail you? What is your e-mail address?

3. Does this school have a computer lab? Can I get a student account?

4. May I bring a computer to class?

5. Is there a library in this school? How do I get a library card?

6. Do we have homework every night?

7. What should I do if I don't understand something?

8. What are we going to study in this class?

9. Are there other classes I can take at this school?

10. What should I do if I am absent?

11. What is the school calendar? Do we have any vacation days?

E **Write three more questions about your school or class.** Then, ask your teacher the questions.

Reading

A **Underline the problem(s) each student is having with English.**

> **READING NOTE**
>
> **Comparing the text to your experiences**
>
> As you read, compare the information in the reading to your own experiences.

I work 50 hours a week as a taxi driver, so I talk to people all day. They understand me, but I know I make a lot of mistakes. No one corrects me. My vocabulary is strong. Grammar is my problem. For example, I don't use the past tense. I always say, "I drive him to the office this morning" instead of "I drove him to the office this morning." I'm trying to change little by little.

Ravi

I live in an area where everyone speaks my language. My neighbors and friends speak Spanish. I can speak Spanish at the supermarket, at the bank, and at the post office. I don't work, so it's really difficult to find ways to practice English.

Maria Luisa

I understand the grammar and the readings in my class and I think my writing is good, but I'm very nervous when I speak English. I don't want to make any mistakes because people will think that I'm stupid. Also, my pronunciation isn't good. When I speak, people often say, "What? Say that again."

Lian

X ← I have been in the United States for one year. I'm studying hard and I'm learning grammar, but the vocabulary is difficult. When I listen, I don't understand many of the words. When I try to read, there are two or three new words in every sentence. I feel discouraged.

(I want to give up)

Ketsia

Idea (handwritten)

B **Read the suggestions for learning English.** Add one more suggestion.

1. Watch one TV program in English every day.

2. Listen to songs in English. Sing along. *Speaking* (handwritten)

3. Try to speak English when you go out in the community.

4. Use the Internet. There are several English language learning study sites.

5. Don't worry about mistakes. It's natural to make mistakes when you are learning a language. *(It doesn't matter)* (handwritten)

6. Use English language learning computer programs in your computer lab.

7. Find a study partner. Work together one or two days after school.

8. Make a friend from your school who doesn't speak your language. Meet once a week after class for conversation practice.

9. Read the newspaper in English.

10. Be kind to yourself. Understand that learning English takes time.

11. Keep an English journal. Write a mistake you made while speaking. Then, write the sentence correctly. Or, write new words and sentences you hear.

12. _____

C **Give each student in the reading two or three suggestions from the list in Exercise B.** Write the numbers of the suggestions on the lines next to their names.

Ravi _____4_____ ____11____ ____9____

Maria Luisa ____6____ ____3____ ____9____

Lian _____1_____ ____2____ ____7____

Ketsia ____11____ ____6____ ____4____

D **Write two of your strengths in learning English.** Write two of your difficulties. Which suggestions can you try?

My Strengths — *(making a plan)* (handwritten)

listening - understanding (handwritten)

vocabulary. (handwritten)

My Difficulties

grammer (handwritten)

speaking (pronunciation) (handwritten)

future (Plan) (handwritten)

1. I'm going to ___*use the internet and read the newspaper*___ .

2. I'm going to ___*Try to speak English when I go out in the*___ .
community. (handwritten)

Present continuous (handwritten) { *I'm watching TV right now.* (handwritten)

Writing Our Stories

A **Read Sandra's story.** She is introducing herself to her teacher and class.

> **Start your story on the front of the paper. The red margin is on the left.**

> **Give your story a title. Write the title on the middle of the line.**

> **WRITING NOTE**
> Look carefully at the correct composition format. Refer to it when you write a composition.

> **Skip a line between the title and the story.**

> **Indent each paragraph.**

> **Put a space between paragraphs.**

> **Put your name and the date at the top or bottom of your composition.**

(title)

Hello

space

  My name is Sandra and I am from Bogotá, Colombia. I came to the United States five years ago. My sister, Gloria, is here with me, but my mom and dad and my six brothers all live in Colombia. I miss them a lot, but we e-mail each other all the time.

  I work full time at a small printing company. I do several jobs at this company. Sometimes, I do data entry. At other times, I am a press operator.

  I don't have much free time, but I enjoy music, especially rock and romantic music. On Saturday afternoons, I play tennis with the tennis club at my school.

  Right now, I'm studying English. I plan to major in communications and work in the TV industry. *Producing* I have many dreams. Someday I would like to live in Florida and have a family.

Sandra Martinez
September 10

B **Before Sandra wrote her story, she organized her ideas.** Look at the composition and complete her notes.

My Family	My Work	My Interests	My Future
Gloria	printing company	rock music	TV industry
six brothers	full time	romantic music	live in florida
Mom and Dad	data entry	tennis	have a family
	press operator	study English	

C **Correct the mistakes with the singular and plural nouns.**

1. I have two ~~brother~~ *brothers* and three ~~sister~~ *sisters*.
2. I work in *a* clothing store.
3. I'm *a* cashier.
4. I'm *a* student at *an* adult school.
5. I'm taking four class*es*
6. I have *a* computer.
7. I work part time, twenty hour*s* a week.
8. I came to the United States two year*s* ago.

> **WRITING NOTE**
>
> **Singular and Plural Nouns**
>
> 1. Use an article with a singular noun.
> 2. Use *an* with nouns that begin with a vowel sound: *a, e, i, o,* and sometimes *u.*
> 3. Do not use an article before proper names: *Tom, California.*
> 4. Plural nouns end in *-s* or *-es.* Some irregular plurals are *men, women,* and *children.* Do not use *a* or *an* with a plural noun.

D **Organize your ideas in the chart.** Then, write a story to introduce yourself to your teacher and your class.

My Family	My Work	My Interests	My Future
three brothers	student	light music	work at big company
mom and Dad		karateh	
my husband		study English	

E **Sharing Our Stories** **Work with a small group of students.** Share your stories with each other. Ask each other questions.

A **Look through this textbook and complete the information.** Then, share your answers with the class.

> When you open a new textbook, it's a good idea to look through the book quickly. You can see how the book is organized and where helpful information is located.

1. There are __274__ pages in this textbook.

2. Look at the table of contents. There are __15__ units in this textbook.
Two topics in the textbook are __Around the world__ and __moving__.

3. There is a grammar chart section that begins on page __240__.
The grammar charts for the past tense are on page __247__.

4. If I need spelling rules, I can look on page __252 to 253__
Write the third person simple present tense of these verbs:
fix __fixes__   wash __washes__
cry __cries__   buy __buys__

5. I can look up the irregular form of the past verbs on page __117__.
Write the past tense of these verbs:
break __broke__   fly __flew__
teach _____   ride _____

6. The audio script begins on page __258__.
The audio for Exercise A on page 34 is on CD __1__, track __8__.

7. The map of the United States is on page __274__.
There are __5__ states that border the Gulf of Mexico.
The four states on the border of the United States and Mexico are
__Texas__, _____, __Florida__, and __new mexico__.

8. The map of the world is on page __273__.
The names of the countries **are / are not** on the map.
Kanada - USA - mexico There are __3__ countries in North America.

9. Every unit ends with an **English in Action** section. Look at Unit 9, page 130.
The topic of Unit 9 is __natural Disasters__ مَدْرَسَة
The **English in Action** section presents _____.

A **Discuss the pictures and the study suggestions.** Add more study suggestions.

Grammar

- Look at the charts and examples.
- Read some of the sentences. Then, repeat them out loud without looking at the book.
- Write some of your own sentences using the new grammar.
- Review any mistakes you made in class or in your homework. Write the sentences correctly.
- Help from computer or Internet

Speaking

- Ask each other questions from the unit.
- Practice conversations from the unit.
- Do your homework together.
- Talk about the unit, school, your families, your jobs, and your lives!
- _____

Listening

- Listen to the audio several times.
- Answer the questions about the story.
- Listen again and look at the audio script.
- Do a dictation of some of the sentences.
- watch Tv and listining internet class

Vocabulary

word

- In a small notebook or on your cell phone, write two or three words each day that are new for you.
- Look up the words in a dictionary or ask someone the meaning.
- Write each new word in a sentence.
- Review a few words each day.
- _____

Unit
2 The Average American

A **Read about the average American.** Guess and circle the correct information.

1. The average American lives in a **house / an apartment / a condo**.

2. The typical American family has **one / two / three** children.

3. Most people eat **eggs / cereal / toast** for breakfast.

4. The average person drinks **one / two / three** cup(s) of coffee a day.

5. Most Americans **take a bus / walk / drive** to work.

6. The average American eats **one / two / three** hamburger(s) a week.

7. The average family has **one / two / three** TVs.

8. The average American watches TV **two / three / four** hours a day.

9. The average American changes jobs every **four / seven / ten** years.

10. The average person moves **five / eight / eleven** times in his or her lifetime.

B (Circle) **or add to the statements about your life.** Then, read your sentences to a partner.

1. I live in a **house / an apartment / a condo**.

2. My family has **one / two / three /** _____ children.

3. I eat **eggs / cereal / toast /** _____ for breakfast.

4. I **take a bus / walk / drive /** _____ to work.

5. I eat **one / two / three /** _____ hamburger(s) a week.

6. My family has **one / two / three /** _____ TVs.

7. I watch TV **two / three / four /** _____ hours a day.

C **Listen.** Charlie is talking about himself. Complete the chart. Then, compare Charlie to the average American male.

CD1·TR4

> The average American male gets married at 27. Charlie is 32, and he is still single.

Charlie	The Average American Male
32 - single	gets married at 27
is ____' ____" tall	is 5'10" tall
weighs ____ pounds	weighs 170 pounds
likes / doesn't like his job	likes his job
works ____ hours a day	works eight hours a day
earns $_____	earns $40,200
lives in an _____	lives in a house
_____ to work	drives to work
has / doesn't have a pet	has a pet

Active Grammar

Affirmative Statements	
I	
You	work.
We	eat breakfast.
They	
He	works.
It	eats breakfast.

Negative Statements		
I		
You		work.
We	don't	eat breakfast.
They		
He		work.
It	doesn't	eat breakfast.

The simple present tense describes routines and activities that happen every day, every week, every month, and so on.

A **Complete.** Use the correct form of the verb. Some of the verbs are negative.

1. I (drink) _drink_ two cups of coffee a day. My wife (drink) _____ tea.

2. We live near the elementary school, so our children (walk) _____ to school. They (take) _____ the bus.

3. She is a vegetarian. She (eat) _____ meat. She (eat) _____ a lot of fruits and vegetables.

4. Marco (get up) _____ late every morning, so he (eat) _____ breakfast.

5. My family is large. I (have) _____ five sisters, but I (have) _____ any brothers.

B **Interview a classmate.** What is the same about your day? What is different?

	You	Your Partner
1. Do you eat breakfast every day?		
2. Do you work full time?		
3. Do you take the bus to school?		
4. Do you use a computer every day?		
5. Do you cook for your family?		
6. Do you have a TV in your bedroom?		
7. Do you go to bed before midnight?		

Yes, I do.
No, I don't

C Pronunciation: Final s. Listen and repeat.

CD1 · TR5

/s/	/z/	/iz/
likes	owns	watches
wants	drives	uses
takes	studies	dances

  D Circle the sound you hear.

CD1 · TR6

1. /s/ (/z/) /iz/   **4.** /s/ /z/ /iz/   **7.** /s/ /z/ /iz/

2. /s/ /z/ /iz/   **5.** /s/ /z/ /iz/   **8.** /s/ /z/ /iz/

3. /s/ /z/ /iz/   **6.** /s/ /z/ /iz/   **9.** /s/ /z/ /iz/

 E Working Together Student to Student.

Student 1: Turn to page 254. Read the sentences in Set A.

Student 2: Listen and write the sentences under *Josh* or *Sam*.

Then, change roles. Student 2, turn to page 254 and read the sentences in Set B. Student 1, write the sentences under *Josh* or *Sam*.

Josh

1. _____

2. _____

3. _____

Sam

1. _____

2. _____

3. _____

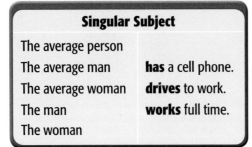

Singular Subject	
The average person	
The average man	**has** a cell phone.
The average woman	**drives** to work.
The man	**works** full time.
The woman	

Plural Subject	
Most Americans	
Most people	**have** cell phones.
Fifty percent of people	**drive** to work.
The men	**work** full time.
The women	

A **Complete the sentences.** Use the correct form of the verb.

1. The average woman (earn) _____earns_____ $35,745 a year.

2. Most full-time workers (receive) _____ a paid vacation.

3. About 30 percent of teenagers (work) _____ full or part time.

4. Most Americans (drive) _____ to work.

5. The average person (sleep) _____ 6.7 hours a night.

6. Women (do) _____ 70 percent of the housework in a family.

7. The average person (use) _____ a computer every day.

B **Dictation Your teacher will dictate the sentences on page 256.** Listen and write the sentences that you hear.

WORD PARTNERSHIPS	
50 percent	
half	of the students
about half	of the men
more than half	of the women
fewer than half	

Do you rent or own your home?

With sugar 63%

Black; no sugar 37%

1. _____

2. _____

3. _____

4. _____

5. _____

6. _____

C Working Together Work with a partner. Write sentences about each chart.

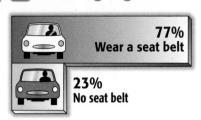

Do you wear a seat belt?

1. <u>The average person wears a seat belt.</u>

2. _____

Do you eat breakfast?

3. _____

4. _____

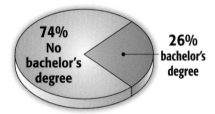

Do you have a bachelor's degree?

5. _____

6. _____

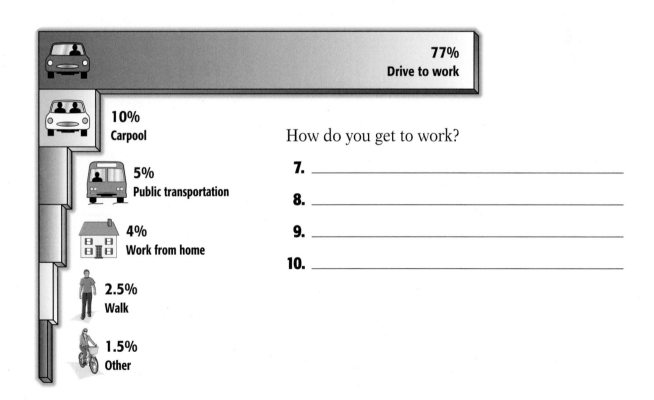

How do you get to work?

7. _____

8. _____

9. _____

10. _____

every morning	once a week	on the weekend	in the summer
every day	twice a month	on Sundays	in the winter
every night	three times a year		

Put time expressions at the end of a sentence.

A **Complete the sentences about yourself.** Use time expressions.

1. I study English _____.

2. I go to work _____.

3. I work overtime _____.

4. I go to the dentist _____.

5. I take a vacation _____.

6. I sleep late _____.

7. I buy new clothes _____.

8. I pay my bills _____.

9. I get a haircut _____.

10. I rent a movie _____.

B **Talk with a partner.** How often do you do each activity listed?

I go dancing every weekend.

I go dancing once a year!

1. go dancing

2. eat out

3. call my native country

4. order a pizza

5. do the laundry

6. eat at a fast-food restaurant

7. exercise

8. go to a party

9. read a magazine

10. check my e-mail

11. go to the beach

12. watch TV

always	100%
usually	80–90%
often	70–75%
frequently	
sometimes	50%
hardly ever	1–15%
never	0%

Put adverbs of frequency before most verbs.

I **often** <u>walk</u> in the park.
He **never** <u>takes</u> a taxi.

Put adverbs of frequency after the verb *be*.

I <u>am</u> **never** late for work.
She <u>is</u> **rarely** sick.

A **Put the words in the correct order.**

1. always / homework / do / I / my _____

2. tired / in the morning / He / always / is _____

3. her / She / seldom / sister / calls _____

4. class / is / interesting / usually / This _____

5. drives / He / always / too fast _____

6. weather / is / Florida / usually / in / The / beautiful _____

7. wear / They / their / always / seat belts _____

B **Talk about yourself.** Use an adverb of frequency in each sentence. Add two sentences of your own.

I always eat breakfast.

I never eat breakfast. I'm not hungry in the morning.

1. I eat breakfast.

2. I am polite.

3. I am homesick.

4. I get headaches.

5. I think about my future.

6. I am worried.

7. I go to bed early.

8. I do my homework.

9. I am late for class.

10. I take a taxi.

11. I am busy.

12. I lose my keys.

13. _____

14. _____

A Look at the pictures of an American family. What do you know about the family?

1.

Hours:
_____
Salary:
$ _____

Hours:
_____
Salary:
$ _____

2.

Time to work:
_____
minutes

Time to work:
_____
minutes

3.

$ _____

4.

5.

6.

CD1·TR7

B Listen. On the pictures, write the missing information about the Shaw family.

C **Read about the average American family.** Then, compare with the Shaw family.

1. The average family income is $67,300 a year.

   The Shaws' family income is $120,000 _____.

2. Most husbands earn more than their wives.

   _____.

3. Most workers drive to work.

   _____.

4. The average family has one pet.

   _____.

5. The average household is a mother and father and one or two children.

   _____.

6. The average family takes a vacation twice a year.

   _____.

7. Most families have three TVs.

   _____.

D **Complete.** Use the correct form of the verb. Some of the verbs are negative.

1. Mr. Shaw (drive) _*doesn't drive*_ a minivan.

2. Mr. Shaw (work) _____ close to home.

3. Mrs. Shaw (take) _____ public transportation to work.

4. Mr. and Mrs. Shaw (have) _____ one child.

5. Mr. and Mrs. Shaw (live) _____ in an apartment.

6. Andy's parents (work) _____ part time.

7. Mrs. Shaw (work) _____ in an office.

8. The family (eat) _____ out once a week.

9. Andy (have) _____ a pet bird.

10. The Shaws and the grandparents (live) _____ in the same house.

> The word **family** is singular, but people often use **they** to talk about family.
>
> The **family** eats out on Friday night. **They** like Chinese or Italian food.

A **Discuss.** Then, read.

1. Where do you attend class—at a community college, an adult school, a high school, or another kind of school?

2. What community college is nearest to your home?

3. What programs does the community college offer?

The Average Community College Student

About 40 percent of all college students in the United States attend community colleges. Community colleges are schools that offer two-year associate degrees, and certificates and licenses in a large number of careers such as paralegal, office assistant, and information technology. The 1,195 community colleges in the United States also **train** students for new jobs and offer courses in many subjects, including English as a second language.

Most community colleges have open admissions; they **accept** almost all students who apply. These students are often the first ones in their families to attend college. Most students need one or more **basic skills** courses in reading, writing, or math to prepare them for college-level classes. Eighty percent of students work either full or part time, so it is difficult to attend school full time. Two-thirds of all students attend school part time. The tuition at a community college is more **affordable** than at a four-year school. The average tuition is $2,400 a year, and about half of the students receive some financial aid. Many of the students who begin at a community college **transfer** to a four-year college for their junior and senior years.

Emily is a typical community college student. She attends school part time. As a young woman, she is part of the 60 percent of all community college students who are women. She is 29 years old, the average age of a community college student. Emily's parents and her older brother graduated from high school, but she is the first person in her family to begin college.

Emily works full time in the admissions office in the county hospital. Her **goal** is to become a registered nurse. She is taking pre-nursing courses and has been accepted to the nursing program. More than half of all nurses in the United States receive their degrees from community colleges.

Emily is a second semester student. During her first semester, she needed to take a course in basic math. This semester she is taking three courses. In the fall, Emily will attend school full time and work on the weekends. She applied for financial aid and is going to receive $1,000 a semester next year.

Most students take four years or more to **complete** their degrees at a community college. Emily hopes to have her nursing degree by the time she is 32.

B Word Builder (Circle) the correct word or phrase.

1. The program will **train** him to be a **police officer / student**.

2. The school **accepts** many **students / classes** each semester.

3. The student needed a **basic skills** course in **reading / financial aid**.

4. The tuition at an **affordable** school is **reasonable / expensive**.

5. Some students **transfer** from a two-year college to a **four-year college / job**.

READING NOTE

Finding Examples

A reading often gives facts about a topic. Then, it tells a story to give specific examples.

6. Emily's goal is to **become a nurse / apply to college**.

7. Most students need four years or more to **complete** their **degrees / tuition**.

C **Read the facts about community college students.** Find examples in the story to show that Emily is a typical community college student.

1. Community college students are often the first ones in their families to attend college.

~~Emily's parents didn't go to college~~ .

2. Most students need one or more basic skills courses.

_____.

3. Most students work full or part time.

_____.

4. Two thirds of all students attend school part time.

_____.

5. About half of the students receive some financial aid.

_____.

D **Look at the information about community college students in the reading.** (Circle) the chart that shows the correct information.

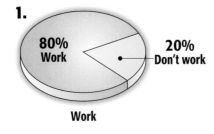

1.
80% Work
20% Don't work

Work

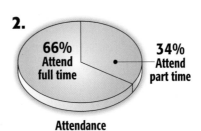

2.
66% Attend full time
34% Attend part time

Attendance

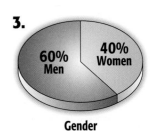

3.
60% Men
40% Women

Gender

A **Read.**

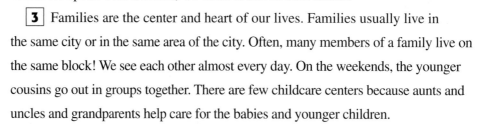

1 We are from Brazil. Brazil is the largest country in South America and one of the largest countries in the world. The people of Brazil speak Portuguese.

2 Brazilians are outgoing, expressive people. When people meet, they kiss each other on both cheeks. Men pat one another on the back or give each other a hug. When we speak with a friend, we often touch or hold hands.

3 Families are the center and heart of our lives. Families usually live in the same city or in the same area of the city. Often, many members of a family live on the same block! We see each other almost every day. On the weekends, the younger cousins go out in groups together. There are few childcare centers because aunts and uncles and grandparents help care for the babies and younger children.

4 The main meal is in the early afternoon, usually at 1:00. We have rice and beans with every meal and we know how to cook them many different ways. There is also meat or fish and a vegetable or salad at the meal. On Sundays, the whole family often eats together with fifteen or twenty people or more talking and laughing and enjoying each other.

5 People in Brazil enjoy sports, especially volleyball, basketball, and tennis. But the most popular sport is *futebol* (soccer in the United States). We think that our teams and players are the best in the world. Brazil has won the World Cup five times.

6 One of our favorite activities is going to the beach. The beaches are free. We put down our blankets, take out our suntan lotion, and turn on our stereos—loud! People walk along the beach selling food, drinks, hats, jewelry, and many other things. As the day continues, we begin to dance and it becomes like a party on the beach. We stay at the beach until late at night. Brazilians enjoy celebrations and parties. When you visit our country and receive your first invitation to a party, remember to come at least an hour late. In Brazil, we are very relaxed about time.

B Write the topic of each paragraph in the reading.

1. _____ introduction _____

2. _____ greetings _____

3. _____

4. _____

5. _____

6. _____

C Work with a group of students from your native country (if possible). Talk about the lives of average people in your country. Here are some topics you can discuss:

greetings	education
families	holidays
sports	weekend activities
food	religion
transportation	work

D Write a paragraph about the lives of average people in your native country. Choose three or four topics to write about. Give many details and examples.

E If there is a mistake with the underlined verb, correct the mistake. If the verb is correct, write *correct*.

1. Most Americans <u>drives</u> to work. _____ drive _____

2. Many Americans <u>take</u> public transportation. _____ correct _____

3. Most American women <u>doesn't get</u> married before age 25. _____

4. The average American <u>have</u> a computer. _____

5. The average American <u>doesn't eat</u> a large breakfast. _____

6. Most American families <u>has</u> one or two children. _____

7. Americans <u>eats</u> their main meal in the evening. _____

A **Read the information.** Complete the charts.

1. There are twenty students in a class. Half of the students drive to school. Five of the students take the bus. Five students walk.

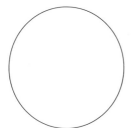

2. There are twenty students in a class. Ten of the students work full time. Eight of the students work part time. Two students don't work.

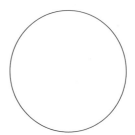

3. There are twenty students in a class. Fifty percent of the students study two hours a day. Twenty-five percent of the students study one hour a day. Twenty-five percent don't study.

4. There are twenty students in a class. Forty percent drink coffee in the morning. Thirty percent drink tea. Twenty percent drink juice. Ten percent drink water.

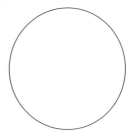

5. There are twenty students in the class. Six of the students are from Mexico. Four students are from China, three are from Ecuador, and three are from India. There are two students from Haiti, and one student each from Poland and Egypt.

B **Take a class survey.** Write the information about your class.

- One student is the leader and will ask each question to the entire class.
- Students will raise their hand to show their answers to each question.
- Two students are the counters. They will count each answer, including their own.
- Write the answers in your book.

1. Number of students in our class: _____

2. Seat belts

Who wears a seat belt? _____

Who doesn't wear a seat belt? _____

3. Work

Who works part time? _____

Who works full time? _____

Who doesn't work? _____

4. How many hours do you watch TV?

Who doesn't watch TV? _____

Who watches TV one hour a day? _____

Who watches TV two hours a day? _____

Who watches TV three hours a day? _____

Who watches TV four or more hours a day? _____

5. What country are you from?

Country	Number of Students
_____	_____
_____	_____
_____	_____
_____	_____
_____	_____
_____	_____
_____	_____

 C **Working Together** **Work in a small group.** Use the information in Exercise B. Draw five charts about your class to show the results of your survey.

3  Spending and Saving

A **Complete the sentences.** Use words from the box.

withdraw	loan	deposit
interest rates	charge	mortgage
budget	late fee	debt

1. When you put money into the bank, you _____ it.

2. When you take money out of the bank, you _____ it.

3. When you borrow money from the bank, you take out a _____.

4. When you borrow money to buy a house, you have a _____.

5. Many people don't use cash at the store. They _____ things on their credit cards.

6. Many people are in _____ because they charged too much on their credit cards.

7. Credit cards charge high _____.

8. If you don't pay your bills on time, you have to pay a _____.

9. To control expenses, many people have a _____.

B **Discuss.**

1. Where do you bank? Do you have a checking account? A savings account?

2. How many credit cards do you have? What is the interest rate on your cards?

3. Do you bank online?

4. Do you shop online? What sites do you like?

5. Not including housing, what is your biggest expense each month?

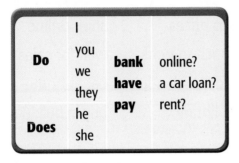

 A **Read the conversation.** Then, practice it with a partner.

Tom: Do you have a bank account?

Len: Yes, I do. I have a checking account.

Tom: Do you have an ATM card?

Len: Yes, I do.

Tom: Do you bank online?

Len: No, I don't. I pay my bills by check.

 B **Working Together** **Find someone who . . .** Walk around the classroom and ask the questions about spending and saving. If a student answers "Yes," write that student's name. If a student answers "No," ask another student the question.

Questions	Student's Name
1. Do you have more than three credit cards?	_____
2. Do you know the interest rate on your credit cards?	_____
3. Do you bank online?	_____
4. Do you have a budget?	_____
5. Do you compare prices?	_____
6. Do you know how you spend your money?	_____
7. Do you send money to your family?	_____
8. Do you go to the mall every weekend?	_____
9. Do you shop at garage sales?	_____
10. Do you spend too much money on clothes?	_____

C Complete the questions and answers about how the people save money.

Kendra	Jake	Tuan and Lana
uses coupons	compares prices	shop online
shops at garage sales	brings lunch to work	wait for sales
has a budget	pays credit card in full	eat at home
doesn't buy bottled water	uses the library	buy in bulk (large sizes)

1. __Does__ Kendra ____use____ coupons? ____Yes, she does.____

2. __Do__ Tuan and Lana ____eat____ out a lot? ____No, they don't.____

3. _____ Jake _____ prices? _____

4. _____ Kendra _____ her lunch to work? _____

5. _____ Tuan and Lana _____ online? _____

6. _____ Jake _____ the library? _____

7. _____ Kendra _____ bottled water? _____

8. _____ Jake _____ his credit card in full? _____

9. _____ Kendra _____ a budget? _____

10. _____ Tuan and Lana _____ in bulk? _____

D **Working Together** **Work with a group.** Make a list of five more ways to save money. Share your ideas with the class.

1. _____

2. _____

3. _____

4. _____

5. _____

Where	do	I you we they	work? study? save?
When			
Why	does	he she	

A **Match.**

___i___ **1.** Where does Liza work?

_____ **2.** What does she do?

_____ **3.** What time does she get up?

_____ **4.** How does she get to work?

_____ **5.** What does she wear to work?

_____ **6.** What time does the bank open?

_____ **7.** What benefits does she get?

_____ **8.** What time does the bank close?

_____ **9.** How do you know Liza?

_____ **10.** Does she like her job?

a. At 6:30 A.M.

b. Yes, she does.

c. A dress or a suit.

d. At 9:00 A.M.

e. She takes the bus.

f. She works at my bank.

g. She's a teller.

h. Medical benefits.

i. She works at State Bank.

j. At 4:00 P.M.

B **Ask and answer questions about the bank employees.** Use your imagination.

1.

Frank
security guard

2.

Derek
loan officer

3.

Juana
programmer

C **Listen and take notes about how Laura spends money each day.** Add up the total.

Expenses	Amount
Coffee and donut	$4.00
Total	

D **Complete the questions about Laura's daily expenses.**

1. What _does Laura buy at the coffee shop_ ? A coffee and a donut.

2. How far _____? About a mile.

3. Why _____? Because she gets up late.

4. How much _____? About $8.00.

5. What _____? A soda.

6. How much _____? $4.00 a day.

7. What _____? A lottery ticket.

8. _____? No, she doesn't have a budget.

E **Read the conversation.** Then, write a conversation about some of your daily or weekly expenses. You can use some of the ideas in the word box. Present your conversation to the class.

A: Do you know how you spend your money?

B: Not really.

A: How do you get to work?

B: I drive. I spend about $20 a week on gas.

A: How much do you spend a day on lunch?

B: I usually spend six or seven dollars.

A: What else do you buy every day?

B: I always get a cup of coffee on my way to work.

lunch
coffee
gas
clothes
bus / train
lottery tickets
childcare
clothes

1.

Apartment
Housing: $1,000 a month

2.

Gym: $30 a month
Three times a week

3.

College / part time:
$2,000 a semester

4.

Car loan: $400 a month
Insurance: $1,200 a year

5.

Dinner: $60
Every Saturday night

6.

Savings: $20 a month

1. _Where do they live?_ _____

2. _How much do they pay for housing?_ _____

3. _____

4. _____

5. _____

6. _____

7. _____

8. _____

9. _____

10. _____

When *who* is the subject of a sentence, it is always singular.		When *who* is the object of a sentence, it can be singular or plural.	
Who works at City Bank?	**Laura** does.	**Who** does he drive to work?	He drives **his brother** to work.
Who saves money every month?	**Henry and Ivan** do.	**Who** do they send money to?	They send money **to their parents**.

 A **Working Together** **Work with a group and answer the *Who* questions.** Then, make sentences about your group.

1. Who has more than three credit cards?

2. Who lives in an apartment?

3. Who has a mortgage?

4. Who banks online?

5. Who buys lottery tickets?

6. Who walks to school?

7. Who works at night?

> None of us has more than three credit cards.
>
> One of us has more than three credit cards.
>
> Three of us have more than three credit cards.

B **Write questions with *Who*.**

1. Molly drives _____ to school.

   <u>Who does Molly drive to school</u>?   She drives her daughter to school.

2. _____ wants to be a nurse.

   <u>Who wants to be a nurse</u>?   Nidia does.

3. _____ saves $100 a week.

   _____?   Josh does.

4. Carlos calls _____ every night.

   _____?   He calls his girlfriend.

5. Martin sends money to _____ every month.

   _____?   He sends money to his brother.

6. _____ belongs to a health club.

   _____?   Sofia does.

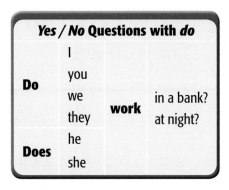

	Yes / No Questions with *do*		
Do	I you we they	**work**	in a bank? at night?
Does	he she		

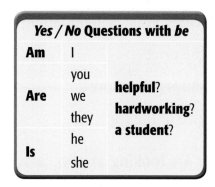

	Yes / No Questions with *be*	
Am	I	
Are	you we they	**helpful**? **hardworking**? **a student**?
Is	he she	

A Complete the questions with *Am, Are, Is, Do,* or *Does.*

1. __Do__ you have a credit card?

2. __Does__ he spend a lot of money?

3. __Am__ I careful with my money?

4. _____ she sometimes late with her bills?

5. _____ he work full time?

6. _____ gas expensive?

7. _____ you shop at the mall every weekend?

8. _____ they pay taxes?

9. _____ you good at saving money?

10. _____ he compare prices?

B Ask and answer questions with a partner.

1. you / work in a bank?

2. you / get up early in the morning?

3. you / a serious student?

4. your teacher / from the United States?

5. this class / difficult?

6. you / talkative?

7. your teacher / give a lot of homework?

8. you / always do your homework?

> Do you work in a bank?

> No, I don't.

A **Discuss.** What is important to you when you are buying a car? Check (✓).

☐ the price

☐ miles per gallon

☐ size of the car

☐ the resale price

☐ the car company

☐ reputation of the car dealer

B **You are looking at new cars.** Write three questions you would ask the car salesperson.

1. _____

2. _____

3. _____

 C **Listen to the conversation between Oscar Bravo, a new car buyer, and Dion Williams, a car salesman.** Complete the sentences with the correct number.

CD1·TR9

1. This car's engine has _____ cylinders.

2. Oscar drives about _____ miles a day.

3. The hybrid gets _____ miles per gallon.

4. Oscar's car gets _____ miles per gallon.

5. A hybrid would save Oscar _____ dollars a day.

6. The warranty for the hybrid car is _____ years.

CD1·TR10

D **Listen to the conversation between Oscar Bravo, a new car buyer, and Gloria Grayson, a loan officer at First City Bank.** Complete the car loan application.

Car Loan Application

Name: __Oscar__ __H__ __Bravo__
(First) (Middle Initial) (Last)

Present Address: __27 Mills Drive Apt 12__ __Dallas__ __Texas__ __75206__
(Street) (City) (State) (Zip Code)

Date of Birth: __5/12/77__ Social Security #: __123-45-6789__

Status: Single ☑ Married ☐ Separated ☐ Divorced ☐

Employer: __Park Industries__ Position: __Manager__ Phone: __765-555-1212__

Time at Job: _____ Salary: _____

Home: Own ☐ Rent ☐ Monthly Payment: _____

Loan for: Used Car ☐ New Car ☐ Loan Amount: _____ Term: ☐1 ☐2 ☐3 ☐4
(Years)

Down Payment Amount: _____ Account #: _____

E **Complete the sentences.** Use words from the box.

1. Mr. Bravo is talking to a _____ .

2. His _____ is $4,000.

3. His _____ is $800.

4. Mr. Bravo needs a _____ of $12,000.

5. Mr. Bravo's _____ for the car is $8,000.

6. Mr. Bravo has a _____ at this bank.

7. The _____ of the loan is three years.

monthly salary
checking account
term
down payment
loan
loan officer
rent

F **Discuss each statement about car buying in the United States.** Compare the information to car buying in your native country.

1. Most families in the United States have two cars.

2. The average price of a new car is $28,000.

3. People bargain with the car dealer when they buy a car.

4. Most people take out a loan when they buy a car.

5. Buyers check the car loan rates at different banks.

WORD PARTNERSHIPS

| take out | a loan |
| pay off | |

CULTURE NOTE

A 401(k) plan is a retirement savings plan sponsored by your company. From every paycheck, a small part of your pay goes into the plan. Often, your company matches part of your contribution. For example, if you put $50 a week into your plan, your company puts in $50 also. Your 401(k) plan is yours, even if you leave the company. This is money for retirement; you cannot use it until you retire.

READING NOTE

The organization of an article

Sometimes readings are organized so that readers can quickly see the main ideas. The most important ideas are in bold print.

A **Before you read the article, look at the title and headings.** Answer the questions.

1. What is the article about?

2. How many money saving tips are in the article?

3. Which tip talks about credit cards?

B **Word Builder** Match.

__b__	**1.** expense	**a.** an organized plan
_____	**2.** system	**b.** money that you spend
_____	**3.** tips	**c.** to reduce the amount
_____	**4.** record	**d.** work to reach a goal
_____	**5.** cut	**e.** ideas or suggestions
_____	**6.** effort	**f.** a written statement of money spent

Money Saving Tips

In 1970, Omar got his first job. His yearly salary was $4,000. His parents told him, "Put 10 percent of your paycheck away for your future." Omar put $400 in the bank. Over the years, Omar continued to save 10 percent of his salary. His next employer had a 401(k) plan. Omar continued to save 10 percent of his salary and his employer added four percent. When Omar retired last year, he had $425,000 in his 401(k) retirement plan!

How do people save money? Omar's **system** was simple—put 10 percent of every paycheck into a retirement plan. Here are some savings **tips** from money experts.

1. Keep a budget. This is the first step in any savings plan. How much money comes in every month? Where does it go? For a few months, keep a **record** of your expenses—car payments, gas, phone, rent, utility bills, food, eating out. Don't forget about the large yearly **expenses** like car insurance.

2. Make a plan. Decide what you are saving for. A car? A house? Retirement? How much money do you need for each?

3. Use your credit card wisely. Try to pay for items with cash or a debit card. When you use credit cards, pay them off as soon as possible. For example, if you pay $1,200 in credit card interest a year, that is $1,200 you could save.

4. Buy used. It is possible to buy lightly used items for half or less of the original price. Stop at garage sales and look for furniture and children's items. There are websites for used items in excellent condition. Car dealers offer late model used cars with one-year warranties. These cars are coming off leases and often have low mileage.

5. Cut your spending. Try to figure out how to **cut** your expenses. If you have a cell phone, can you drop your landline? Can you refinance your mortgage? Can you get a better price on car insurance? Do you need two cars?

Saving money is a family **effort**. Sit down with your partner and talk about money. As you start to save, you will feel more secure and satisfied as your dollars start to grow.

 Go online. Use the keywords below to find a basic budget worksheet. Print and bring several worksheets to class. Compare the worksheets and decide which is the most useful.

Keywords

Free budget worksheet

Basic budget planner

Basic budget form

A **Discuss.** Have you ever written a business letter? Why did you write it?

B **Read.**

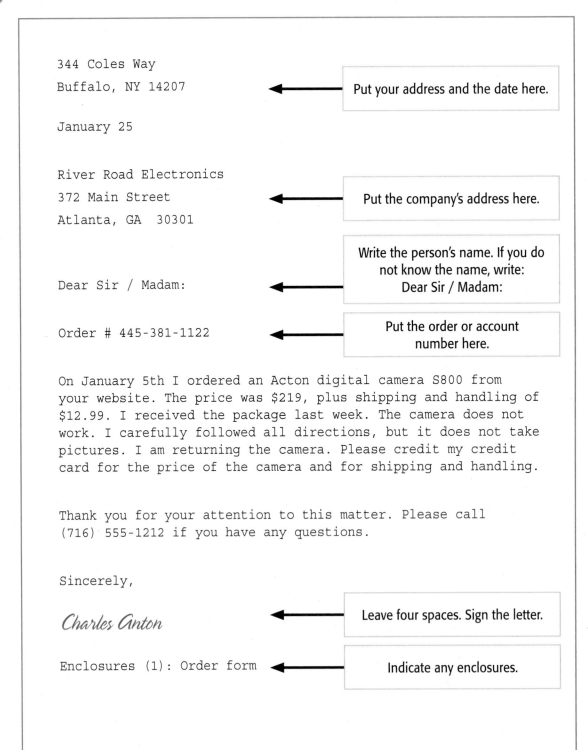

344 Coles Way
Buffalo, NY 14207

January 25

River Road Electronics
372 Main Street
Atlanta, GA 30301

Dear Sir / Madam:

Order # 445-381-1122

On January 5th I ordered an Acton digital camera S800 from your website. The price was $219, plus shipping and handling of $12.99. I received the package last week. The camera does not work. I carefully followed all directions, but it does not take pictures. I am returning the camera. Please credit my credit card for the price of the camera and for shipping and handling.

Thank you for your attention to this matter. Please call (716) 555-1212 if you have any questions.

Sincerely,

Charles Anton

Enclosures (1): Order form

Put your address and the date here.

Put the company's address here.

Write the person's name. If you do not know the name, write:
Dear Sir / Madam:

Put the order or account number here.

Leave four spaces. Sign the letter.

Indicate any enclosures.

C Answer the questions.

1. Who wrote the letter? _____

2. When did he write the letter? _____

3. When did he buy the camera? _____

4. Did he buy the camera from a store? _____

5. Why is he returning the camera? _____

6. Does he want another camera from the company? _____

7. Does he want the company to send him a check? _____

8. What enclosures is he sending to the company? _____

D Edit the addresses. Be sure to capitalize the first letter of all the words.

1. 15 Pine street
   apartment 2
   Edison, nj 08817

2. 921 tenth Avenue
   detroit, MI 48201

3. 56 Gilman road
   Las vegas, Nv 89044

E Write a business letter to a company in your area. Use one of these suggestions or think of another reason.

1. You want to return a product.

2. Your credit card company made a mistake on your bill.

3. The telephone company charged you for a call you did not make.

4. You want to thank a business for excellent service.

5. You want to order a product or request information.

> **WRITING NOTE**
>
> **Business Letters**
> 1. Start all lines on the left.
> 2. Use a business letter format.
> 3. Put spaces between each section of the letter.
> 4. Make sure the letter is short and clear.
> 5. Sign the letter.
> 6. Include the names of any enclosures.

A **Oscar Bravo needs a $12,000 car loan.** He is looking at car loan rates and terms at different places. Look at the charts and write the amounts.

Town Bank — Interest Rate: 6%

Number of Years	Monthly Payment	Total Interest Paid	Total Cost of Car
2	$531.85	$764.34	$12,764.34
3	$365.06	$1,142.28	$13,142.28
4	$281.82	$1,527.38	$13,527.38
5	$231.99	$1,919.62	$13,919.62

City Bank — Interest Rate: 9%

Number of Years	Monthly Payment	Total Interest Paid	Total Cost of Car
2	$548.22	$1,157.21	$13,157.21
3	$381.60	$1,737.48	$13,737.48
4	$298.62	$2,333.78	$14,333.78
5	$249.10	$2,946.02	$14,946.02

Car Dealer — Interest Rate: 12%

Number of Years	Monthly Payment	Total Interest Paid	Total Cost of Car
2	$564.88	$1,557.16	$13,557.16
3	$398.57	$2,348.58	$14,348.58
4	$316.01	$3,168.29	$15,168.29
5	$266.93	$4,016.00	$16,016.00

1. _____ offers the lowest interest rate.

2. The monthly payment for a three-year loan at Town Bank: _____

3. The monthly payment for a three-year loan at City Bank: _____

4. The monthly payment for a three-year loan at the car dealer: _____

5. The total interest for a five-year loan at Town Bank: _____

6. The total interest for a five-year loan at City Bank: _____

7. The total interest for a five-year loan at the car dealer: _____

8. The total cost of a four-year loan at Town Bank: _____

9. The total cost of a four-year loan at City Bank: _____

10. The total cost of a four-year loan at the car dealer: _____

B Discuss.

Oscar wants his car payments to be between $350 and $400. Which loan should he choose? _____

C Name six items that people take out loans for.

1. _____

2. _____

3. _____

4. _____

5. _____

6. _____

> **CULTURE NOTE**
>
> **Loan Advice**
> - Shop around to find the bank or store that offers the lowest interest rates.
> - Be sure that the interest rate will remain the same during the life of the loan.
> - Pay off the loan in the shortest time possible.
> - Do not miss a loan payment. If you miss a payment, it will be more difficult to get another loan in the future.

D Go online. Find a loan calculator. Use the calculator to complete the chart for a $5,000 loan. Then, choose a different amount and complete the chart.

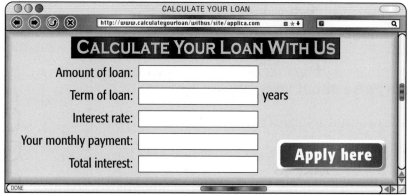

Loan amount: $5,000	Loan amount: _____
Term: 2 years	Term: 2 years
6%: _____	6%: _____
9%: _____	9%: _____
12%: _____	12%: _____

Volcano

mt. St. Helens (1980)

Unit

4

The States

A **Discuss.** Give an example of each of these geographical features in the United States: a lake, a river, a mountain range, a seaport, an island, and a canyon.

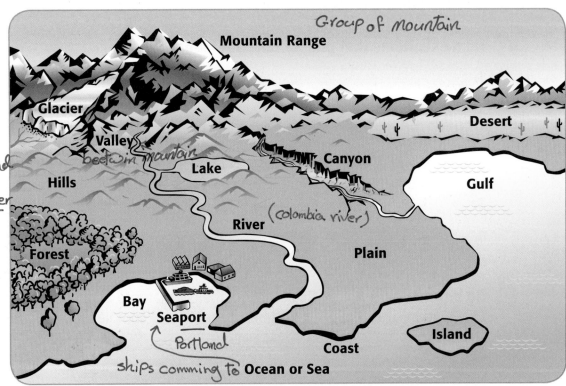

Group of mountain

Mountain Range

Glacier

Valley

bedroin mountain

Lake

Hills

rivers in Portland is willamete river

Canyon

Desert

Gulf

River *(colombia river)*

Plain

Forest

Bay

Seaport

Portland

Island

ships comming to **Ocean or Sea**

Coast

B (Circle) *True* or *False* about your city.

1. We can see mountains from our school.   (True)   False

2. This city / town is on a river.   (True)   False

3. If I drive an hour, I can see the Atlantic or the Pacific Ocean.   *next to*   (True)   False

Salem **4.** This city is the capital of the state.   True   (False)

5. There is a desert near here.   True   (False)

6. This city / town is near a lake.   (True)   False

7. There is a large forest near here.   (True)   False

8. This city / town is also a seaport.   (True)   False

> **Count nouns** are people, places, or things that we can count individually (one by one).
> Count nouns can be singular or plural.
> Expressions with *one of the*, *every*, and *each* are singular.
>   **Every** state **has** a capitol building.
> Expressions with *a few of the*, *some of the*, *many of the*, *all of the*, etc., are plural.
>   **All of the** states **have** capitol buildings.

A **Write *S* next to the singular nouns.** Write *P* next to the plural nouns.

1. __S__ a desert
2. __P__ mountains
3. __S__ a forest
4. __P__ rivers
5. __P__ seaports

6. __S__ one of the cities
7. __S__ a mountain range
8. __P__ a few of the parks
9. __S__ every national park
10. __P__ many of the people

11. __S__ each of the farms
12. __P__ all of the states
13. __P__ millions of tourists
14. __S__ every state
15. __P__ several of the islands

B **Circle the correct form of the verb.**

1. A plain **(is)** / **are** a large area of flat land.

2. A range **(is)** / **are** a group of mountains.

3. Canyons **is** / **(are)** long, deep cracks in the earth's surface.

4. Glaciers **is** / **(are)** large rivers of slow-moving ice.

5. Every major city **(has)** / **have** a lot of traffic.

6. Many of the rivers **begins** / **(begin)** in the mountains.

7. Millions of tourists **visits** / **(visit)** the national parks every summer.

8. Every dairy farm **(produces)** / **produce** milk.

9. Every state **(has)** / **have** interesting places to visit.

10. All the states **has** / **(have)** interesting places to visit.

11. Each farm **(grows)** / **grow** many kinds of vegetables.

12. All road maps **shows** / **(show)** cities and highways.

13. Most cities **has** / **(have)** skyscrapers.

a skyscraper

The States · **51**

A Map of the United States

 A **Pronunciation: Syllables and Stress** **Listen and repeat.**
CD1·TR11

1. the At·lán·tic Ó·cean
2. the Ap·pa·lá·chian Móun·tains
3. the Mis·sis·síp·pi Rí·ver

 B **Listen and mark the stress.**
CD1·TR12

1. Ca·na·da
2. Mex·i·co
3. the U·ni·ted States
4. the Rock·y Moun·tains
5. the Grand Can·yon
6. A·las·ka
7. Ha·wai·i
8. the Pa·ci·fic O·cean
9. Death Val·ley

 C **Listen.** Point to each location on the map.
CD1·TR13

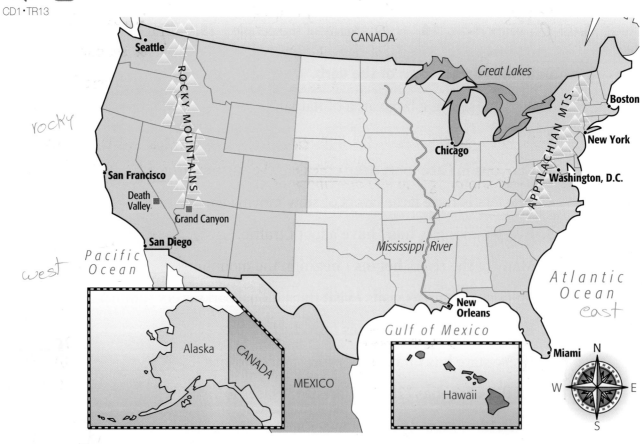

There	is	**a**	seaport	on the <u>coast</u>.ساحل
	isn't		desert	in the North.
	are	**a few**	seaports	in the South.
		several	mountains	in the East.
		many	rivers	in the West.
		a lot of	forests	in the central part of the country.
	aren't	**any**	farms	

 A **Make sentences about the map of the United States.**

> There are many seaports on the coast.

> There is a high mountain range in the West.

1. farms

2. national parks

3. major cities

4. mountain range

5. ranches

6. large lakes

7. major river

8. seaport

9. desert

B **Working Together** **Work with a partner.** Plan the perfect island. On the map, draw the features you would like, such as mountains, a river, a lake, and farms. Then, join another group and describe your island.

> There is a seaport in the East, and there's a small town on the seaport. To the north of the seaport is a plain; there are a few farms there.

scenery → منظره - چشم‌انداز   *Pollution* → آلودگی   *scrape* → ۲

industry → صنعت   *ranch* → مزرعه‌پرورش اشیاء ۱

Active Grammar — Count and Non-count Nouns

> **Count nouns** are items that we can count individually (one by one): lake—lakes. They can be singular or plural.
> **Non-count nouns** cannot be counted. They are always singular.
> 1. Liquids or gases: water, oil, oxygen, rain
> 2. Items that are too small or too numerous to count: sand, corn, rice
> 3. General categories: traffic, scenery, music, tourism
> 4. Ideas: information, beauty, work
>
> *Note:* Some words can be both count and non-count: crime—crimes, industry—industries.

A Write the words under *Count Nouns* or *Non-count Nouns*.

mountain C   seaport C   museum C   university C
industry both   farm C   snow N-C   ranch C
pollution N-C   crime both   skyscraper C   tourism N-C
tourist C   river C   factory C   rain N-C
unemployment N-C   noise C   traffic N-C   country C

Count Nouns	Non-count Nouns
mountain	industry
industry	pollution
tourist	unemployment
seaport	crime
farm	snow
crime	traffic
river	tourism
noise	rain
museum	noise
skyscraper	
factory	
university	
ranch	
country	

WORD PARTNERSHIPS

air	
water	pollution
noise	

54 · Unit 4

		no	traffic	in this city.
There	is	**a little**	pollution	in this city.
		a lot of	rain	in my country.
	isn't	**any**	crime	in the United States.
		much	industry	

A **Complete the sentences about the city.** Use *there is, there isn't, there are,* or *there aren't.*

1. ___There are___ a lot of factories in the city, so ___there is___ a lot of pollution.

2. ___There is___ a lot of traffic in the city, so ___there is___ a lot of noise.

3. ___There are___ a lot of large companies in the city, so ___there isn't___ much unemployment.

4. ___There is___ a large seaport near the city, so ___there is___ a lot of traffic in the bay.

5. ___There are___ many museums, restaurants, and shows, so ___there is___ a lot of tourism.

6. ___There are___ many police officers, so ___there isn't___ much crime.

there aren't much crimes

B **Talk about the city or area that your school is in.**

> There are a few colleges and universities near here.

> There is a lot of tourism in this city.

1. colleges and universities
2. tourism
3. factories
4. crime
5. museums
6. ethnic restaurants

7. traffic
8. nightclubs
9. unemployment
10. fast-food restaurants
11. noise
12. hospitals

| How many | museums parks | are | there | in your city? |
| How much | snow traffic | is | | in your country? |

 A **Working Together** **Complete the questions.** Use *How much* or *How many*. Then, talk with a group of three or four students about your native countries. If possible, each student should be from a different country.

1. What country are you from?

2. ___How many___ skyscrapers are there in your country?

3. ___How much___ tourism is there in your country?

4. ___How much___ traffic is there in your country?

5. ___How many___ immigrants are there in your country?

6. ___How many___ farms are there in your country?

7. ___How much___ snow is there in your country?

8. ___How many___ mountain ranges are there in your country?

9. ___How many___ crime is there in your country?
    much

10. ___How many___ universities are there in your country?

> I'm from Japan. There are many skyscrapers in my country.

 B **Working Together** **Student to Student.** Ask and answer questions about Canada and Mexico. Use *How much* or *How many*. Complete the chart.

Student 1: Turn to page 254. Complete the chart about Canada.

Student 2: Look at the chart below. Complete the information about Mexico.

How many deserts are there in mexico?
How many
How many
How much

	Mexico	Canada
Tourism	a lot	a lot
Deserts	nine	one
Mountains	many	many
National parks	64	42
Snow	very little	a lot
Ski resorts	one	many
Official languages	one	two

> How much tourism is there in Mexico?

> There is a lot of tourism in Mexico.

56 · Unit 4

complain →r

~~There are~~ too ma~~n~~y rain in this city.
is   much

Active Grammar — Too many, too much, not enough

There are too many homeless people.
There is Too much Traffic (in) downtown.

There	is	**too much**	rain.
		not enough	industry.
	are	**too many**	fast-food restaurants.
		not enough	parks.

We often use not enough and too many / too much to talk about problems or to complain.

not enough = less than you want or need

There are**n't enough** farms in that country. There is**n't enough** food.

too many, too much = more than you want or need

There are **too many** cars on the road. There is **too much** traffic.

My Teacher ask me to many questions.

(Persian handwritten annotation)

A Listen to the complaints about world problems. Complete the sentences. Use the words in the box.

CD1·TR14

There are not enough good People in our world.
There is   "   "

| aren't enough | are too many | isn't enough | is too much |

1. There __isn't enough__ rain.

2. There __aren't enough__ jobs.

3. There __are Too many__ homeless people.

4. There __isn't enough__ food for everyone.

5. There __isn't too much__ snow.

6. There __is too much__ traffic.

7. There __isn't enough__ public transportation.

8. There __are too many__ plastic bottles.

B Working Together **Work with a group.** Make a list of five things you like and five things you don't like about the area where you live.

There are lots of good restaurants.

There is too much crime.

Things we like	Things we don't like
1. *There i_ _ _ _ _ _*	1. *There is too much rain*
2.	2. *There is too many homeless People*
3.	3. *There isn't enough money for all Peopl*
4.	4.
5.	5.

A **Discuss the feature map of Montana.**

1. What are Montana's borders?

2. What is the capital?

3. What geographical features do you see on this map?

land

summer ball

🔊 **B** **Look at the map and listen.** As you listen, point to each location on the map. Then, make statements. Use the words in the box.

CD1•TR15

The Forth largest

GENERAL AND SPECIFIC STATEMENTS
General statements: There is a large national park in Montana. Specific statements: Glacier National Park is in Montana. Do not say: There is Glacier National Park in Montana.

are in the east of montana

There is alot of rain in the western montana

there are many native Americans in Montana.

rain	horse ranches	tourism
the Rocky Mountains	the Missouri River	lakes
Native Americans	rivers	Fort Peck Lake
Indian reservations	Glacier National Park	Canada
Helena *is the*	national park	snow

Capital of Montana.

many Native Americans live on reservations.
the Missouri River is in Montana.

beach
bitch → femal. dog

C **Circle** the letter of the correct answer.

1. What is to the north of Montana?

    a. Wyoming **b.** Canada **c.** Glacier National Park

2. What is the weather like in the western part of Montana?

    a. It's cold and wet. **b.** It's cold and dry. **c.** It's hot and wet.

3. What is the weather like in the eastern part of Montana?

    a. It's cold and wet. **b.** It's cold and dry. **c.** It's hot and dry.

4. Why is the eastern part of Montana dry?

    a. Because it is so far north. **b.** Because the mountains stop the clouds.

5. Where are there many horse ranches?

    a. in the eastern part of the state **b.** in the western part of the state

6. What is one of Montana's major industries?

    a. fishing **b.** manufacturing **c.** tourism

make sth

D **Complete the sentences.** Use the correct form of the verb.

1. The Missouri River (begin) _____ begins _____ in Montana.

2. The western part of Montana (receive) _____ receives _____ a lot of snow.

3. Montana (have) _____ has _____ very cold winters.

4. Thousands of tourists (visit) _____ visit _____ Montana.

5. The Rocky Mountains (stop) _____ stop _____ the rain clouds.

6. Many of the Native Americans (live) _____ live _____ on reservations.

7. Snow (cover) _____ covers _____ the mountains. *(put it over) → cover*

E **Listen and write the questions you hear.** Then, ask and answer the questions with a partner.

CD1·TR16

1. How many _____ rivers are there in montana ? _____

2. How many _____ Indian reservation are there ?   7 reservation

3. How much _____ snow is there _____ in rocky mountains?

4. _____ " ~ industry is there in montana ?

5. _____ " ~ Tourism is There ?

6. _____ " ~ Traffic is there in montana ?

The States · **59**

Reading

Death Valley

A What do you know about deserts? (Circle) *True* or *False*.

1. A desert receives very little rain.   (True)   False

2. The only plants in the desert are different kinds of cactuses.   True   (False)

3. Animals cannot live in the desert.   True   (False)

4. Summer is the best time to visit the desert.   True   (False)

B Word Builder Match.

___f___ **1.** sea level   **a.** a show or display of art, plants, or animals

___c___ **2.** precipitation   **b.** to change or adjust to new conditions

___g___ **3.** varieties   **c.** rain or snow

___d___ **4.** roots   **d.** the part of the plant that grows into the earth
                                    and brings in water

___b___ **5.** adapt
                                e. to stay away from
___e___ **6.** avoid
                                f. at the same height as the sea or ocean
___a___ **7.** exhibit
                                g. kinds or types

Death Valley National Park is the largest national park in the continental United States. This 3.3 million acre park in southern California is the lowest, hottest, and driest place in North America. The lowest point is 282 feet (86 meters) below **sea level**. In the summer, the average temperature is 115° (46° Celsius), and the highest temperature ever recorded here was 134° (56.6° Celsius). There are some summers when Death Valley receives no rain, and the average yearly **precipitation** is less than two inches.

into and out of   The first visitors to this desert area were different tribes of Native Americans. They walked through this area but did not stay.   *generation*

In 1849, people heard about the discovery of gold in California. Thousands of people began the long trip to the west. This large desert area was so difficult to cross that it received the name Death Valley.

Today, tourists and nature-lovers from all over the United States travel to Death Valley
containing   to enjoy its natural beauty. There are over one thousand **varieties** of plants in this desert, including many kinds of cactuses and flowers. Cactuses, with their interesting and unusual shapes, need very little rain. Their **roots** are close to the surface of the ground so they can quickly collect any
rain - shower   rainfall. A few days after the first rain in the spring, thousands of wildflowers cover the desert.

There are also many animals that have learned to **adapt** to this hot climate. Most are active at night, sleeping during the day

Prickly pear cactus

weather
sky

to **avoid** the hot desert sun. For example, the kangaroo <u>rat</u> sleeps deep underground while the sun is out. It can live its <u>entire</u> life without drinking any water, getting its water from the food it eats.

mouse

    If you are planning a trip to Death Valley, <u>winter is the</u> best time to visit. There are <u>nine campgrounds</u> with more than fifteen hundred <u>campsites</u>. The main visitor area is Furnace Creek with nature **exhibits**, a museum, and a bookstore. Be sure to watch the <u>informative</u> film on desert life. After that, you can <u>explore</u> the desert by car, by bike, or on foot. Park <u>rangers</u> offer programs on desert life, the <u>history</u> of Death Valley, and the desert sky at night. If you are planning a trip to Death Valley, don't forget these four essentials: a sun hat, sun block, lots of water, and a camera.

Kangaroo rat

READING NOTE

Supporting Details

When an article makes a statement, it usually gives specific information to support the <u>statement</u>.

C   **Write a detail from the reading to support each fact.**

Statement	Supporting Detail
1. Death Valley is the largest park in the <u>continental</u> United States.	**1.** It is a 3.3 million acre park.
2. It is the lowest place in North America.	**2.** It is 282 feet (86 meters) below sea level.
3. It is the hottest place in North America.	**3.** California is hottest place in north America.
4. It is the driest place in North America.	**4.** Death Valley No rain

D   **Match the two parts of each sentence.**

_c_ **1.** Visitors need to bring sun block   **a.** because it is cooler at this time.

_e_ **2.** Native Americans didn't stay in Death Valley   **b.** because it was very difficult to cross.

_a_ **3.** Desert animals are active at night   **c.** to protect their skin from the sun.

_f_ **4.** Cactus roots are near the surface   **d.** millions of <u>wildflowers</u> cover the desert.

_b_ **5.** This area was named Death Valley   **e.** because they needed a lake or river for water.

_g_ **6.** This area is so dry   **f.** to quickly collect rainwater.

_d_ **7.** After the first spring rain,   **g.** because high mountains block the rain clouds.

whole-all

stove—oven

instructor's

necessary—needed

Population → How many people live in state. eap: oregon

animal → what is state animal?

The States · 61

Writing Our Stories

A Read the student report about California.

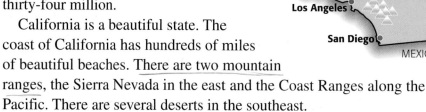

California is on the west coast of the United States, and it's the third largest state. Its borders are Oregon to the north, Nevada and Arizona to the east, Mexico to the south, and the Pacific Ocean to the west. Sacramento is the capital. The population is over thirty-four million.

California is a beautiful state. The coast of California has hundreds of miles of beautiful beaches. There are two mountain ranges, the Sierra Nevada in the east and the Coast Ranges along the Pacific. There are several deserts in the southeast.

Two of the major cities are San Francisco and Los Angeles. San Francisco is on the hills over San Francisco Bay. Tourists visit Chinatown and ride up and down the hills on the cable cars. Los Angeles is in southern California. It is the home of Hollywood and the movie industry.

For most of the year, the weather along the coast is sunny and mild. In the winter, there is snow in the mountains. In the south, the weather is hot and dry.

Agriculture and tourism are two of the major industries. California grows more than half of the nation's fruits and vegetables. Many Californians also work in the tourist industry in the cities, parks, and resorts.

B Write a report.

1. Choose a state in the United States. Each student should choose a different state.

2. Draw a map of the state. Show the borders, the capital, and major geographical features.

3. Complete the chart on page 63. Look up information on the Internet, in an almanac, or in an encyclopedia.

4. Write a short report.

5. Each student will make a short class presentation (see pages 64 and 65).

State	
Location	
Borders	
Capital	
Population	
Geography	
Two major cities	
Weather	
Industries	

WRITING NOTE

Capital Letters
Use capital letters for the names of specific locations and geographical features:

Country names: the **U**nited **S**tates, **M**exico

State names: **A**laska, **N**ew **Y**ork

City names: **C**hicago, **S**an **D**iego

Bodies of water: the **P**acific **O**cean

Mountain Ranges: the **R**ocky **M**ountains

Parks: **G**rand **C**anyon **N**ational **P**ark

Tourist Attractions: the **S**tatue of **L**iberty

C **Edit the paragraph.**

Florida is the most popular tourist destination in the united states. During the winter, visitors enjoy a break from the cold and snow. Florida offers hundreds of miles of beaches along the atlantic ocean and the gulf of mexico. Families enjoy tourist attractions such as disney world, universal studios, and sea world. Florida's cities such as miami, tampa, and fort lauderdale offer great restaurants and exciting night life. Florida's most popular park is everglades national park where visitors can birdwatch, fish, or take boat tours and see alligators and crocodiles.

A **Read the steps for giving a successful class presentation about the state you researched.**

1.

2.

3.

4.

5.

6.

1. Prepare your materials: large map, notes, pictures.

2. Practice your presentation at home.

3. Stand in front of the class and look at your classmates.

4. Show the map to the class. Tell your classmates the name of the state and explain the location. Speak loudly, clearly, and slowly.

5. Point to the capital. Spell the capital. Tell the class the population of the state.

6. Point to two places of interest on the map. Tell the class one or two things that people can enjoy at each location. Do not read your report. Use notes.

B **Listen to one student's report.** Discuss the questions.

1. How did this student prepare?

2. How large was the map? Could the students see the words on the map?

3. How many times did the student repeat the population?

4. What two places of interest did the student talk about?

5. How long was the presentation?

6. How do you feel when you stand in front of a group?

7. How can you best prepare to talk in front of the class?

C **Give a classroom presentation about the state you researched.** As each student speaks, complete the chart about the state.

State	Capital	Population

alone

lonely —→ feels bad
feeling

Technology

A **Label the electronic equipment.**

digital camera	MP3 player	game station
laptop computer	GPS	cell phone

1. _____

2. _____

3. _____

4. _____

5. _____

6. _____

 B **Complete the sentences.** Then, discuss your answers.

1. I **have / don't have** a computer.

2. I **have / don't have** Internet access at home.

3. The school **has / doesn't have** a computer lab for students.

4. I spend about _____ hours a day on the computer.

5. I have the following electronic equipment: _____

6. I'd like to buy the following electronic equipment: _____

7. I can use the following software: _____

8. My favorite Web site is _____.

I	am		send**ing** an e-mail.
You	are		order**ing** a movie.
He	is	(not)	mak**ing** reservations.
It	is		work**ing**.
They	are		play**ing** a video game.

1. The present continuous talks about an [action that is happening now.]
   He **is using** his computer.
2. The present continuous talks about an [action that is temporary.]
   He **is living** with his brother.
   (He expects to move soon.)

 A Complete the sentences. Use the present continuous form of the verb.

1. Li-Ping (write) <u>is writing</u> an e-mail to her brother in China. She (tell)

   _____ him about her new job at a dot-com company.

2. Raul (take) _____ a virtual tour of an art museum. He (look) _____ at paintings by Picasso and Dalí.

3. Mr. and Mrs. Chan (plan) _____ a day in the city. They (check)

   _____ the reviews of several restaurants. They (make) _____

   reservations for a show.

4. Lauren (take) _____ a course at work this month. She (learn) _____ to use the company's new software program.

B Read each sign. Imagine that a person does not see the sign. What is he or she doing?

> That man doesn't see the sign. He is taking a picture.

1.

2.

3.

4.

5.

6.

7.

8.

Am	I	tak**ing** a picture?
Are	you	send**ing** an e-mail?
Is	she	listen**ing** to music?
Is	it	work**ing**?
Are	we	study**ing**?
Are	they	mak**ing** reservations?

Yes, you **are**.	No, you **aren't**.
Yes, I **am**.	No, I'm **not**.
Yes, she **is**.	No, she **isn't**.
Yes, it **is**.	No, it **isn't**.
Yes, we **are**.	No, we **aren't**.
Yes, they **are**.	No, they **aren't**.

 A **Ask and answer questions with a partner.**

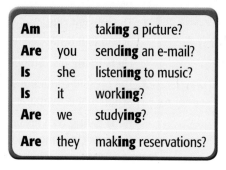

> Are we sitting in the classroom?

> Yes, we are.

1. we / sit in the classroom?

2. you / speak your native language?

3. we / speak English?

4. teacher / take a break?

5. you / look out the window?

6. it / rain?

7. students / take a test?

8. we / look at our books?

9. we / sit in the back of the classroom?

10. you / drink water?

 B **Listen to each speaker.** Ask questions and guess what he / she is doing. Then, listen again and compare your questions.

CD1·TR18

1. *Is he taking a picture?* _____

2. _____

3. _____

4. _____

5. _____

6. _____

7. _____

What	**am**	I	do**ing**?
Which movie	**are**	you	order**ing**?
How	**is**	it	work**ing**?
Where	**are**	they	go**ing**?

You're check**ing** prices.
I'm order**ing** *Space Age*.
It's work**ing** well.
They are go**ing** to the lab.

The present continuous tense can talk about specific future plans.
I**'m leaving** at 2:00.

A **Complete the questions.**

Conversation 1

A: What Web site ___is___ he ___looking at___?

B: He's looking at Wings Airlines.

A: What ___ he ___?
   1   2

B: He's buying an airline ticket.

A: Where ___ he ___?
   3   4

B: He's going to Atlanta.

Conversation 2

A: What site ___?
   1

B: She's looking at Sunrise Greeting Cards.

A: What ___?
   2

B: She's designing a birthday card.

A: Who ___?
   3

B: She's sending the card to her brother.

A: How old ___?
   4

B: He's 21.

 B **Listen to the conversation.** Then, practice it with a partner.

CD1·TR19

A: What are you doing?

B: I'm writing a report.

A: What software are you using?

B: I'm using Write Now.

A: How's it coming?

B: Very slowly. And it's due tomorrow.

Pronunciation: *Wh-* questions **Listen and repeat.**

CD1·TR20

> *Wh-* questions have a rising / falling intonation.

1. Where is he going?

2. Who are you texting?

3. What is she studying?

4. Who is she calling?

5. What are you listening to?

6. Which game is she playing?

7. What are you ordering?

8. Which site are you using?

  Working Together **In your notebook, write ten questions about the people in the picture.** Then, work in a group. Ask and answer the questions.

1. <u>What is Ahmed printing</u> ?

> When **Who** is the subject of a sentence, it is always singular.
>
> **Who is** buying a computer? Laura **is**.
> **Who is** fixing the computer? Henry and Ivan **are**.
>
> When *Who* is the object of a sentence, it can be singular or plural.
>
> **Who is** Max calling? He **is** calling his sister.
> **Who are** Ali and Kim talking to? They **are** talking to their friends.

A **Answer the questions.** Use your imagination.

Marie

1. Who is taking a photo? _____Marie is_____.

2. Who is she taking a photo of? ___Her daughter___.

Joseph

3. Who is writing an e-mail? _____.

4. Who is he writing to? _____.

Margo / Paul

5. Who is driving? _____.

6. Who is Paul driving to work? _____.

B **Working Together** **Two students will act out the situations below.** Ask two *who* questions about each situation.

1. Student 1 is giving a book to Student 2.

2. Student 1 is taking a picture of Student 2.

3. Student 1 is helping Student 2 with homework.

4. Student 1 is inviting Student 2 to a party.

5. Student 1 is texting Student 2.

6. Student 1 is talking to the teacher.

Carla   Lin

> Who is giving a book to Carla?

> Who is Lin giving a book to?

Some verbs in English do not usually take the present continuous tense. They are called **non-action verbs**. These verbs often show feelings, senses, beliefs, and possession.

agree	hate	love	seem
believe	have	need	smell
belong	hear	own	sound
cost	know	prefer	taste
feel	like	remember	think
forget	look	see	understand

Some verbs can show both action and non-action.

I **have** a computer.   I'm **having** a good time.

She**'s having** a party.

I **think** he's a good teacher.   I'm **thinking** about my boyfriend.

A **Complete the sentences.** Then, work with a group and compare your responses.

1. I belong to _____.

2. I believe that _____.

3. I don't own a _____.

4. Our teacher seems _____ today.

5. I feel _____ today.

B **Complete the sentences.** Use the present or the present continuous form of the verb in parentheses.

1. Which word processing program (prefer) _*do*_ you _____*prefer*_____?

2. I (remember - negative) _____ my password for this site.

3. I (try) _____ to find a good recipe for banana cake. This one (sound) _____ good.

4. They (save) _____ money to buy a computer. Their children (need) _____ one for school.

5. Hannah (sit) _____ at her computer. She (look) _____ confused. She (know - negative) _____ how to use this software.

Time Expressions with Present Continuous	Time Expressions with Simple Present	Adverbs of Frequency
now	once a day	usually
right now	every day	never
at this moment	every morning	always
at this time	all the time	sometimes

A **Circle** the correct time expression.

1. Linda is checking her e-mail **now** / **in the morning**.

2. She receives about five e-mails **right now** / **every day**.

3. Shanta is looking at her horoscope **now** / **every day**. She checks her horoscope **now** / **every morning**.

4. Bill **at this moment** / **always** makes his airline reservations online.

5. Sarah just finished her report for science. She is using the computer program's spell check **right now** / **in the evening**.

6. Stanley is taking a break **at this moment** / **twice a day**. He's playing a card game.

7. My Internet connection **at this moment** / **always** works very slowly.

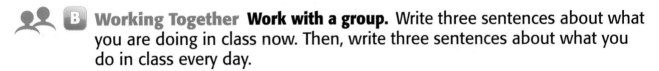

B **Working Together** **Work with a group.** Write three sentences about what you are doing in class now. Then, write three sentences about what you do in class every day.

C **Ask and answer the questions with a partner.**

> Yes, I am.
> No, I'm not.

> Yes, I do.
> No, I don't.

1. Do you have a computer?

2. Are you using a computer now?

3. Do you have a cell phone with you?

4. Are you talking on your cell phone?

5. Are you carrying a wallet?

6. Do you have a credit card?

7. Are you working with a partner?

8. Do you often work with a partner?

9. Are you writing now?

10. Are you talking with the teacher?

A **Word Builder** **Match each word or phrase with its definition.**

_c_	**1.** site	**a.**	fix errors in a computer program
	2. update	**b.**	working well
	3. design	**c.**	a location on the Internet
	4. debug a program	**d.**	plan
	5. up and running	**e.**	add new information
	6. go down	**f.**	travel company with ships
	7. cruise line	**g.**	stop working

 B **Listen to the first part of the story. Discuss.**

CD1•TR21

1. What information can people find on the Cruise*away.com Web site?
2. What does this company do?

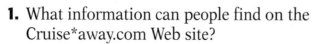

WORD PARTNERSHIPS	
Internet	site
	connection
	company
	provider

C Listen to the second part of the story. What is each employee at Cruise*away.com doing? Complete the sentences.

CD1·TR22

1. Megan _is updating information about a cruise line_.

2. Samip _____.

3. Michael _____.

4. Antonio _____.

5. Lee _____.

D Circle *True* or *False*.

1. Cruise*away.com is an Internet site. (True) False

2. People use this site to plan their cruise vacations. True False

3. If people need more information, they can call this site. True False

4. Cruise*away.com designed and programmed this site. True False

5. Samip is the manager of the company. True False

6. All the employees work from 9:00 to 5:00. True False

7. Lee starts work at 8:00. True False

8. It's important that the site is always working. True False

E Complete the sentences. Use the present or present continuous form of the verb in parentheses.

1. Megan ___is playing___ with a stress ball now. She often _____ with a stress ball while she works. (play)

2. At this moment, Antonio _____ a break. He _____ four or five breaks a day. (take)

3. Lee _____ at work now. He _____ at 10:00 every morning. (arrive)

4. Michael _____ with six or seven cruise lines a day. He _____ with a cruise line now. (talk)

5. Samip _____ jeans today. He always _____ jeans. (wear)

A Discuss.

1. How many hours a day do you spend on the computer?

2. What is an addiction? What are some examples of addictions?

3. What do you think "computer addiction" means?

"Larry used to be an excellent student. Now, he's falling asleep in class. He's not completing his class work. He didn't finish his science report. He's always on the computer playing video games. Even at one and two o'clock in the morning, I can hear him playing video games in his room."   —a mother's report

1 An addiction is an activity or a habit that a person cannot control and that is **harmful** to them. Some psychologists are talking about a new kind of addiction—computer addiction. A person with a computer addiction can't stop using the computer—checking e-mail, playing video games, chatting with "friends," surfing the Internet.

2 Do you know a computer addict? This person cannot control the time he spends on the computer. Some days, the morning, afternoon, and evening pass, and the person is still sitting at the computer. The person is upset when someone **interrupts** his computer use. He feels nervous or depressed when he isn't on the computer. When he can finally turn the computer on, he feels **relieved** and comfortable again. He **neglects** his family and his friends. At times, he doesn't take care of himself; for example, he misses meals or doesn't shower.

3 Computer addiction can cause both social and physical problems. Socially, the addict spends less and less time with his family and friends. "Cyber friends" are more important than real friends. Physically, computer addicts can **develop** dry eyes, backaches, and headaches. Many computer addicts don't eat properly, and many have sleep problems.

4 If you think you are becoming a computer addict, there are some steps that you can take. First, admit that you have a problem and talk to your family about it. Explain that you are trying to **limit** your computer time. These ideas might help:

- Set an alarm clock for one or two hours. When the alarm clock rings, turn off the computer.
- Choose a time that you will turn off the computer at night. For example, turn off your computer at 11:00 every night.
- Only use the computer in the family room or living room. Family members can remind you that you have been on the computer too long.
- Find other activities that you enjoy. Go out to lunch with friends, take a class, begin to exercise.
- If these ideas don't help, you might need professional help.

B Word Builder (Circle) the letter of each correct answer.

1. Eating too much _____ is **harmful** to your health.

   a. fruit   **b.** junk food

2. You **interrupt** someone who is reading when you _____.

   a. walk by quietly   **b.** start to talk to her

3. You feel **relieved** when your teacher tells you that _____.

   a. you passed the test   **b.** you failed the test

4. If you **neglect** your health, you _____.

   a. will get sick   **b.** will feel better

5. If you read without your glasses, you will **develop** a _____.

   a. good story   **b.** headache

6. If you **limit** the time you watch TV, you watch _____.

   a. more TV   **b.** less TV

C Write the number of the correct paragraph next to the topic of the paragraph.

   __2__ The signs of computer addiction

   _____ Ways to control computer addiction

   _____ Problems that computer addiction can cause

   _____ The definition of computer addiction

> **READING NOTE**
>
> **Identifying the topic of a paragraph**
> The topic of a paragraph tells what the paragraph is about.

D Answer the questions.

1. What is one sign of computer addiction?

_____

2. What is one problem that computer addiction can cause?

_____

3. What is one way to help a person limit the use of the computer?

_____

A Read the e-mail message.

NEW MAIL

New Mail | Reply | Forward | Print | Delete | Address Book | Spell

From: lidiav@state*u.edu

To: dianagt@yellow*bird.com

Subject: My new computer

Hi Diana,

I'm sitting in my dorm room with my new computer and I'm writing my first e-mail to you. Mom and Dad gave me this new laptop for my birthday. They also gave me a pen tablet. I can draw on the tablet and see the picture on the computer. I can also manipulate my photos with different software. This tablet is amazing!

I love college. I'm taking twelve credits this semester. I'm enjoying my art classes the most. I'm taking a painting class and a graphic design class. I'm spending my life in the art studios! I'm rooming with a girl from California. She's majoring in art, too.

How are you? Are you still going out with David? Are you still managing the pet store? E-mail me!

Ciao,
Lidia

B Answer the questions.

1. Who wrote this e-mail?

2. Who did she send the e-mail to? What is their relationship?

3. What is the writer's e-mail address?

4. What does *.edu* mean?

5. What is Lidia majoring in?

C Find and correct the mistakes.

1. She is ~~send~~ *sending* an e-mail message.

2. She learning how to use new software.

3. The school have a computer lab.

4. She sits in the computer lab now.

5. You writing an e-mail to your friend?

6. How everything with you?

7. What classes she is taking?

8. Does she has a computer?

9. She meet a lot of people.

10. You still going out with David?

D Write an e-mail message to a friend or a classmate.

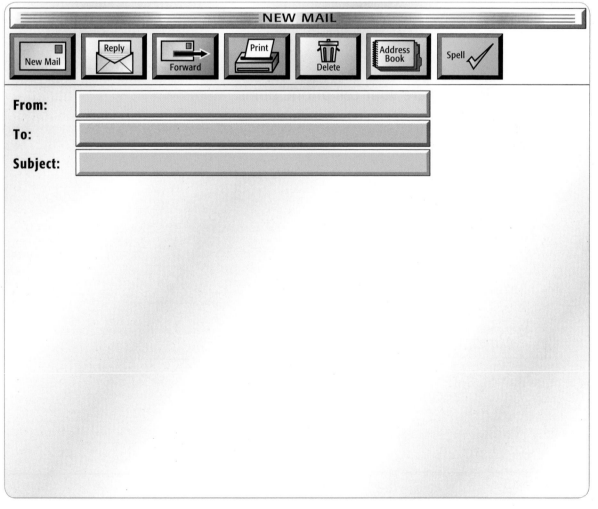

A **Discuss.** Complete the information about your cell phone. Then, talk about the features you use most often on your cell phone.

1. I have a _____ phone.

2. I talk on my phone about _____ minutes a day.

3. My reception is **great / good / fair**.

4. My cell phone has these features (Check [✓] all that apply):

☐ I can make international calls.　　☐ I can check the weather.

☐ I can check my e-mail.　　☐ I can use a GPS.

☐ I can go online.　　☐ I can set an alarm.

☐ I can play games.　　☐ I can keep my calendar.

☐ I can listen to music.　　☐ I can use it as a credit card.

☐ I can take photos.　　☐ I can _____.

B **Working Together** **Work with a group of three students.** Complete the chart. Then, compare your cell phone plans.

	Student 1	Student 2	Student 3
Company			
Number of phones			
Number of minutes			
Features			
Quality of reception			
Cost			

A **Read the directions for setting an alarm on a cell phone.** How are these directions the same or different for your cell phone?

> **To set an alarm:**
> 1. Press **Clock.**
> 2. Press **Alarm.**
> 3. Press **Add Alarm.**
> 4. Enter the time you want the alarm to ring.
> 5. Select **A.M.** or **P.M.**
> 6. Press **Save.**

press

enter

choose

select

tap

B **Choose one of the cell phone features below or a favorite feature on your cell phone.** Write step-by-step directions on how to use the feature.

a. how to take a photo and e-mail it to a friend

b. how to write a text message and send it

c. how to enter a new contact on your phone

d. how to enter a new event on your calendar

e. how to record a voice message

Directions

1. _____

2. _____

3. _____

4. _____

5. _____

6. _____

C **Working Together** **Give your cell phone to a classmate.** Carefully explain your directions. Can your partner follow your directions?

A **Discuss the pictures.** Where is each person? What is happening? What else happens during a physical examination at the doctor's office?

have a physical	give a vaccine	write a prescription	floss her teeth
read an eye chart	get a vaccine	order a test	examine
fill a cavity	check his cholesterol	check his blood pressure	take an X-ray

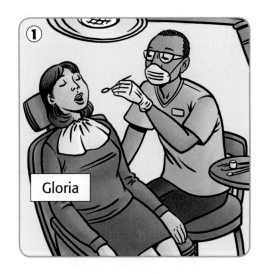

Gloria

Mark

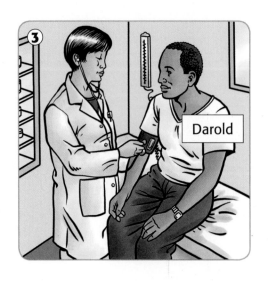

Darold

Tom

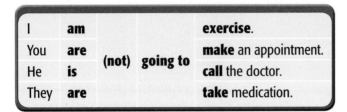

I	am			exercise.
You	are	(not)	going to	make an appointment.
He	is			call the doctor.
They	are			take medication.

A **Read about Gloria.** <u>Underline</u> the verbs in the *going to* future.

    Gloria is at the dentist. This is her first visit in two years. Gloria has four cavities. The doctor is filling two cavities today. He <u>is going to fill</u> two more cavities next week. Gloria is going to take better care of her teeth. She isn't going to drink soda with every meal. She isn't going to eat chocolate every day. She is going to floss her teeth every evening.

B **Complete the sentences with the *going to* future.**

1. I (go) _____ to the dentist next week.

2. Many people (get) _____ flu vaccines.

3. Jack fell and hurt his leg. The doctor (take) _____ an X-ray.

4. The baby has an ear infection. The doctor (write)

_____ a prescription for an antibiotic.

5. My husband and I have high cholesterol. We (eat)

_____ less fat. I (buy) _____

more fruit and vegetables.

CD1·TR23

C **Pronunciation: Medical Specialists Listen.** Mark the stressed syllable. Then, listen again and repeat.

súr·geon   ob·ste·tri·cian

car·di·ól·o·gist   der·ma·tol·o·gist

oph·thal·mol·o·gist   gy·ne·col·o·gist

pe·di·a·tri·cian   al·ler·gist

fam·i·ly doc·tor   psy·chi·a·trist

> **CULTURE NOTE**
>
> If a person needs a specialist, his family doctor can suggest one. People also find the name of a specialist by asking their friends or co-workers. What kind of doctor is in each picture on page 82?

D **Ayumi has the flu.** Talk about her day. What is she going to do? What isn't she going to do?

> She isn't going to go to work.

go to work
stay in bed
take aspirin
use a heating pad
drink a lot of fluids
take a hot shower
take a walk
do the food shopping
cook
sleep most of the day

 E **Working Together** **Talk with a partner about your plans for today.** Write your partner's response and your response to each question.

1. What are you going to do after school?

_____ *is going to* _____.
(Your partner's name)
I am going to _____.

2. What are you going to do this evening?

_____.

_____.

3. When are you going to do your homework?

_____.

_____.

4. What time are you going to go to bed?

_____.

_____.

Are	you		**see** the doctor?
Is	she	**going to**	**stay** home from work?
Are	they		**get** a flu vaccine?

Yes, I **am**.	No, I'**m not**.
Yes, she **is**.	No, she **isn't**.
Yes, they **are**.	No, they **aren't**.

A **Write the questions and answers.** Use the words in parentheses.

1. Mary has a headache. (take some aspirin)

Is she going to take some aspirin?_____ Yes, ___she is___.

2. Joseph has a toothache. (call the dentist)

_____ Yes, _____.

3. Carol has the flu. (go to work)

_____ No, _____.

4. I have a sore throat. (you / drink some tea)

_____ Yes, _____.

5. My brother is in the hospital. (you / visit him)

_____ Yes, _____.

B **Working Together** **Find someone who . . .** Walk around the classroom and ask your classmates the questions below. If a student answers "Yes," write the student's name. If the student answers "No," ask another student the question. Try to find a student who answers "Yes" for each question.

Are you going to join a health club?   No. (Ask another student!)

Are you going to join a health club?   Yes. (Write the student's name.)

1. join a health club?   _____

2. have a physical examination?   _____

3. get a flu shot?   _____

4. change jobs?   _____

5. move?   _____

6. get a driver's license?   _____

7. get married?   _____

8. visit your native country?   _____

When	**am**	I		
Where	**are**	you	**going to**	**exercise?**
Why	**is**	he		
	are	they		

CD1·TR24

A **Discuss the new vocabulary.** Then, listen to the conversation between Mr. West and the doctor. Answer the questions.

| broken leg | swollen | painkiller | ice pack |
| cast | swelling | crutches | |

1. What's the matter with Jimmy?

2. Is the doctor looking at the X-rays?

3. What is the nurse putting on Jimmy's leg? Why?

4. How long is Jimmy going to stay in the hospital?

5. When is the doctor going to put a cast on his leg?

6. How long is Jimmy going to be in a cast?

7. What are they going to give him for pain?

B **Complete the questions about George.** He sprained his ankle while playing basketball.

1. What <u>is George going to put on his ankle</u>?

He's going to put an ice pack on his ankle.

2. How long _____?

He's going to use an ice pack until the swelling goes down.

3. When _____?

He's going to use a heating pad in two or three days.

4. What _____?

He's going to take aspirin for pain.

86 · Unit 6

5. _____?

Yes, he is. He's going to use crutches.

6. How long _____?

He's going to use the crutches for a week.

7. What _____?

He's going to put a bandage on his ankle during the day.

8. How long _____?

He's going to stay home from work for two days.

👥 **C** **Working Together** **Student to Student**

Student 1: Turn to page 255. Read the questions to Student 2. Then, listen to Student 2 and write the questions.

Student 2: Listen to Student 1 and write the questions. Then, turn to page 255 and read the questions to Student 1.

1. _____

2. _____

3. _____

4. _____

5. _____

👥 **D** **Working Together** **Write a conversation between a patient and a friend who is visiting him / her in the hospital.** Use the questions in Exercise C. Act out your conversation for the class.

| How are you feeling, Marie? | Well, I feel much better than yesterday. | How's your back? Are you going to need an operation? |

I	will	**walk** every day.
She		**join** a health club.
They	won't	**change** jobs.

Use *will* to express an offer to help.
I'll drive you to school.
Use *will* to make predictions.
You**'ll** get the job.

CD1 · TR25

A **Pronunciation: *I'll* Listen and repeat.**

1. I'll help you.

2. I'll call her.

3. I'll drive you.

4. I'll make dinner.

5. I'll visit you.

6. I'll take you to the doctor.

7. I'll pick up your prescription.

8. I'll see you tomorrow.

B **George went to the doctor with chest pains.** Read the doctor's advice. Do you think George will follow his recommendations?

George will change his diet.

I don't agree. George won't change his diet. He loves fried food.

I agree.
I don't agree.

Change your diet.
Stop smoking.
Get more sleep.
Start to exercise.
Use less salt.
Lower your cholesterol.
Get a pet.
Cut down on sweets.
Walk to work.
Lose weight.

C **Your sister has a broken leg and needs help for a few weeks.** Offer to help her. Use *it, them, him,* or *her* for the underlined words.

1. I can't drive <u>the children</u> to school.

2. I can't make <u>dinner</u>.

3. I can't do <u>the laundry</u>.

4. I can't do <u>the food shopping</u>.

5. I can't answer <u>the phone</u>.

6. I can't make <u>the beds</u>.

7. I can't wash <u>my hair</u>.

8. I can't return <u>those library books</u>.

9. I can't deposit <u>my paycheck</u>.

10. I can't walk <u>the dog</u>. [Note: Use *him* or *her* in the answer.]

11. I can't change <u>that light bulb</u>.

12. I can't mail <u>these letters</u>.

> I can't drive <u>the children</u> to school.
> I'll drive **them**.
> I can't make <u>dinner</u>.
> I'll make **it**.

  D **Working Together** **Work in groups.** Make predictions about your class and your school. Then, share your predictions with the class.

The school will build a new cafeteria.

All the students will get 100% on the next test.

The teacher won't give us any homework tonight.

The Big Picture

A **Discuss the new words.** Which words do you see in the picture?

blanket	concussion	pale	stretcher
bleeding	confused	pressure bandage	windshield
blood pressure	intersection	stitches	witness

B **Look at the picture and complete the sentences.**

1. The man's arm is _____ heavily, so the emergency

   worker is applying a _____.

2. Another emergency worker is taking the man's _____.

3. The woman is lying on a _____.

4. The _____ of the woman's car is broken.

5. A _____ called 911.

 C **Listen to the story of the accident.**

CD1·TR26

90 · Unit 6

D **Answer the questions.**

1. What are Luis's injuries?

2. What are the emergency workers doing?

3. What treatment is Luis going to receive at the hospital?

4. What are the woman's injuries?

5. Whose injuries are more serious?

6. What treatment is the woman going to receive at the hospital?

WORD PARTNERSHIPS	
I was in I had	an accident.
It was my fault.	

E **Listen again and (circle) True, False, or NI (Not Enough Information).**

CD1 • TR26

1. Luis went past the stop sign.	True	(False)	NI
2. The accident was the woman's fault.	True	False	NI
3. Luis called 911 for emergency help.	True	False	NI
4. Luis has a broken arm.	True	False	NI
5. Luis is going to need stitches in his arm.	True	False	NI
6. The woman is telling the workers her phone number.	True	False	NI
7. The woman probably hit her head on her windshield.	True	False	NI
8. The woman is going to stay in the hospital for a week.	True	False	NI

F **Complete the sentences.** Use the *going to* future or the present continuous.

1. Luis (lie) _____is lying_____ by the side of the road.

2. An emergency worker (apply) _____ a pressure bandage.

3. In a few minutes, the workers (take) _____ him to the hospital.

4. Luis (need) _____ thirty stitches in his arm.

5. The workers (put) _____ the woman in the ambulance.

6. At the hospital, the doctor (examine) _____ her carefully.

7. A police officer (direct) _____ traffic.

8. He (file) _____ an accident report.

G **Dictation** **Your teacher will dictate the sentences on page 256.** Listen and write the sentences you hear. Refer to the words in the box for spelling.

stayed	insurance	lawyer
overnight	report	sue

A Healthy Lifestyle • **91**

A Discuss.

1. Where are your lungs? What do they do?

2. What do you know about asthma?

3. Does anyone in your family have asthma? <u>What treatment is he / she receiving?</u>

4. What is the boy in the picture using? Why?

Ricky Garcia is going to play outside with his friends. He is taking out his inhaler and taking two puffs. Five minutes later, he's in the park with his friends, running after a soccer ball. Ricky has asthma, but he knows how to control it.

Asthma is a lung disease. The airways of the lungs become swollen and **inflamed**, making it difficult to breathe normally. A person with asthma may have wheezing, coughing, a tight feeling in the chest, or shortness of breath. Serious breathing problems are called **asthma attacks**. They can be mild or very serious, requiring immediate medical attention.

Asthma can begin at any age. Childhood asthma, often beginning when a child is younger than ten years old, is one of the most common childhood diseases. Doctors report that the number of young people with asthma is **increasing**. Over four million children have the disease and the number is growing. It is the number one cause of absence from school. Asthma is often **genetic**. If a parent has asthma, the children are more likely to develop the disease. Children with asthma need to be under a doctor's care. They and their parents can learn to understand this disease and learn how to control it.

It is important to find out the "**triggers**" for asthma. In other words, what causes the attack? The most common triggers are exercise, viral infections, stress, and **irritants** like dust, pollen, or animals. Once a child learns the triggers, he can help prevent future attacks.

There are two kinds of asthma medications—control drugs and quick-relief drugs. Children take control drugs once or twice a day to help prevent asthma attacks. If a child begins to have an asthma attack, he needs immediate help, so a **quick-relief** drug is necessary. This is often an inhaler. School-aged children usually carry their inhalers with them. This medication works quickly and children begin to breathe more easily in a few minutes. If a child has a serious asthma attack, he may need emergency care at a hospital or doctor's office.

About half of all children **outgrow** asthma, and their asthma attacks stop when they are teenagers. However, many people live with the disease into adulthood.

B (Circle) *True* or *False*.

1. A child with asthma has breathing problems.   True   False

2. Asthma can begin when a child is two or three years old.   True   False

3. If a parent has asthma, all his / her children will have asthma.   True   False

4. Exercise can trigger asthma.   True   False

5. Every year, more children have asthma.   True   False

6. An inhaler can help if a child is having an asthma attack.   True   False

7. Parents must take the child to the hospital for every asthma attack. True   False

8. Many children with asthma need to take medication every day.   True   False

---

READING NOTE

Vocabulary in Context

When you are reading, you will see new words. The meaning, or definition, of a new word is often in the same sentence or in the sentence before or after.

1. The airways of the lungs become swollen and **inflamed**.

    Inflamed means swollen.

2. Asthma is often **genetic**. If a parent has asthma, the children are more likely to develop the disease.

    Genetic means that a parent can pass a health problem to a child.

C Word Builder **Write the definition of the words from the article.** The definition is in the same sentence as the word or in the sentence before or after it.

1. asthma attack _____

2. increasing _____

3. triggers _____

4. irritants _____

5. quick-relief _____

6. outgrow _____

A **Take the survey.**

Health Questionnaire

	YES	NO
1. Do you smoke?	☐	☐
2. Do you drive everywhere?	☐	☐
3. Do you exercise three or more times a week?	☐	☐
4. Do you eat fresh fruit and vegetables every day?	☐	☐
5. Do you eat a lot of fried food?	☐	☐
6. Do you always put salt on your food?	☐	☐
7. Do you take vitamins?	☐	☐
8. Do you drink a lot of caffeine?	☐	☐
9. Do you drink a lot of soda?	☐	☐
10. Do you eat a lot of sweets?	☐	☐
11. Do you sleep at least seven hours a night?	☐	☐
12. Do you drink six or more glasses of water a day?	☐	☐

B **Read a student's composition about her lifestyle.**

In general, my lifestyle is healthy. However, there are a few things I **need to change**.

In the morning, I eat a good breakfast. I always have fruit and then I have cereal or yogurt. There's a small cafeteria at work and I order soup or a salad for lunch. For dinner, I usually stir-fry some vegetables and meat and eat that with rice.

But my diet isn't perfect. First, I **love to put** salt on my food. I put soy sauce on everything I cook. I have a salt shaker on my kitchen table, and I add more salt to everything on my plate. From now on, I'm going to buy light soy sauce. Also, I will buy salt-free seasoning and try it. Second, I drink three or four cups of coffee every day. I need a cup of real coffee in the morning. I'm going to **try to drink** decaf in the afternoon and evening.

Unfortunately, I don't exercise enough. I work and go to school, so it's hard to find the time. I like to walk. There's a park near my house. I will try to walk there for thirty minutes on Saturday and Sunday. At school, my classroom is on the third floor. I usually take the elevator, but from now on I **plan to take** the stairs.

WRITING NOTE

Verb + infinitive

Many words take the infinitive form. Use an infinitive after *try, need, plan, like,* and *love.*

An infinitive is *to* + the base form of the verb.

> There are a few things I <u>need</u> **to change**.
>
> I <u>love</u> **to put** salt on my food.

C **Complete each sentence with an infinitive after the verb.**

1. I will (try / exercise) __try to exercise__ more.

2. I (plan / walk) _____ to work.

3. I (love / eat) _____ sweets, especially chocolate.

4. I (need / lose) _____ twenty pounds.

5. I will (try / go) _____ to bed earlier.

D **Complete the chart.** This student organized her ideas before she wrote. She listed three things she wanted to change. Then, she made a plan for each thing. Complete her last box.

Things to change	Plans for change
Salt	use light soy sauce try salt-free seasonings
Coffee	one cup regular coffee decaf in the afternoon and evening
Exercise	walk 30 minutes on weekends take the stairs to class

E **In a chart, write two or three things you would like to change about your lifestyle.** Then, make notes about your plans for change. You don't need to write complete sentences.

F **Write a composition.** Describe your lifestyle. Then, write about the changes you want to make and your plans for change.

A **Discuss.**

1. Have you ever called 911? Describe the situation.

2. For what kinds of emergencies can you call 911?

B **Check (✓) the situations that are emergencies for a 911 call.**

☐ **1.** You see a bad car accident.

☐ **2.** Your neighbors are having a loud party.

☐ **3.** Someone stole your bicycle.

☐ **4.** You burned yourself badly.

☐ **5.** Your mother is confused and dizzy.

☐ **6.** There's a fire in your kitchen.

☐ **7.** You are locked out of your house.

☐ **8.** Your car won't start.

☐ **9.** Someone is screaming for help.

☐ **10.** Someone is robbing a store.

C **Write the number of each emergency under the correct picture.**

1. My daughter took my medication.

2. My husband fell. I think he broke his leg.

3. I'm in bed. I hear someone in my house.

4. I cut my hand. I'm bleeding a lot.

5. My friend is choking.

6. I think my father had a heart attack.

a. _____

b. _____

c. _____

d. _____

e. _____

f. _____

Dispatcher

CD1·TR27

D **Listen to the conversation between a caller and a 911 dispatcher.** Answer the questions.

1. What is the emergency?

2. Who is calling?

3. What did the dispatcher ask the caller?

4. What directions did the dispatcher give?

E **Working Together** **Choose one of the situations from Exercise B or C.** Write a conversation between a caller and a 911 dispatcher. Then, act out your conversation for the class. You can use some of the sentences and questions from the box below.

What's the emergency?

Is anyone hurt / injured?

How old is your daughter / father?

Where are you?

What is your location?

Are you safe?

Are you in any danger?

Is your door unlocked?

Is the person breathing?

Stay on the line.

Stay calm. / Calm down.

The police are on the way.

Unlock the door.

WORD PARTNERSHIPS

Help is	
The police are	on the way.
An ambulance is	

Around the World

A **Write the location under each picture.**

Willis Tower, Chicago   An alligator, Louisiana   Denali, Alaska
Niagara Falls, New York   ~~Mt. Waialeale, Hawaii~~   O₂, London

1. Mt. Waialeale, Hawaii

2. _____

3. _____

4. _____

5. _____

6. _____

B **Read the facts about the United States.** <u>Underline</u> the adjectives.

1. Alaska is <u>larger</u> <u>than</u> Texas.

2. Florida receives more visitors than any state in the United States.

3. The rainiest location in the United States is Mt. Waialeale in Hawaii.

4. The O_2 in London, England, is the largest dome in the world.

5. Willis Tower is the tallest building in the United States.

6. Denali is the highest mountain in the United States.

7. Louisiana has more alligators than any other state in the country.

8. Niagara Falls in New York is one of the most popular tourist attractions in the United States.

Type of Adjective	Comparative Form		
One-syllable adjectives	old**er than**	larg**er than**	
...le adjectives ...in -y	bus**ier than**	sun**nier than**	
...ore-syllable ...es	**more** populated **than**	**more** interesting **than**	
...orms	good – **better than**	bad – **worse than**	far – **farther than**

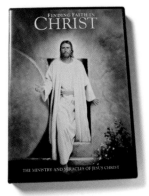

...e adjectives in the correct column.

	long	tall	dry	safe	friendly
...ated	noisy	beautiful	expensive	famous	cold

...yllable ...ctives	Two-syllable adjectives ending in -y	Two-or-more-syllable adjectives not ending in -y
...ong	busy	populated

B Write the comparative form of each adjective from Exercise A.

One-syllable adjectives	Two-syllable adjectives ending in -y	Two-or-more-syllable adjectives not ending in -y
longer than	busier than	more populated than

C Pronunciation: Comparative Adjectives **Listen and repeat.**

CD1·TR28

1. busier	**4.** noisier	**7.** rainier
2. taller	**5.** friendlier	**8.** higher
3. larger	**6.** farther	**9.** sunnier

D **Complete the sentences.** Use the comparative form of the adjectives.

1. Florida is (sunny) _____*sunnier than*_____ Washington State.

2. New Jersey is (crowded) _____ any other state.

3. Chicago is (busy) _____ Columbus.

4. Louisiana is (humid) _____ Nevada.

5. Arizona is (dry) _____ Pennsylvania.

6. Santa Fe is (old) _____ Orlando.

7. For surfers, Hawaii is (popular) _____ Maine.

8. New York City is (noisy) _____ Dallas.

E **Circle** **the adjective that compares your native country and/or city to the United States.** Then, work in a group and talk about your answers.

1. My country is **larger / smaller** than the United States.

2. My country is **more populated / less populated** than the United States.

3. The weather in my native city is **hotter / colder** than the weather in this city.

4. My native city is **rainier / drier** than this city.

5. The traffic in my native city is **heavier / lighter** than the traffic in this city.

6. My native city has **more / less** crime than this city.

7. Houses in my native city are **more expensive / less expensive** than houses in this area.

8. Gasoline is **more expensive / less expensive** than in the United States.

9. The cost of living here is **higher / lower** than in my country.

F **Working Together** **Work with a partner.** Compare yourselves, using the adjectives in the box. Then, tell the class two of your comparisons.

young	quiet
hair / long	talkative
hair / short	busy
tall	nervous
short	athletic

I am quieter than Sofia.

Active Grammar

		more	universities		
New York	has	**fewer**	jobs	**than**	Chicago.
Los Angeles		**more**	traffic		Dallas.
		less	noise		

Use *more* and *less* with non-count nouns.
Use *more* and *fewer* with count nouns.

A **Describe the differences between a city and a town.**
Complete the sentences with *more, less,* or *fewer*.

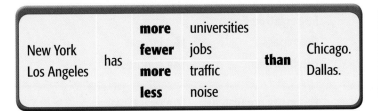

1. A city has _____more_____ skyscrapers.

2. There is _____ traffic in a town than a city.

3. Because of the traffic, there is _____ noise in a city.

4. A city offers _____ job opportunities.

5. There are _____ stores and restaurants in a town.

6. There are _____ tourists in a city than a town.

7. A town has _____ crime than a large city.

8. A town usually has _____ factories than a city.

 B **Write two comparative sentences about each fact in your notebook.**

1. Tourists to France: 82 million   Tourists to Italy: 44 million
France has more tourists than Italy.
Italy has fewer tourists than France.

2. Cars in Italy: 35 million   Cars in France: 30 million

3. Native speakers of Spanish: 332 million   Native speakers of English: 322 million

4. Saudi Arabia: produces 21 percent of the world's oil   Kuwait: produces 8 percent of the world's oil

5. Internet users in Japan: 95 million   Internet users in Germany: 53 million

6. People in the United States watch four hours of TV a day.   People in Australia watch three hours of TV a day.

Type of Adjective	Superlative Form		
One-syllable adjectives	**the** old**est**	**the** larg**est**	
Two-syllable adjectives ending in -*y*	**the** bus**iest**	**the** sunn**iest**	
Two-or-more-syllable adjectives not ending with -*y*	**the most** populated	**the most** interesting	
Irregular forms	good – **the best**	bad – **the worst**	far – **the farthest**

A **Write the adjectives in the correct column.**

rainy   high   fast   friendly   clean   healthy
expensive   noisy   modern   populated   popular   hot

One-syllable adjectives	Two-syllable adjectives ending in -*y*	Two-or-more-syllable adjectives not ending in -*y*
high	rainy	expensive

B **Write the superlative form of the adjectives in the correct column.**

One-syllable adjectives	Two-syllable adjectives ending in -*y*	Two-or-more-syllable adjectives not ending in -*y*
the highest	the rainiest	the most expensive

CD1・TR29

C **Pronunciation: Superlative Adjectives** **Listen and repeat.**

1. the busiest
2. the tallest
3. the largest
4. the noisiest
5. the friendliest
6. the farthest
7. the rainiest
8. the highest
9. the sunniest

D **Complete the sentences.** Use the superlative form of the adjectives.

1. Alaska is (cold) _____the coldest_____ state in the United States.

2. Florida is (popular) _____ state for retired people.

3. (high) _____ city in the world is Wenchaun, China.

4. The Great Pyramid of Giza is one of (famous) _____ structures in the world.

5. (large) _____ dome in the world is O₂ in London, England.

6. The Louvre in Paris is one of (interesting) _____ museums in the world.

7. Ojos del Salado is (tall) _____ volcano in the world.

E **Match the place and the feature.** Then, make a sentence about each place.

Places	Features
__c__ **1.** Greenland	**a.** (large) desert
_____ **2.** Everest	**b.** (cold) place
_____ **3.** The Sahara	**c.** (large) island
_____ **4.** Vatican City	**d.** (long) river
_____ **5.** The Nile	**e.** (high) waterfall
_____ **6.** Antarctica	**f.** (deep) ocean
_____ **7.** The Pacific	**g.** (low) place
_____ **8.** Asia	**h.** (large) continent
_____ **9.** The Dead Sea	**i.** (tall) mountain
_____ **10.** Angel Falls	**j.** (small) country

Greenland is the largest island in the world.

F **Work with a small group.** Talk about students in your class.

Zhen is one of the friendliest students in our class.

We often use *one of the _____* to talk about one of a group.

friendly	serious	young	talkative	organized
tall	athletic	quiet	funny	(good) singer

China France	is	**as interesting as** **as beautiful as**	India. Italy.

Colombia Ecuador	isn't	**as populated as** **as large as**	Brazil. Mexico.

Use **as** _____ **as** to show that two people, places, or things are the same.

Use **not as** _____ **as** to show that two people, places, or things are not the same.

Florida is **not as large as** Texas. = Texas is **larger than** Florida.

Silver is **not as expensive as** gold. = Gold is **more expensive than** silver.

China

India

A Dictation **Your teacher will dictate the sentences on pages 256–257.** Listen and write the sentences you hear.

1. _____

2. _____

3. _____

4. _____

5. _____

6. _____

 B Give your opinion. Use (*not*) *as* _____ *as* or a comparative adjective.

1. art museums / history museums / interesting

2. Chinese food / Italian food / tasty

3. traveling by car / traveling by train / comfortable

4. English / Mandarin Chinese / difficult

5. people in the city / people in the country / friendly

6. a week in New York City / a week in a national park / expensive

> Art museums are not as interesting as history museums.

> I think art museums are more interesting.

A **Complete the sentences.** Use the correct form of the adjectives.

1. New York is (large) _____the largest_____ city in the United States.
   But Mexico City is (large) _____larger than_____ New York City.

2. At this time, China is (populated) _____ India. But
   by 2025, India will probably be (populated) _____
   country in the world.

3. London has (long) _____ subway system in the
   world. But Tokyo has (busy) _____ subway system
   in the world.

4. Coffee is (popular) _____ hot beverage in the United
   States. In many countries, tea is (popular) _____
   coffee.

B **Working Together Work in a group of
four or five students.** Complete the sentences
about yourself. Then, compare yourself to other
students.

> Maria has two brothers and five sisters.
> She has the most brothers and sisters.

1. I have _____ brothers and sisters.   4. I live about _____ miles from school.

2. My house has _____ TVs.   5. I can speak _____ languages.

3. I get up at _____ in the morning.   6. I sleep _____ hours a night.

C **Discuss.** Use adjectives in some of your answers.

> Brazil has the best soccer
> team in the world.

> No way! Italy is better
> than Brazil.

> Spain has the strongest
> team this year.

1. What is the best soccer team in the world?

2. What is the busiest road in your area?

3. Who is the most famous leader in the world?

4. What is the best movie this year?

5. Which coffee is the tastiest?

6. What is the most interesting place to visit in your area?

7. What is the most difficult language to learn?

A Discuss.

1. What is the largest city in your native country?

2. Are cities diverse in your country?

3. Is unemployment high or low in your country?

4. How do most people commute to work?

Chicago

Los Angeles

New York

  B **Listen.** Complete the chart with information about New York City.

CD1·TR30

	Chicago	**Los Angeles**	**New York**
Population	2,837,000	3,834,000	
Percent of population that is Hispanic	28%	49%	
Unemployment rate	9.7%	12.2%	
Average household income	$44,684	$40,844	
Average home price	$282,000	$392,000	
Average commute time	39 minutes	32 minutes	
Percent of people who drive to work	51%	66%	
Museums	61	94	
Yearly rainfall	34 inches	13 inches	
Yearly snowfall	34 inches	None	
Sunny days per year	189	284	

C Complete the sentences using the information from the chart in Exercise B.

1. The population of New York is (high) _____higher than_____ the population of Chicago.

2. New York is (populated) _____ city in the United States.

3. Los Angeles has (high) _____ percentage of Hispanics of the three cities.

4. A house in Los Angeles is (expensive) _____ a house in Chicago.

5. A house in Chicago is (expensive) _____ a house in New York.

6. Chicago has (high) _____ household income.

7. Workers in New York have (long) _____ commute to work.

8. The Statue of Liberty is one of (popular) _____ tourist attractions in New York.

D Working Together Student to Student Listen and circle the correct city.

Student 1: Turn to page 255. Read the questions in **Set A.**

Student 2: Listen and circle the correct city below.

Change roles. Student 2 will turn to page 255 and read the questions in **Set B.** Student 1 will listen and circle the correct city.

1. Chicago   Los Angeles   New York
2. Chicago   Los Angeles   New York
3. Chicago   Los Angeles   New York
4. Chicago   Los Angeles   New York
5. Chicago   Los Angeles   New York
6. Chicago   Los Angeles   New York
7. Chicago   Los Angeles   New York

E Discuss.

1. Would you rather live in a large city or in a small town?

2. Where in the world would you like to live?

3. Which of the three cities in the chart would you like to visit?

4. What other countries or cities in the world would you like to visit?

A **Discuss.** Then, read.

1. What is the closest airport to your home?

2. What is the busiest airport in your native country?

3. Do you know anyone who works at an airport? What is the person's job?

> **CULTURE NOTE**
>
> Many airlines offer frequent flier programs. A frequent flier is a person who often flies on a particular airline. Each time the passenger flies, the airline gives the passenger "miles." The passenger can use the miles to get free flights, to upgrade to business or first class, or to shop.

Three of the busiest airports in the world are in the United States. Los Angeles Airport (LAX) is located in Los Angeles, California. O'Hare Airport (ORD) is in Chicago, Illinois, and Hartsfield Atlanta International Airport (ATL) is in Atlanta, Georgia. These are the three busiest airports because of the large number of passengers that pass through these airports every year. In addition, these airports move a great deal of cargo (packages, equipment, and so on) through the cargo airlines that also fly from the airports.

LAX was established in 1928. It is now one of the busiest airports in the world, with 50 passenger and cargo airlines that use the airport. In 2009, more than 56 million passengers flew into or out of LAX. About 53,000 employees work at the airport. The employees work at a number of places throughout the airport, including airline counters, coffee shops, bakeries, and one of the 55 stores where passengers can shop. LAX is a pet-friendly airport with a small pet park where passengers can walk their dogs.

More than 70 million passengers passed through O'Hare in 2009, another one of the busiest airports in the world, with 78 airlines using its facilities. O'Hare was established in 1945. Today many frequent fliers know O'Hare because flights often stop in Chicago on the way to other parts of the country or the world. Because so many passengers spend significant time in the airport, O'Hare offers a number of services, such as a hair salon, a children's museum, an athletic club, and a post office. There are 72 restaurants and stores, which are operated by the airport's 50,000 employees.

Established in 1925, Hartsfield has become the busiest airport in the world. A quarter of a million passengers pass through the airport each day. In 2009, more than 90 million passengers arrived or departed through its gates. Fifty passenger and cargo airlines use the airport. Fifty-six thousand employees work for the airlines, the 114 restaurants, and 91 shops. In fact, the airport is the largest employer in Georgia. To help people move from terminal to terminal, or from a terminal to one of the 30,000 parking spaces, the airport has an underground people mover, which connects all the airport terminals.

B Scan the reading and complete the chart.

Airport	Number of passengers in 2009	Year established	Number of airlines	Number of employees	Facilities offered
Los Angeles Airport (LAX)	56 million				
O'Hare Airport (ORD)					
Hartsfield Atlanta Airport (ATL)					

C Correct the information. Write the name of the correct airport.

1. ~~LAX~~ ATL is the busiest airport in the world.

2. ORD is the oldest airport of the three.

3. ATL employs the fewest workers of the three airports.

4. ORD is the most pet-friendly airport of the three.

5. LAX handles the most passengers.

6. LAX hires the most employees.

> **READING NOTE**
>
> **Scanning for Information**
> When you scan an article, you do not need to read every word. You look through the article quickly to find the information you need.

A Read.

Dear Friend,

You should come to visit my country, Peru. It is one of the most interesting countries in South America. It has one of the most unusual places—Machu Picchu. Machu Picchu is one of the new Seven Wonders of the World. It is an ancient Inca site, located high in the Andes Mountains. Machu Picchu was the estate of the Inca emperor Pachacuti. You can visit the ruins of over 200 buildings, including houses, temples, and public buildings. One of the most famous places there is the Temple of the Sun. It has wonderful architecture. Don't miss the Temple of the Three Windows. It has a fantastic view of the Andes Mountains.

The best time to visit Peru is from May to September. That is the driest period. The busiest time is during our national holiday, July 28th, so it is better to travel before or after that date. If you come in the wintertime, you can experience one of our most exciting festivals, the Festival of the Sun.

See you in Peru,
Marco

B Add commas to the sentences in the correct places.

1. Airport employees work at airline counters, stores, and restaurants.

2. The three largest countries in the world are Russia Canada and the United States.

3. There are three countries in North America: Canada the United States and Mexico.

4. In my country, you can listen to the best music at nightclubs in restaurants or at the university.

5. New York City has the most art museums on the East Coast. For example, you can visit the Museum of Modern Art the Whitney Museum or the Guggenheim.

> **WRITING NOTE: COMMAS**
>
> Add commas (,) in a list of three or more people, places, or things.
>
> The Amazon, the Nile, and the Yangtze are the three longest rivers in the world.
>
> O'Hare, LAX, and Hartsfield are the three busiest airports in the United States.
>
> O'Hare has many restaurants and stores. (No comma)

C **Your friend is trying to decide where to go for vacation.** Write a letter to your friend. Explain why your native country is a good place for a vacation. Use some superlatives. Here are some questions you can answer:

- Why should your friend visit your country?

- When is the best time to visit your country?

- What is one of the most popular places to visit? Describe it.

- What is one of the most historic places?

- What is one of the best beaches, lakes, or rivers? Why is it "the best"?

- What is the most interesting place? Why?

- What is the most fun activity to do in your country?

D **Find and correct the adjective mistake in each sentence.**

1. Canada is the large country in the world.

2. China is more populated then Russia.

3. The Nile River is more longer than the Yangtze River.

4. The New York subway system is much more longer than the Boston subway system.

5. The Great Wall of China is one of most popular attractions in the world.

6. The most hot inhabited place in the world is Dallol, Ethiopia.

7. California is not as larger as Alaska.

 E **Sharing Our Stories** **Give a short presentation to your classmates about an interesting destination in your native country.** If possible, bring in a few pictures of the place.

> One of the most interesting places in my country is...

A Discuss.

1. What Internet search engine do you use?

2. What kinds of information do you look up on the Internet?

3. What websites do you often use?

4. Is most information on the Internet up to date?

5. How do you know if the information on the Internet is true?

B Word Builder Write the full name of each of these domains.

1. .edu _____ *education* _____

2. .com _____

3. .net _____

4. .org _____

5. .gov _____

6. .mil _____

WORD PARTNERSHIPS	
look up	information
	a word
	the meaning
	the definition
	the address

Internet Search Tips: Keywords

1. Be specific.
   Example: Who won the World Series in 2000?
   Type: World Series 2000.

2. Put the most important words first.

3. Use three keywords or more:
   heart: too general
   heart disease: too general
   heart disease causes: good – specific keywords

4. Put complete titles and phrases in quotes:
   "Blue Ridge Parkway"

5. Try different search engines.

6. At times, click on *Images* or *Maps* or *Videos* to get
   a visual look at the information you want.

C **Go online.** Find the information in the charts. Work in a group of two or three students. Write one more question for number 6.

URL = Universal Resource Locator or
     = Internet address

1. What is the weather forecast for Barcelona, Spain, tomorrow?

Keywords:	
URL:	
Answer:	

2. What is the population of Moscow, Russia?

Keywords:	
URL:	
Answer:	

3. How much is a ticket from the airport nearest you to Honolulu, Hawaii?

Keywords:	
URL:	
Answer:	

4. Who won the gold medal in men's tennis in the 2008 Summer Olympics?

Keywords:	
URL:	
Answer:	

5. What are the hours of the Shedd Aquarium in Chicago? How much is an adult ticket?

Keywords:	
URL:	
Answer:	

6. Question:

Keywords:	
URL:	
Answer:	

D **Compare your information as a class.**

1. Does every group have the same information?

2. Did every group use the same website?

3. Are some websites more reliable than others?

Unit 8

Moving

A **Read and complete.** The average American moves eleven times during his or her life. What is your experience with moving?

1. In my native country, I _____.

   a. never moved   **b.** moved once   **c.** moved _several_ _____ times

2. I came to the United States in _____.

3. I **had / didn't have** family in the United States.

4. Since I came to the United States, I have _moved once_

   a. never moved   **b.** moved once   **c.** moved _____ times

5. In the United States, I have lived in _____ and _____.
                                          (city or state)   (city or state)

6. I moved because _____.

7. Now I live in ___*Portland*___. In the future, I would like to live in
                 (city or state)
___*california*___.
   (city or state)

8. In the future, I **will / won't** return to my native country to live.

در دفتر نوشته شده !

I	**lived**	in Taiwan.
He	**moved**	to the United States.
They	**signed**	a lease.

1. Regular past tense verbs end in
   -*d* or -*ed*.
   (See Spelling Rules Appendix, page 253.)
2. The form is the same for singular and
   plural subjects.

A **Read the story.** Write the verbs in the past tense.

خوانده بود ✗

Miguel and Ana were unhappy in their last apartment. The apartment
had only one bedroom and the kitchen was very small. They (want)
_____wanted_____ an apartment with two bedrooms and a large
                1
kitchen. They (look) _____looked_____ in the newspaper and (talk)
                              2
_____talked_____ to friends. Finally, they found an apartment they (like)
          3
_____liked_____ . They (sign) _____signed_____ a lease and paid a
        4   5
security deposit. Miguel and Ana (pack) _____packed_____ their clothes,
                                              6
books, and kitchen items into boxes. Miguel (rent) _____rented_____ a small
                                                              7
truck. On moving day, several of their friends (help) _____helped_____ them
                                                                8
move. They (carry) _____carried_____ furniture and boxes out of the old
                          9
apartment and into their new home.

B Pronunciation: Final -ed Listen. Write the number of syllables you hear. Then, listen again and repeat.

CD1·TR31

> After most consonants, **-ed** is pronounced as /t/ or /d/.
> After /d/ and /t/, **-ed** is pronounced /əd/. This adds a syllable to the verb.

1. changed ___1___   5. liked ___1___   9. lived ___1___
2. rented ___2___   6. wanted ___2___   10. painted ___2___
3. looked ___1___   7. helped ___1___   11. signed ___1___
4. needed ___2___   8. called ___1___   12. waited ___2___

C Pronunciation: Linking -ed + vowel sound Listen and repeat.

CD1·TR32

> The final *t* or *d* sound is often linked with the first vowel in the next word.

1. He lived‿in a small apartment.   4. He signed‿a lease.
2. He looked‿at many apartments.   5. He packed‿all his things.
3. He filled‿out a rental application. 6. He borrowed‿a van.

D Talk about the things Miguel and Ana did when they moved into their new apartment.

> They registered their son in school.

1. register their son in school
2. introduce themselves to their neighbors
   They introduced themselves to their neighbors.
3. file a change of address form in the post office
   They filed change of address from in the post office.
4. open a bank account *opened a bank account.*
5. paint the kitchen *Painted the kitchen*
6. wash the windows
7. try a few restaurants in town
8. call the telephone company
9. change the address on their drivers' licenses
10. apply for a library card

Befor I moved I Packed my suitcase – I bought ticket – I went to the our
friend's hom to say good bye.

E Make a list of five things you did before or after you moved. Share your list with a partner.
I came with aircraft. I
I introduce with my neighbors.
I began study English.
made sure my husband with me.

A **Listen and repeat.**

CD1·TR33

[handwritten notes in Persian/Farsi in the margins]

Discuss different ways to memorize the irregular past tense verbs.

Simple Form	Past	Simple Form	Past	Simple Form	Past
be	was / were	fly	flew	run	ran
become	became	forget	forgot	say	said
begin	began	get	got	see	saw
bite	bit	give	gave	sell	sold
break	broke	go	went	send	sent
bring	brought	grow	grew	sit	sat
buy	bought	have	had	sleep	slept
come	came	hear	heard	speak	spoke
cost	cost	know	knew	spend	spent
do	did	leave	left	steal	stole
drink	drank	lose	lost	take	took
drive	drove	make	made	teach	taught
eat	ate	meet	met	tell	told
fall	fell	pay	paid	think	thought
feel	felt	put	put	wake	woke
fight	fought	read	read	wear	wore
find	found	ring	rang	write	wrote

B **Ask and answer the questions.** Use a verb from the list above.

1. When did you come to the United States?
   I came to the United States 4 months ago.
2. How did you come? *I came by aircraft. airplane*
3. How much did you pay for your ticket?
   I paid 1,200 $.
4. What did you bring with you?
5. Who met you at the airport? *my friend met me.*
6. How did you feel? *our felt were exited.*
7. Did you know anyone in the United States? *yes, we did. we knew several people.* *we got to know some new People*
8. Where did you go when you left the airport? *we went to the our friend's home.*
9. What did you buy your first week in the United States? *we didn't buy anything.*
10. When did you find your first job? *I didn't found any job.*
11. When did you begin to study English? *I began soon.*

sold every thing I had.
Packed my suitcases.   unpacked my suitcases.

Moving · 117

Active Grammar

Past Time Expressions

Yesterday	Last	Ago
yesterday morning	last night	a few minutes ago
yesterday afternoon	last week	an hour ago
yesterday evening	last weekend	a week ago
	last Saturday	two years ago
	last month	
	last year	

در دفتر نولتَه شره !

Use a time expression at the beginning or the end of a sentence.

A **Complete the sentences.** Use *yesterday*, *last*, or *ago*.

خوانده شود ✗

1. We moved _____ **last** _____ year.

2. My brother visited us _____ last _____ month.

3. I graduated from high school six years _____ ago _____ .

4. My sister broke her arm _____ last _____ Tuesday.

5. He got his driver's license _____ last _____ August.

6. The teacher left the classroom a few minutes _____ ago _____ .

7. I went to the dentist _____ yesterday _____ morning.

8. We got married five years _____ ago _____ .

9. I paid my rent _____ yesterday _____ afternoon.

10. I came to the United States a year _____ ago _____ .

B **Talk about the last time you did the things listed below.**

2. I took a vacation yesterday morning.

3. we came to class late last week.

4. I watched a movie yesterday afternoon.

5. we ate out yesterday evening.

> I bought a new camera last year.

خوانده شود ✗

1. buy a new camera

2. take a vacation

3. come to class late

4. watch a movie

5. eat out

6. give someone a present

7. go to a party

8. lose something

9. wake up late

10. get a traffic ticket

Simple Past Tense: Negatives

دردفترنوشته شده !

I	**didn't live**	in the city.
We	**didn't have**	a garden.
He	**didn't lock**	his doors.
They	**didn't take**	the bus to school.

Use *didn't* and the simple form of the verb to form the negative.

A **Complete the sentences about the place where you grew up.**

خوانده شود ✗

1. I (live) _____lived_____ in the city.

2. I (live) _____didn't live_____ in a small town.

3. I (grow up) _didn't grow up_ on a farm. *I didn't walk*

4. When I was a child, I (walk) _____walked_____ to school.

5. I (have) _____had_____ my own bedroom. *I didn't have …*

6. We (know) _didn't know_ our neighbors. *I knew …*

7. We (feel) _____felt_____ safe in our neighborhood. *didn't feel …*

8. We (lock) _didn't lock_ our doors. *we locked …*

B **Working Together** **Compare your life now with life in your native country.**

خوانده شود ✗

> In my country, I watched TV two or three hours a day. Now, I'm too busy. I only watch TV on the weekends.

+ In my country I ate Iranian food Now, I have many kinds of food to choose.

1. watch TV   **6.** eat _____ food

2. wear a warm coat   **7.** go to the market every day

3. study English   **8.** work

4. have a computer   **9.** know my neighbors

5. drive   **10.** eat at fast-food restaurants

C **In your notebook, make a chart.** Write three differences between your life now and your life in your native country.

Then	Now
I didn't eat at fast-food restaurants.	I eat at a fast-food restaurant once a week.

in my country, I didn't eat fastfood Now, I don't eat fastfood either

in my country, I ate fastfood. Now, I eat fast food also too

D Talk about your first year in the United States.

> I arrived at Kennedy Airport.

> I didn't fly here. I drove across the border at Tijuana.

1. arrive at an airport
2. live with a relative
3. begin to study English *this Term*
4. like the weather
5. like the food
6. miss my family
7. visit relatives

8. come to the United States with my family
9. find a job
10. call my family a lot
11. meet new friends
12. get a driver's license
13. travel
14. go to high school here

CD1·TR34

E Jarek is talking about some important events in his life. Listen and complete the time line.

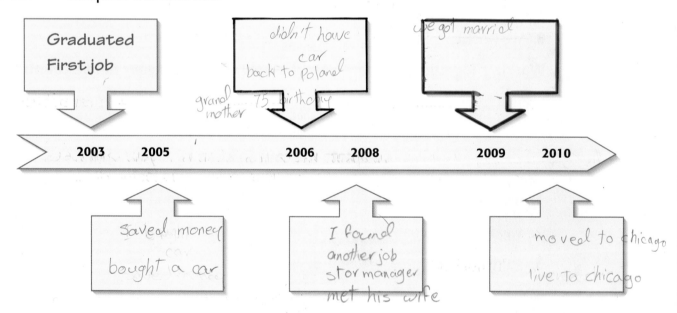

Graduated
First job

didn't have car
back to Poland
grand mother 75 birthday

we got married

2003   2005   2006   2008   2009   2010

Saved money bought a car

I found another job stor manager
met his wife

moved to chicago
live to chicago

F Working Together Draw a time line with six or seven important dates in your life. Share your time line with another student. What events did you both include on your time line? What events are different?

Active Grammar

(handwritten note in Persian) X خوانده شود

Present Tense of *Be*	Past Tense of *Be*
I **am** busy.	I **was** busy.
You **are** lonely.	You **were** lonely.
He **is** friendly.	He **was** friendly.
It **is** safe.	It **was** safe.
They **are** noisy.	They **were** noisy.

1. *Was* and *were* are the past tense of *be*.
2. The negative forms are *wasn't* and *weren't*.
   I *wasn't* busy.
   You *weren't* lonely.

The neighbors were unfriendly.

A **Boris did not like his old apartment. Explain the reasons.**

(handwritten note in Persian) X خوانده شود

1. neighbors / unfriendly
2. apartment / small
3. appliances / old
4. neighbors / noisy
5. elevator / usually broken

6. neighborhood / (negative) safe
7. apartment / dark
8. rent / high   *reviews*
9. landlord / (negative) helpful   *furnishing help*
   giving aid useful
10. apartment / (negative) near public transportation

B **Working Together Complete the conversation with your own ideas.**
Then, practice it with a partner. Act out your conversation for the class.

(handwritten note in Persian) در دفترنوشته شده !

A: Why did you move?

B: I didn't like my old apartment!

A: Why not? What was the problem?

B: _The appliances were too old._

A: How about your neighbors?

B: _my neighbors were noisy. (they weren't quiet)_

A: How much was the rent?

B: _It was $600 a mounth.   It was too high._

A: How do you like your new apartment?

B: I love it! It's _big, new_ and _doesn't ✓ noisy. neighbors ._   *have*

A **Why do people move?** Add five more reasons to the list.

✓ 1. They get a new job.

✓ 2. They want better schools for their children.

3. They find better land for staying.

4. They need To new house.

5. They want friendly neighbors.

6. They have logical reason for themselves.

7. They are happier than ever.

✓ They want to less rent.
Pay

B **Listen to the conversation between Yolanda and a new friend.** Take notes about the reasons she and her husband moved and the places they moved to.

CD1·TR35

why? where?

Reason		Place	
1. She got married.		1.	5 times
2.	liked neighbors	2.	wasn't helpful
3.		3.	always broken
4.	we hade baby	4.	To small
5.	chang job	5.	lots room
	transfort him here		rent appartment

C **Put the sentences in order.** Use your notes from Exercise B to help you.

_8_ **a.** Diego's company transferred him to Atlanta.

_1_ **b.** Yolanda and Diego got married.

_10_ **c.** They just moved into their first house.

_3_ **d.** They rented a one-bedroom apartment in Easton.

_5_ **e.** They moved to an apartment in Dover.

_4_ **f.** The building had many problems.

_6_ **g.** Yolanda had a baby and they needed a larger apartment.

_9_ **h.** They lived in apartment for a year to get to know the area.

_2_ **i.** They moved to the United States.

_7_ **j.** They moved back to Easton.

D **Dictation Your teacher will dictate the sentences on page 257.** Listen and write the sentences you hear. The verb in each sentence is negative.

1. _Yoland and Diego weren't happy on the first apartment._
2. _The landlord didn't fix things._
3. _They didn't like the location of the second apartment._
4. _The apartment wasn't near Diego's job._
5. _They neighors weren't friendly._
6. _After they had a baby their apartment wasn't big enough._
7. _When they moved to Atlanta they didn't know anything about the area._

E **Complete the chart with information about the moves you have made.**

Year	Location	Reason You Moved

F **Working Together Talk with a partner about the information in your chart.** Write a conversation about your moves and the reasons you moved. Join with another group and act out your conversation.

A **Discuss.** Then, read.

Have you ever seen the inside of a large recreational vehicle (RV)? Tell the class about the rooms, the furniture, and the equipment.

How often do Mark and Joan LaPlant move? Three or four times a year!

Mark and Joan are full-timers, that is, they live in their recreational vehicle full time. In the winter, Florida is their home. In the summer and fall, they travel around the country, visiting national parks, oceans, and forests. Mark and Joan retired when they were fifty, sold their home, and have been "moving" since then. They tell their friends that it is the perfect lifestyle for them, pointing to its many advantages. First, they love the independence. They follow the warm weather and have visited forty states in their travels. They don't miss home **ownership**. Mark says he doesn't need to think about cutting the lawn, raking the leaves, or painting the house. According to Joan, their lifestyle is healthier than before. They walk, hike, and enjoy the outdoors almost every day. Mark and Joan also say that it's easy to make friends. At an RV park, your neighbors are fellow travelers. You soon find yourself sharing adventures and the names of interesting places to visit. Mark and Joan stay **in touch with** their family and friends on the Internet. Their children live in North Carolina and in Texas, so these two states are major stops on their travels.

However, there are some disadvantages to RV life. Space is **limited**. Joan and Mark sold or gave away their furniture and many of their personal **belongings**. Joan says, "I don't buy anything anymore—there's no place for it. Last year, my only purchase was a new set of towels." There is less **privacy**, too. You can't walk into another room and just be alone for a time. Next, a large RV can be difficult to **maneuver**. Mark reports, "I enjoy driving on the highway, but you don't want to drive this to the supermarket. Backing up is difficult and finding a parking space is impossible!" Most full-timers tow a car behind their RV. With the high price of gas, moving an RV has become expensive. A full-size RV gets five to ten miles per gallon. Mark and Joan used to move five or six times a year, but now they only move three times.

Mark and Joan have a word of advice for anyone considering a full-time RV lifestyle. Don't sell your house and buy an RV. Rent an RV and try it out first.

B Read the article again. List three more advantages and three more disadvantages of a full-time RV lifestyle.

— They don't buy any thing any more.

Advantages	Disadvantages
1. Independence. _freedom_	1. Space is limited.
2. _Don't miss home ownership_	2. _- No place for their personal belongings_
3. _Doesn't need think about cutting the lawn, raking the leaves_	3. _- less privacy_
4. _healthier than before_	4. _- difficult to maneuver_ _- Backing up is difficult_ _- Finding a parking space_

or Painting the house

C Word Builder Circle the meaning of each underlined word.

1. They don't miss home <u>ownership</u>.

   a. life   **b.** possession   **c.** expenses

2. Mark and Joan stay <u>in touch with</u> their family and friends on the Internet.

   a. near   **b.** interested in   **c.** connected with

   keep in touch / stay in touch

   WORD PARTNERSHIPS

stay	
keep	in touch

3. Space is <u>limited</u>.

   a. large   **b.** small   **c.** comfortable

4. Joan and Mark sold or gave away their furniture and many of their personal <u>belongings</u>.

   a. pictures   **b.** friends   **c.** things

5. There is less <u>privacy</u>, too.

   a. time   **b.** friendship   **c.** space to yourself

6. A large RV can be difficult to <u>maneuver</u>.

   a. buy   **b.** take care of   **c.** drive

D Discuss.

1. Would you like to live an RV lifestyle? Explain why or why not.

2. What places would you like to visit?

خطیقلمسر ✗

A **Read Lidia's story about her first year in the United States.**

Inter

My arrival in the United States was a family affair. *event*
My mother and father and four brothers and I came to
the United States from Peru together. My two older
brothers met us at the airport. They had been here for
many years and they were finally able to sponsor us.

We arrived in October, not able to speak any English. By
January, I was studying English at the local adult school.

One of my brothers helped me find a job in a nail polish factory. I didn't
like it at all because the salary was very low, and new workers came and
went every few weeks. After a year, I was able to attend beauty school and
get a manicurist license. When I finished, I got a job at a nail salon. Many
of my customers were American, so I was able to become more confident
speaking English.

The first summer we were here, my brother taught me how to drive. I passed
my driving test on my first try! At first, I only drove near my house, but now
I can go a little farther.

I think the first year in this country is difficult and a little scary, but it's
also exciting. It really helps if your family is together and you can help
each other.

Lidia

– I didn't like my job, so I quit. *ترسیدن*
– I quit my job because
  I didn't like it

WRITING NOTE

Using *so*

Use *so* to show the result of an action or a situation.

I didn't speak English, **so** I couldn't find a good job.

We didn't like the cold weather, **so** we moved to Arizona.

B **Match the two parts of each sentence.**

__b__ **1.** I didn't like my job,   **a.** so I went to live with him.

__a__ **2.** My brother already lived here,   **b.** so I quit. *ترک*

__c__ **3.** I couldn't speak English,   **c.** so I registered for English class.

__e__ **4.** English was very difficult,   **d.** so I rented one with a friend.

__d__ **5.** Apartments were very expensive,   **e.** so I studied very hard.

becaus apartments are expensive.

C **Complete the sentences.**

1. I didn't have a car, so ___I take a bus.___ *(took)* *(out)*
2. My neighborhood wasn't safe, so ___I went with my dad___ *always*

D **Check (✓) the information that is true about your first year in the United States. Complete the sentences.**

☐ **1.** I came to the United States alone.

☑ **2.** I came to the United States with my family.

☐ **3.** I found a job at _____.

☑ **4.** I didn't find a job.

☑ **5.** I began to study English.

☑ **6.** I got my driver's license.

☑ **7.** I moved from ___Iran___ to ___United States___.

☐ **8.** I traveled to _____.

☑ **9.** I bought a ___car___.

E **Write about your first year in the United States.** For ideas, look at the checklist in Exercise D and your time line on page 120. Include one or two sentences with *so*.

F **Find and correct the mistakes.**

1. I came to *the* United States in 2001.
2. I ~~not have~~ *didn't* any family in this country.
3. I ~~live~~ *lived* with some friends for a month.
4. I found a job, but I ~~no~~ *didn't* like it. So, I quit soon.
5. In my country I ~~have~~ *had* a better job. So, I don't know what am I doing now?
6. At first, I ~~am~~ *was* very lonely. So, I'm not lonely either.
7. I ~~miss~~ *missed* my family a lot, so I called them every week.
8. My first year was difficult because I ~~don't~~ *didn't* speak English. So, I comfortable now.
9. I ~~begin~~ *began* to study English at an adult school.

A Write the letter of the housing problem under the correct picture.

a. The faucet is leaking.
b. The lock is broken.
c. There are cockroaches.
d. The paint is peeling.
e. The air conditioner isn't working.
f. We don't have any heat.

1. _____

2. _____

3. _____

4. _____

5. _____

6. _____

CD1·TR36

B **Listen to the conversations.** Write the problem and the apartment owner's response.

Conversation 1

Problem: _____

Response: _____

Conversation 2

Problem: _____

Response: _____

C **Write four more housing problems.**

1. _____.

2. _____.

3. _____.

4. _____.

CULTURE NOTE

If you have an apartment, keep a record of your calls with the landlord. Write the date, the time, and the name of the person you spoke to. Keep a copy of any notes you send. If possible, take a photograph of the problem.

D **Read the conversation.** Then, discuss the questions with a partner.

Landlord: Bob Parker here.

Tenant: Hi, Mr. Parker. This is Linda Torres from Apartment 320. We don't have any hot water.

Landlord: Oh, I'm sorry. Do you have cold water?

Tenant: Yes, we have cold water, but no hot water.

Landlord: It might be the hot water heater. I'll come by later today. Will you be home at about 3:00?

Tenant: No, I don't get home until 4:00.

Landlord: Okay. I'll be there sometime between 4:00 and 5:00.

Tenant: Thanks. I'll see you then.

1. What is the tenant's problem?

2. What does the landlord think is the cause of the problem?

3. When will the landlord come to the apartment?

4. Do you think Mr. Parker is a good landlord? Why or why not?

E Working Together **Write a telephone conversation between a tenant and a landlord.** Then, act out your conversation for the class.

Natural Disasters

CD2·TR1

A **Listen and repeat the natural disaster or event.** Then, write the correct word under each picture.

hurricane	heat wave	forest fire
flood	drought	snowstorm / blizzard
earthquake	volcanic eruption	tornado

a. _____

b. _____

c. _____

d. _____

e. _____

f. _____

g. _____

h. _____

i. _____

B **Write the letter of the event from Exercise A next to its description.**

____d____ **1.** We saw a large black cloud in the sky and we ran into the basement.

_____ **2.** The rain was very heavy and the wind was terrible. It knocked down thousands of trees in our area. We lost part of our roof.

_____ **3.** We could see the flames and the smoke for fifty miles.

_____ **4.** The house shook. I quickly got under the table. Some of our pictures fell off the walls.

_____ **5.** The water in the river kept rising and rising. We had to evacuate our house.

_____ **6.** For days before, the mountain made loud noises and smoke came out of the top. Then, there was a terrible explosion and rocks shot up in the air. The lava started to flow down the mountain.

_____ **7.** It was very hot for weeks. The city issued a warning that people should not exercise. We had our air conditioner on all day.

_____ **8.** It snowed for two days. We had three feet of snow. School closed for three days. It took us two days to shovel our driveway.

_____ **9.** There was no rain all summer. The city declared water restrictions. We couldn't water the lawn or wash our cars.

C **Discuss.**

1. What is a "natural" disaster? Can you think of any other natural disasters?

2. Have any of these natural disasters ever occurred in your state?

3. Look at the map of the United States on page 274. What areas of the United States are more likely to have hurricanes? snowstorms? earthquakes? tornadoes?

4. Which of these events or disasters sometimes occur in your native country?

5. Have you ever experienced a natural disaster? Tell the class about the event.

Were you home?	Yes, I **was.**	No, I **wasn't.**
Was he cold?	Yes, he **was.**	No, he **wasn't.**
Was it windy?	Yes, it **was.**	No, it **wasn't.**
Were they scared?	Yes, they **were.**	No, they **weren't.**

Where were you?	I **was** at home.
Why was she scared?	Because the fire **was** near her house.
Where was the forest fire?	It **was** in California.

CD2·TR2

A **Complete the questions and answers.** Then, listen and check your work.

1. How deep __was__ the water?   It __was__ six feet deep.

2. How strong _____ the wind?   It _____ a hundred miles per hour.

3. _____ you in Texas during the drought?   Yes, I _____.

4. How long _____ the drought?   It _____ five months long.

5. _____ there any rain?   No, there _____.

6. Where _____ the tornadoes?   They _____ in Nebraska.

7. _____ you at home?   No, I _____. I _____ in my car.

8. How many tornadoes _____ there?   There _____ four.

9. When _____ the earthquake?   It _____ last year.

10. How strong _____ the earthquake?   Thankfully, it _____ strong.

11. _____ the children in school?   Yes, they _____.

12. _____ any children hurt?   No, they _____.

Did	you	**evacuate**?	Yes, I **did**.	No, I **didn't**.
	he	**go** to work?	Yes, he **did**.	No, he **didn't**.
	it	**rain** all week?	Yes, it **did**.	No, it **didn't**.
	they	**lose** power?	Yes, they **did**.	No, they **didn't**.

CD2·TR3

A **Pronunciation: *Did you* Listen and repeat.**

> In conversation, *Did you* sounds like /*Diju*/ or /*Didja*/.

1. Did you see the tornado?

2. Did you watch the storm on TV? **4.** Did you have any damage?

3. Did you evacuate? **5.** Did you feel the earthquake?

B **Last month, there was a heat wave in Texas.** It was over 100°F every day. Call your friend in Texas and ask about his experience. Use the words and pictures below.

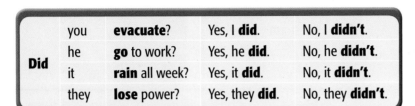

Did people exercise outside?

No, they didn't. They exercised at the gym.

1. people / exercise outside

2. people / drink a lot of water

3. the power / go out

4. you / take long cool showers

5. you / keep your air conditioner on all day

6. you / turn off your air conditioner at night

 C **Write five more questions to ask your friend about the heat wave.**

When	did	the storm	begin?
Where	did	you	stay?
How many days	did	it	rain?
How much damage	did	you	have?

A **Write the words in the correct order to make questions.**

1. the tornado / did / What time / hit / ?

   What time did the tornado hit?

2. you / were / Where / ?

   _____

3. warning / have / How much / you / did / ?

   _____

4. see / tornadoes / did / How many / you / ?

   _____

5. do / did / you / What / ?

   _____

6. did / in the basement / you / How long / stay / ?

   _____

7. have / you / Did / any damage / ?

   _____

 B **Working Together Use the questions in Exercise A.** Practice a conversation between two friends about a tornado. Act out your conversation for the class.

What time did the tornado hit?

It hit at 2:30 in the afternoon.

C **Read.** Then, complete the questions and answers.

A forest fire that burned 15,000 acres was finally brought under control on Wednesday morning. The fire began Sunday in Black Bear State Park.

On Monday, the mayor ordered all residents to leave their homes. The police evacuated more than 500 residents. The fire destroyed twenty homes in the area and caused heavy damage to forty others. There were no injuries. Officials estimated the damage to homes and cars at two million dollars. The governor declared the town a disaster area.

The fire spread quickly in the hot, dry conditions. It was difficult to fight the fire because of the strong winds.

Police closed Route 40 to traffic on Tuesday because of heavy smoke conditions. Thousands of travelers had to drive an hour north to Route 28 to pass the fire area.

Some residents did not follow the evacuation order. Paul Grayson sent his wife and two children to safety, but he stayed to hose down his roof with water. As flames came near his house, he started thinking, "Am I crazy? Did I stay here too long, just for a house?"

1. How many acres _did the forest fire burn_____?

It burned 15,000 acres.

2. When _____?

It started on Sunday.

3. Where _____?

It began in Black Bear State Park.

4. How many residents _____?

The police evacuated more than 500 residents.

5. How many homes _____?

The fire destroyed twenty homes.

6. How much _____?

There was about two million dollars in damage.

7. Why _____?

It was difficult to fight the fire because of the strong winds.

8. Which road _____?

The police closed Route 40.

9. Why _____?

He wanted to hose down the roof of his house.

D **Working Together** **Work with a group.** Write ten questions about the snowstorm. Then, join another group. Ask and answer your questions.

Buffalo, New York, is located on Lake Ontario. Cold air from Canada moves across the lake, bringing heavy snow. In one storm in 2001, it snowed for three days, and 81 inches of snow (2 meters) fell in the city.

1. How many inches of snow did Buffalo get? _____
2. _____
3. _____
4. _____
5. _____
6. _____
7. _____
8. _____
9. _____
10. _____

Who helped a neighbor after the flood?	Jack **did.**
Who saw the tornado?	Ivan and Raisa **did.**
Who was at home when the earthquake hit?	Ursula **was.**

In these questions, *Who* is the subject.

 Kim and Don Vo live in southern California. There was a large forest fire near their home.

 Carla lives in Kansas. Last week, she saw a tornado coming toward her house.

 Brian lives in Buffalo, New York. After the last snowstorm, there was three feet (one meter) of snow on the ground.

 Marisa and Marco live in Florida. They listened to the reports of the hurricane coming toward their city.

 A **Ask and answer questions with *Who*.**

Who shoveled the driveway?

Brian did.

1. shovel the driveway

2. run down to the basement

3. evacuate

4. have an accident in the snow

5. listen to the weather channel

6. see the fire in the distance

7. hear the tornado warning

8. pack the car and leave

B **Work with a group of five or six students.** Ask and answer the questions.

1. Who watched the news last night?

2. Who had a big breakfast today?

3. Who read the newspaper today?

4. Who listened to the weather report this morning?

5. Who called a family member last night?

6. Who got up late this morning?

7. Who took the bus to school?

8. Who went to bed after midnight last night?

No one did.
I did.
Two of us did.
A couple of us did.
A few of us did.
All of us did.

A **This family is preparing for a hurricane.** Explain what they are doing and why.

 B **Listen to the conversation.** Then, answer the questions.

1. Where does the couple live?

2. How much warning did they have before the hurricane?

3. What did they put in the garage? Why?

4. What did they buy at the store?

5. Why did they need a power saw?

6. Why do you think they filled the bathtub with water?

7. How strong was the wind?

8. How long was the power out?

9. What damage did their neighbor have?

10. Where did the woman stay during the hurricane?

C Complete the questions with *Did* or *Was*. Then, write the answers.

1. <u>Did</u> they listen to the weather forecast?   <u>Yes, they did.</u>

2. _____ there enough warning?   _____

3. _____ they buy water?   _____

4. _____ the wind strong?   _____

5. _____ they evacuate their home?   _____

6. _____ the woman scared?   _____

7. _____ she stay in the bathroom?   _____

8. _____ her husband relaxed?   _____

9. _____ the rain heavy?   _____

10. _____ a tree fall on their house?   _____

D Complete the conversation.

A: How much warning <u>did you have</u> _____?

B: We had warnings for about a week.

A: Where _____?

B: We put everything in the garage.

A: What _____?

B: We bought extra food, batteries, and a power saw.

A: _____?

B: No, we didn't evacuate. We stayed in the house.

A: How strong _____?

B: It was 80 miles per hour.

A: _____?

B: Yes, we lost electricity for two days.

A: _____?

B: No, we had very little damage.

A: _____?

B: I was so scared! I stayed in the bathroom most of the time.

A **Read each statement about tornadoes.** (Circle) *True* or *False*. Then, read the article and check your answers.

1. Tornadoes can be weak or strong.   True   False

2. There are more tornadoes in the United States
   than in any other country.   True   False

3. Tornadoes form over the water.   True   False

4. Tornadoes only last a few minutes.   True   False

A tornado, also called a twister, is a **violent**, spinning cloud that reaches from the **ground** up to storm clouds in the sky. Most tornadoes are weak, lasting only a few minutes, and have winds of less than 110 mph. But the strongest tornadoes can last more than an hour and have wind speeds of 200 mph or more. They can destroy houses in seconds, turn over cars, and pull people, trees, and furniture into the air.

The United States has more tornadoes than any other country in the world. In a typical year, there are 800 to 1,000 tornadoes in the United States. Most **occur** in the middle part of the country. Tornadoes **form** when warm and cool air meet. In the Midwest, the warm air from the Gulf of Mexico often meets the cold air from Canada.

Tornadoes can occur at any time of year, but the usual tornado season is from March through May. Tornadoes form most often in the afternoon and early evening. There is often little **warning** of a tornado. People who live in the Midwest know the signs of tornado activity. The sky becomes dark, often a greenish color. Dark clouds appear in the sky and there is often large hail. Suddenly, there is a loud sound, like a train or a jet plane. Sometimes, tornadoes occur in groups. Two, three, five, or ten or more tornadoes can form over a large area.

A large group of tornadoes hit Oklahoma and Kansas in May 1999. The day was stormy, with violent thunderstorms in the afternoon. As the wind and rain continued, tornadoes began to form. More than thirty tornadoes hit towns and neighborhoods. Some tornadoes stayed on the **ground** for several hours, destroying everything they touched. The tornadoes killed 43 people and injured 600 others. They destroyed thousands of homes and businesses. In some areas, not one home was standing. In other areas, the tornadoes destroyed every home on the left side of the street but didn't touch any homes on the right side. Tornadoes **lifted** people and cars into the air and then threw them back down to earth. One family explained that they were all in the living room, on the sofa and chairs. The storm lifted up the house around them but left them all **unharmed**, still sitting in the living room.

The safest place to be during a tornado is in a safety shelter, a small underground room that people build to protect their families. Other safe places are basements or the first floor bathroom, which is often the most solid room in the house.

B Word Builder **The first word in each line is from the reading. (Circle) the word with a similar meaning.**

1. violent: (strong)   dark   **5.** warning: typical   sign

2. ground: earth   storm   **6.** lifted: picked up   destroyed

3. occur: happen   area   **7.** unharmed: injured   safe

4. form: active   develop

C **Complete each sentence with one of the numbered words from Exercise B.**

1. A _____ tornado can cause loss of life and property.

2. The tornado destroyed our house, but we were all _____.

3. Weather forecasters can predict a hurricane a week or two in advance, but there is often no _____ of a tornado.

4. Tornadoes can _____ any time of year.

5. The tornado was so strong that it _____ the car off the ground.

READING NOTE

Analyzing *True / False* statements

In a *True / False* statement, be careful of words like *all, every, always,* and *never.* These statements are often false.

Sentences with words like *many, some, sometimes,* and *often* are usually more accurate.

Look at the difference:

All tornadoes cause damage.	False
Many tornadoes cause damage.	True

D **(Circle) *True* or *False*.**

1. All tornadoes can destroy homes.	True	False
2. Some tornadoes cause millions of dollars of damage.	True	False
3. Tornadoes always occur in the afternoon or early evening.	True	False
4. Tornadoes never occur at night.	True	False
5. More tornadoes occur in the United States than in any other country.	True	False
6. All families in the Midwest have safety shelters.	True	False
7. People always know when a tornado is going to occur.	True	False
8. Tornadoes can come in groups of two, three, or more.	True	False

A **Look at the notes about Hurricane Katrina.** Then, read the report.

Notes:

Formed late August 2005, near the Bahamas

Moved across Florida into Gulf of Mexico

Became stronger – category 5

Hit Louisiana and Mississippi on August 29th as a category 4

Heavy wind and rain – 8 to 12 inches

New Orleans – very low, below sea level

Strong walls called levees protected the city.

The water went over the levees and flooded the city.

80 percent of city – under water. Destroyed most of city.

1,000 people in New Orleans died.

Damage – $80 billion

More than 100,000 people did not evacuate.

Thousands rescued by boat, helicopters

More than a half-million people – left city for other cities

Today – New Orleans – slowly rebuilding

Hurricane Katrina was one of the worst hurricanes in the history of the United States. On August 29, 2005, Katrina hit the city of New Orleans as a category 4 hurricane. New Orleans is located below sea level. Strong walls, called levees, protect the city from water. The water broke the levees and flooded the city. The water flooded 80 percent of the city. Boats and helicopters rescued thousands of people, but more than 1,000 died. After the storm, more than 500,000 people left the city for other areas. Today, New Orleans is slowly rebuilding.

B **Write a report.** On December 26, 2004, a terrible tsunami hit Indonesia. Use these notes to write a short report about the disaster. Choose the facts you would like to include.

> Notes:
>
> December 26, 2004
>
> Strong earthquake in Indian Ocean
>
> This earthquake caused tsunami
>
> Tsunami – giant wave, wall of water
>
> No warning system to tell people about oncoming tsunami
>
> Tsunami hit many countries around Indian Ocean, especially Indonesia,
>
> Sri Lanka, India, Thailand
>
> Waves – 100 feet high (30 meters) hit beaches and towns
>
> First wave: 10:00 A.M. More waves followed.
>
> 230,000 people died
>
> 1000s of homes and buildings were destroyed
>
> People and countries all over world – helped the victims

C **Find and correct the mistakes.**

1. There were a lot of rain.

2. There was several tornadoes in Nebraska.

3. Before the hurricane, we listen to the radio.

4. Many people evacuate the city.

5. More than 100,000 people die.

6. A tsunami was a giant wall of water.

7. The tsunami hit the day after Christmas, so many people are on vacation.

WRITING NOTE

Taking notes for a report

When you are preparing to write a report, look at several sources of information: books, encyclopedias, almanacs, newspapers, and the Internet. Take notes on the information you read, but do not copy sentences. In a report, it is important to use your own words. It is not necessary to use all your notes in your report.

 A **How much warning do people usually have for these disasters?** Write each disaster in the correct column. Compare your answers with another group.

snowstorm	forest fire
tornado	hurricane
volcanic eruption	tsunami
earthquake	flood

	WORD PARTNERSHIPS
issue	a flood warning
	a tornado warning
	an evacuation order

Several Days' Warning	Short Warning	Little or No Warning
snowstorm		

 B **Read the emergency directions.** Which disaster in Exercise A do they refer to?

1. Secure your home. Move essential items to an upper floor. Turn off utilities. Disconnect electrical appliances. Do not touch electrical equipment if you are wet or standing in water. _____flood_____

2. Evacuate. If there is time, connect garden hoses. Fill any pools, hot tubs, garbage cans, tubs, or other large containers with water. _____

3. Go to a safe area, such as a basement, or to the lowest building level. If there is no basement, go to the center of an interior room on the lowest level (closet, interior hallway) away from corners, windows, doors, and outside walls. Do not open windows. _____

4. DROP to the ground; take COVER by getting under a strong table or other piece of furniture; and HOLD ON until the shaking stops. Stay away from glass, windows, outside doors and walls, and anything that could fall, such as lighting fixtures or furniture. _____

5. Move inland to higher ground immediately and stay there. Stay away from the beach. _____

C **Working Together** **Your friends have recently moved to a cold climate.** The weather forecast is for three feet of snow! How should they prepare? Write four suggestions.

1. _____

2. _____

3. _____

4. _____

D **Working Together** **Work in a small group.** There is a forest fire near your home. You have thirty minutes to evacuate. You are not sure your home will be standing when you return. Decide on ten items to pack.

I'm going to take my photos and photo albums.

I need my computer.

1. _____   6. _____

2. _____   7. _____

3. _____   8. _____

4. _____   9. _____

5. _____   10. _____

10

Wedding Plans

A **Look at the picture.** Write the number next to the correct word.

___1___ **a.** bride   ___3___ **f.** maid of honor   <u>matron</u>   <u>maid</u>

                                                                                       married   not married

___7___ **b.** wedding gown   ___4___ **g.** best man

___2___ **c.** groom   ___6___ **h.** band

___9___ **d.** tuxedo   ___8___ **i.** guests

___5___ **e.** photographer   ___10___ **j.** wedding cake

B **Work with a group of students from different countries if possible.** Answer the questions about wedding customs in your native country.

1. How old is the average man at marriage? How old is the average woman?

2. How do most couples meet?

3. Do you know any couples who met online?

4. Are marriages ever arranged?

5. Where do most people get married?

6. What does the bride wear?

7. What does the groom wear?

8. Who pays for the wedding?

9. How many people usually come to a wedding?

10. What kinds of gifts do people give?

11. Do couples take a honeymoon after they get married?

12. Does the bride keep her own name, or does she take her husband's name?

WORD PARTNERSHIPS	
get	engaged
	married
	divorced

CD2·TR5

C **Jennifer and Brian are engaged.** It's October, and they're getting married in late August. Listen. Match the month and the task.

___e___ 1. October   **a.** Reserve the ceremony and reception sites.

___a___ 2. November   **b.** Start planning the honeymoon.

___f___ 3. December   **c.** Plan the guest list.

___j___ 4. January   **d.** Order the invitations.

___b___ 5. February   **e.** Announce their engagement.

___c___ 6. March   **f.** Order dresses.

___d___ 7. April   **g.** Hire a florist.

___g___ 8. May   **h.** Apply for a marriage license.

___i___ 9. June   **i.** Mail the invitations.

___h___ 10. July   **j.** Book (reserve) a band.

Wedding Plans · **147**

(handwritten top margin) The family has to...
The couple has to

Active Grammar

I		
You	**have to**	**order** the invitations.
They		**plan** the guest list.
She	**has to**	

Have to and *has to* are modals.
They show necessity or obligation.

A **Complete the sentences.** Use *have to* or *has to* and the verb in parentheses.

1. The bride (select) _has to select_ a wedding gown.

2. The bride and groom (plan) _have to plan_ the ceremony.

3. The bride and groom (reserve) _have to reserve_ a place for the reception.

4. They (select) _have to select_ their wedding rings.

5. The bride (ask) _has to ask_ friends or relatives to be her bridesmaids.

6. The groom (ask) _has to ask_ someone to be his best man.

7. The couple (hire) _has to hire_ a photographer.

B **Pronunciation:** *Have to / has to* **Listen and circle the correct modal.**

CD2·TR6

1. **a.** have to   **b.** has to   4. **a.** have to   **b.** has to
2. **a.** have to   **b.** has to   5. **a.** have to   **b.** has to
3. **a.** have to   **b.** has to   6. **a.** have to   **b.** has to

C **Listen and repeat.**

CD2·TR7

1. I have to go to the laundromat.   4. I have to pay my telephone bill.

2. She has to work overtime tomorrow.   5. He has to get gas on the way home.

3. They have to do their homework.   6. She has to make a doctor's appointment.

(handwritten) have to go
(handwritten) has to go

I have to do my homework.

D **Discuss.**

(handwritten) I have to wake up.

1. Name something you have to do before you come to class.
   (handwritten) he/she has to be 21. / They have to learn about driving.
2. Name something a teenager has to do before she can get a driver's license.
   (handwritten) I have to take clothes, money and vacation tools: water, food, sometimes boat.
3. Name something you have to take with you when you go on vacation.
   (handwritten) my teacher has to teach us and she has to ... us.
4. Name something your teacher has to do every day in class.
   (handwritten) I have to active, I have to responsible and respectful.
5. Name something you have to do when you get to work.

148 · Unit 10

(handwritten) I have to comfortable working as a team member.
(handwritten) I have to be honest.

Active Grammar

Don't have to / Doesn't have to

I			
You	**don't**		**order** the invitations.
They		**have to**	**work** today.
She	**doesn't**		

> *Don't have to* and *doesn't have to* are modals.
>
> They show that an action is not necessary.

A **Listen.** Hannah is talking to an older co-worker. Who does each chore? *is a job*
Write *D* for *Dad*, *M* for *Mom*, or *H* for *Hannah*.

CD2·TR8

___M___ **1.** clean the house   ___M___ **5.** do the food shopping

___H___ **2.** clean her room   ___M-D___ **6.** pay the bills

___D___ **3.** cook   ___H___ **7.** pay the cell phone bill

___M___ **4.** wash the dishes   ___M___ **8.** do the laundry

---

B **With a partner, talk about the things Hannah has to do and doesn't have to do at home.**

> Hannah doesn't have to cook dinner. Her father cooks dinner.

C **With a partner, talk about your family.** What chores do you have to do? What are some chores you do not have to do? How does each person help?

D **With a partner, talk about the things that you have to do or don't have to do in your English class.**

> We have to speak English in class.

1. arrive on time

2. buy books

3. bring a dictionary to class

4. attend school in the summer

5. work in groups

6. pay tuition

7. take tests

8. do a lot of homework

9. raise our hands to speak

10. stand up when we speak

11. turn off our cell phones before class

12. write our compositions on a computer

> We don't have to study in the library.

Do	I you we	**have to**	**study**?
Does	he		**send** a gift?

Yes, you **do**.	No, you **don't**.
Yes, I **do**.	No, I **don't**.
Yes, we **do**.	No, we **don't**.
Yes, he **does**.	No, he **doesn't**.

A **Ask your teacher questions about his or her job.**

1. Do you have to work in the summer?

2. Do you have to work overtime?

3. Do you have to go to many meetings?

4. Do you have to bring your lunch or dinner to school?

5. Do all the teachers have to start work at the same time?

6. Does your boss have to observe your classes?

7. Does the school have to stay open in the summer?

8. Do the teachers have to punch a time clock?

Ask your teacher two more questions about his or her job.

B **Read about weddings in the United States.** Then, write a *yes / no* question about weddings in other countries.

1. The couple has to get a marriage license.

   Does the couple have to get a marriage license?

2. The bride's parents usually pay for the wedding.

   Do the bride's parents have to pay for the wedding?

3. The bride usually wears white.

   Does the bride have to wear white?

4. The groom usually wears a tuxedo.

   Does the groom have to wear a tuxedo?

5. The guests have to arrive at the wedding on time.

   Do the guests have to arrive at the wedding on time?

6. The guests have to give gifts.

   Do the guests have to give gifts?
   they

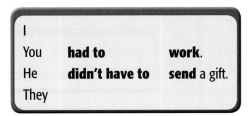

I		
You	**had to**	**work**.
He	**didn't have to**	**send** a gift.
They		

> *Had to* is the past of *have to* and *has to*.
>
> *Didn't have to* is the past of *don't have to* and *doesn't have to*.

A **Complete the sentences about life in your native country.** Use *had to* or *didn't have to*.

1. I _____ didn't have to _____ speak English.

2. I _____ didn't have to _____ work full time.

3. When I lived in my country, I _____ had to _____ wear winter clothes.

4. I _____ didn't have to _____ take public transportation.

5. When I was in high school, we _____ had to _____ do many hours of homework.

6. Students _____ had to _____ pay for their books.

B **Working Together** **Find Someone Who . . .** Walk around the classroom and ask the questions about last weekend. If a student answers "Yes," write that student's name. If a student answers "No," ask another student that question.

> Did you have to go to the supermarket?

Did you have to

Questions	Classmate's Name
1. go to the supermarket?	
2. go to work?	
3. go to the bank?	
4. get up early on Sunday?	
5. clean your home?	
6. do homework?	
7. help someone?	
8. speak English?	

I		
You	**should**	**get married** in the summer.
He	**shouldn't**	**send** a gift.
They		

Should is a modal.
Should gives advice or an opinion.

A **Complete the sentences.** Use *should* or *shouldn't* and the verb in parentheses.

1. Luis and Marta don't have a lot of money. They (have) <u>should have</u> a small wedding. They (take) <u>shouldn't take</u> out a <u>loan</u> to pay for the wedding.

2. I don't think my sister (get) <u>should get</u> married in the park. What will she do if it rains?

3. If you don't have a lot of money, you (hire) <u>shouldn't hire</u> a band. You (hire) <u>shouldn't hire</u> a DJ.

4. Yolanda and Jim are going to get married in a church. They (choose) <u>should choose</u> a reception location near the church.

B **Working Together** **Work in a group of five or six students.** Discuss each statement. Then, write the number of students who agree with the statement and the number of students who disagree with the statement.

Statement	Agree	Disagree
1. People should wait until the age of 21 to get married.		
2. A bride should take her husband's name.		
3. The bride's family should pay for the wedding.		
4. The bride should always wear white.		
5. Money is the best gift to give for a wedding.		

C **Working Together** **Work in a small group.** Talk about how to have a long, happy marriage. Make a list of your five best ideas.

1. You should go out together once a week.
2. <u>you shouldn't fight for every thing.</u>
3. <u>you should support your family. (your husband or your wife)</u>
4. <u>you should be best friend for him/her.</u>
5. <u>you shouldn't be worry about less money.</u>
6. <u>you should change bad behavior to good behavior.</u>

D Complete each sentence with a word or phrase from the box.

should	have to	had to	don't have to
shouldn't	has to	doesn't have to	didn't have to

Mrs. Sullivan is 40 years old. Three years ago, her husband died, leaving her to <u>raise</u> her two sons alone. Now her sons are seventeen and fifteen. Before her husband died, she (work) __didn't have to work__ outside the home. She stayed home and took
                              1
care of her home and family. Mrs. Sullivan (make) __had to__ many
                                              2
lifestyle changes after her husband died. Now, she (work) __have to work__
                                                           3
full time in order to support her family. Her company offers good medical benefits, so she (worry) __doesn't have to__ about doctors' bills. Twice a year,
               4
Mrs. Sullivan goes away on business, so she (find) __should find__
                                                  5
someone to watch her children. Mrs. Sullivan is busy, but she is lonely.

Last year, Mrs. Sullivan started to date a very nice <u>widower</u> in her town. He is 20 years older than she is. He has asked her to marry him. Her sister thinks she (wait) __shouldn't wait__ to get married until her boys are older. Her brother thinks
            6
she (look) __should look__ for a younger man. But her mother has given
            7
her the best advice. "You (listen) __don't have to__ ^listen to anyone else. You
                                  8
(follow) __should follow__ your own heart."
           9

E Read the questions from a wedding planner website. Give each person advice. Use *should*, *shouldn't*, *have to*, or *don't have to*.

1.
> **To: wedding*planner.com**
> **From: A Tight Budget**
>
> My fiancé and I want to have a small wedding with our families and closest friends. We can't afford a big wedding. Do we have to invite our bosses from work?

2.
> **To: wedding*planner.com**
> **From: A Modern Girl**
>
> I'm getting married in six months. My mother wants me to wear the same wedding dress that she wore, but I don't want to wear it. I want to choose my own dress, but I don't want to hurt her feelings.

3.
> **To: wedding*planner.com**
> **From: Second Time Around**
>
> In four months, I'm going to get married for the second time. My first husband and I are divorced, but we are still friends. He's a good father to our two children. Should I invite him to the wedding?

4.
> **To: wedding*planner.com**
> **From: Gotta Dance**
>
> I'm excited about my wedding and the reception. There will be live music at the wedding, and I love to dance. Unfortunately, my fiancé doesn't like to dance. In fact, I've never danced with him. What are we going to do at our wedding reception when they play a special song for us?

A Describe the pictures.

1. What are the people wearing?

2. Where is the ceremony taking place?

3. What season do you think it is?

B Listen to the interview. Complete the sentences.

CD2·TR9

1. Freddy and Louise got married on _____.

2. The wedding ceremony was at _____.

3. There were _____ attendants in the wedding party.

4. There were about _____ people at the church ceremony.

5. Louise has _____ brothers and sisters.

6. Louise's father has _____ brothers and sisters.

7. Louise's friend made the dresses in _____ week(s).

8. Freddy and Louise have been married for _____ years.

C Listen to the interview again. (Circle) *True* or *False*.

CD2·TR9

1.	Freddy's best man was one of his brothers.	True	False
2.	Louise's sister was her maid of honor.	True	False
3.	Many of their relatives were in the wedding party.	True	False
4.	Freddy was very angry at the dressmaker.	True	False
5.	Louise wore her mother's wedding dress.	True	False
6.	Louise was a singer.	True	False
7.	Louise had to pay for a second wedding dress.	True	False

D Ask and answer the questions with a partner.

1. What did the first dressmaker do?

2. What happened to the dresses?

3. When did Louise find out that she didn't have a wedding gown?

4. Who made the dresses?

5. Did Louise's family have to pay for the bridesmaids' second dresses, too?

6. Did Louise contact the police?

7. How did Freddy feel about the second dress?

E Work with a partner. Complete the conversation between Louise and her niece, Claudia, who just got engaged. Present your conversation to the class.

Claudia: Should we have a big wedding or a small wedding?

Louise: _____

Claudia: Should we get married inside or outside?

Louise: _____

Claudia: Should we invite all our relatives?

Louise: _____

Claudia: Should I buy a dress or should I go to a dressmaker?

Louise: _____

Claudia: Should I keep my name or should I take my husband's name?

Louise: _____

Claudia: Where do you think we should go on our honeymoon?

Louise: _____

A Discuss. Then, read.

1. Describe the last wedding you attended.

2. How early did you arrive for the ceremony?

3. Did you bring a gift? What was it?

4. What did you wear to the wedding?

> ### READING NOTE
>
> **Comparing the text to your own experiences**
>
> As you read, compare the information in the reading to your own experiences.
>
> Example: *First of all, respond to the invitation. There is a response card inside the invitation to fill out and return.*
>
> Compare to your experiences:
>
> In my country, we don't have a card. We call the family. I was invited to a wedding last year. I had to ask a friend how to fill out the card.

etiquette = rules of social behavior

You open your mail and you find a wedding invitation. One of your friends is getting married, and you are excited about the wedding because it is your first American wedding. Weddings are different from culture to culture. What are the rules of etiquette for American wedding guests?

First of all, **respond** to the invitation as soon as possible. The bride and groom have to pay for each guest, so it is important to **notify** them that you will attend. Most wedding invitations include a response card. If you cannot attend, it is **polite** to call the couple if you are close friends.

> *Please respond on or before May 30th*
>
> Mr. and Mrs. David Tuller
>
> ✓ Will attend
>
> ___ Will not be able to attend

Read the invitation's envelope carefully. Can you take a guest? Maybe your invitation says, "Marianna Lopez and Guest." That means that you can bring one guest. Only one. You must not bring more than one guest, and that includes your children.

What should you wear to the wedding? Check the wedding invitation for special instructions. For a "black tie" wedding, women wear elegant clothing and men wear tuxedos. "Casual attire" is a casual dress for women and a suit for men. Remember, female guests should not wear white. The guests should be looking at the bride—not at the other guests.

What rules should you follow at the wedding ceremony? The most important rule is to be on time. You should arrive about fifteen minutes before the wedding begins. If you're late, you should enter quietly and find a seat. If something happens during the ceremony that you do not understand, ask the person next to you to explain.

What kind of gift should you buy? Most guests at American weddings do not have to worry about choosing a gift. Many American couples use a wedding gift **registry**. The couple goes to a department store, another type of store, or the Internet in order to register for their gifts. The bride and groom select the items that they need. When guests are ready to buy the gifts, they go to the store or go online and look at the registry. They can find out which items are still available. Then, the store delivers the gift. It is not necessary to bring the gift to the ceremony. In fact, it is more convenient for both you and the wedding couple if you mail the gift.

Wedding couples also **appreciate** gifts of money. In fact, money is the most popular wedding gift. Place the cash or check in a gift card that is specially made for money. Or, put the money in an envelope, and put it in a greeting card.

Have fun at the wedding!

B (Circle) the correct words.

1. Guests **have to / don't have to** respond to the wedding invitation.

2. Guests **have to / don't have to** call the couple about the invitation.

3. Guests **should / shouldn't** take as many friends as they want.

4. Female guests **should / shouldn't** wear white.

5. Guests **have to / don't have to** arrive on time.

6. A guest **should / shouldn't** find out if the couple registered for gifts.

7. A guest **has to / doesn't have to** give money as a gift.

C Word Builder **Match each word to its definition.**

_____ **1.** respond   **a.** a list of gifts

_____ **2.** polite   **b.** to answer

_____ **3.** notify   **c.** to like

_____ **4.** registry   **d.** nice; well-mannered

_____ **5.** appreciate   **e.** to tell

D Discuss the questions with a partner.

1. What are common wedding gifts in your native country?

2. What gifts do most wedding couples in your country appreciate the most?

3. Have you ever attended an American wedding? Compare your experience to the information in the reading.

E Working Together **Bring in photographs of your wedding or that of a family member.** Tell the class about the preparations and the wedding day.

Read.

I am from India, and my family arranged my marriage. I was living in the United States when my uncle found a husband for me. My uncle told my father about a man named Justin, who would be a good husband for me. My family and I went back to India for a meeting with Justin and his family. We stayed for about a month. At the end of the visit, I decided to marry Justin. We got married a year and a half later.

The pre-wedding activities, the ceremony, and the reception lasted about a week. On the first day, my family and Justin's family exchanged gifts. During the week, we had to participate in separate religious services. Some services were at my home, and others were at Justin's home. According to custom, the services were only for our families.

The day before the wedding ceremony, my family had to put up a large tent in our yard. About 100 guests attended our wedding. The guests gave us many gifts, including gifts of gold jewelry. We ate sweets and took many pictures with our family and guests. The guests also gave Justin and me gifts of money, which his sister attached to his clothes.

On the day of the wedding, a priest married us. The ceremony and the reception lasted about seven hours. After the reception, Justin and I left in a car that his family had decorated with a lot of flowers.

Nisha, India

B **Write a story about your wedding or a wedding that you attended.** Include the following information:

Date: _____

Couple: _____ and _____

How the couple met: _____

Relationship to you: _____

Country of the wedding: _____

Location of the ceremony: _____

Number of people in the wedding party: _____

Bride's clothing: _____

Your clothes for the wedding: _____

Size of the wedding: large / small

Number of guests: _____

Location of the reception: _____

Music: _____

Food: _____

WRITING NOTE

Giving Reasons and Results: *so* and *because*

Because gives a reason:

1. The bride had to go back to the dressmaker **because** she lost weight.
2. The groom didn't have to rent a tuxedo **because** he decided to buy a new suit.

So gives a result:

3. The bride lost weight, **so** she had to go back to the dressmaker.
4. The groom decided to buy a new suit, **so** he didn't have to rent a tuxedo.

C **Complete with *because* or *so*.**

1. The bride's sister works at a bakery, _____ they don't have to buy a cake.

2. The groom doesn't own a suit, _____ he is going to rent one.

3. The bride and groom are taking dance classes _____ they aren't good dancers.

4. The bride and groom are saving money _____ they want to go to Europe on their honeymoon.

5. The bride can't find a dress that she likes, _____ she's going to go to a dressmaker for something special.

6. The bride and groom are going to two receptions today _____ they want to check out two different bands.

D **Sharing Our Stories** **Read your partner's story.** Ask about any details that are missing.

A **Discuss these customs in the United States.** Is each custom the same or different in your native country?

1.

Women sometimes hug or kiss a friend once on the cheek when they meet.

2.

Men often shake hands or give a friend a pat on the back when they meet.

3.

People stand a comfortable distance apart when they speak.

4.

People stand in line at buses, stores, and ticket counters. It is not polite to push or cut in line.

 B **Discuss each situation.** Is this a custom in the United States? Is this a custom in your native country?

1. An adult can pat a child on the head to show approval.

2. Two men walk along the street arm in arm.

3. Two women walk along the street arm in arm.

4. Two men bow to one another when they meet.

5. People stand when an elderly person enters a room.

6. People arrive on time or a little early for meetings and appointments.

G **Work in a group.** Talk about customs in your native country.

1. How do friends greet one another?

2. How do co-workers greet one another?

3. How close do you stand to another person when you speak?

4. When you enter a house, do you remove your shoes?

5. When friends visit, what do you offer them to eat or drink?

6. If you are invited to dinner, do you bring a gift for the host?

7. If you are invited to a party that begins at 9:00, what time do you arrive?

8. What U.S. custom do you find very different from your country?

D **Show the hand gestures you use in your native country to express these ideas.** Show the hand gestures that people in the United States use.

1. Yes.

2. No.

3. Okay. Everything is good.

4. Not good. It's not okay.

5. Great! Perfect!

6. Please come here.

7. I hope so.

8. It's expensive.

9. Good-bye.

 E **Working Together** **Discuss.** What does each gesture mean? Is it appropriate in your native country? What other gestures are common in your country?

1. 　**2.** 　**3.**

At Work

A **Look at the photos and write the jobs.**

1. _____   **2.** _____   **3.** _____

B **Match each occupation with the job skill.**

> *Can* is a modal.
> It shows ability.

____c____ **1.** hairdresser   **a.** I can change the locks in a house.

_____ **2.** cable installer   **b.** I can fix sinks, toilets, or showers.

_____ **3.** locksmith   **c.** I can cut and color hair.

_____ **4.** health aide   **d.** I can install Internet service in homes.

_____ **5.** plumber   **e.** I can take a pulse and blood pressure.

_____ **6.** mechanic   **f.** I can give a car a tune-up.

_____ **7.** florist   **g.** I can save money on people's travel plans.

_____ **8.** travel agent   **h.** I can arrange flowers for weddings.

C **Describe a job.** Your classmates will guess what the job is.

I can remodel your kitchen or your bathroom. I can install new cabinets in your kitchen.

Are you a carpenter?

Yes, I am.

Could you please	call Mr. Henderson?
Would you please	check this report?

Could you and *Would you* are modals. Use *Could you* and *Would you* to make polite requests.

> Could you please fill out this form?

A **Restate each sentence as a polite request.**

1. Fill out this form.
2. Take this call.
3. Send an e-mail to the employees.
4. Clean the workroom.
5. Fill this order.

6. Take Ms. Miller's temperature.
7. Bring me some change.
8. Open on cash register 5.
9. Help the next customer.
10. Unpack those boxes.

B **Listen.** Write the request for each item.

CD2·TR10

1.

2.

3.

4.

 C **Pronunciation:** *Would you* and *Could you* **Listen and repeat each request in Exercise B.**

CD2·TR11

 D **In your notebook, write three more requests for each list.**

Student-to-student requests:

Could I please use your dictionary?

Teacher-to-student requests:

Would you please hand in your papers?

I		**wear** a name tag.
You	**must**	**sign** in.
He		**file** a report.

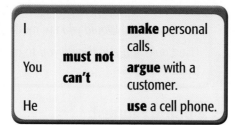

I		**make** personal calls.
You	**must not** **can't**	**argue** with a customer.
He		**use** a cell phone.

Must, must not, and *can't* are modals.

Must states rules, policies, and regulations.

Must not and *can't* show that an action is not allowed or not permitted.

A **Explain each work sign.** Use *must*, *must not*, or *can't*.

> You must wear a hard hat.

1.

2.

3.

4.

5.

6.

7.

8.

9.

10.

11.

12.

 B **Working Together** **Work in a small group.** In your notebook, write six of your school or class rules.

Students must not copy from other students during an exam.

C Talk about the company policies and regulations. Use *must*, *must not*, or *can't*.

> Workers must report to work by 8:00.

WORD PARTNERSHIPS

clock	in
sign	
punch	out
swipe my card	

1. Work hours: 8:00 – 4:00.

2. Punch in and out.

3. If you will be late, call your supervisor.

4. Wear your ID tag at all times.

5. No jeans or athletic clothing.

6. No smoking.

7. No cell phones.

8. Do not bring your children to work.

9. Report unsafe working conditions.

10. No offensive pictures on office walls.

11. Report any accidents immediately.

12. Internet for business only.

13. Customers are our business. Always be polite and helpful.

D Discuss.

1. What are some rules at your workplace?

2. What are some regulations at an airport?

3. What are some laws about children in cars?

4. What are some laws about texting and using cell phones while driving?

5. What are some laws about pets?

6. What are some common apartment regulations?

| I
He
They | **may (not)**
might (not) | **change** jobs.
get a promotion.
take a sick day. |

> *May* and *might* are modals.
> *May* and *might* show possibility.

A **Complete the sentences.** Describe what *may* or *might* happen.

1. Yolanda got to work late today, so the boss might _give her a warning_ .

2. You need a job. A new clothing store is opening in your area, so you might _____ .

3. Nelson has a bad cold. He may _____ to work.

4. The boss is very happy with Mia's work. He might _____ .

5. The economy is bad and our company is not doing very well. The boss might _____ .

6. The economy is very good and our company is doing very well. The boss may _____ .

7. Shelly works full time. She wants to begin college in the fall. She might _____ her job in the fall.

B **Work with a partner.** Talk about the pictures. Then, write two sentences about what *may* or *might* happen in each.

> She might slip on the floor.

> She might fall and hit her head.

1.

2.

3.

4.

5.

6.

I **might go** to nursing school.	*May* and *might* are modals. They show possibility.
Maybe I **will go** to nursing school.	*Maybe* shows possibility. *Maybe* is the first word in a sentence.
I**'m going to go** to nursing school.	*Will* or *(be) going to* show that you are sure or certain.
I **will go** to nursing school.	

A **Rewrite the sentences.** Use *may* or *might*.

1. Maybe I will quit my job. _____ I might quit my job _____.

2. Maybe the boss is going to fire him. _____.

3. Maybe she will get the job. _____.

4. Maybe we are going to have a test. _____.

B **Work in a small group.** Talk about your future plans. Use the future tense if you are sure of your plans. Use *may*, *might*, or *maybe* if you are not sure of your plans.

1. change jobs
2. get a dog
3. visit my native country
4. open a small business
5. continue to study English
6. take a computer class
7. take out a loan
8. go on a cruise
9. buy a new TV
10. move
11. paint my bedroom
12. visit friends

> I might change jobs.

> Maybe I will change jobs.

> I don't like my job. I will change jobs soon.

C **Work with a partner.** Ask and answer the questions. Use *may*, *might*, or the future tense.

1. What are you going to have for dinner tonight?
2. What are you going to do this weekend?
3. Where are you going to go on your next vacation?
4. When are you going to give a party?
5. When are you going to go to the dentist?

Modal	Use to show . . .	Example
have to	obligation necessity	I **have to do** my homework.
(not) have to	something is not necessary	I **don't have to get up** early on Sunday.
should	advice opinion	You **should apply** for the job. You **should wear** a suit.
must	necessity a rule or policy	I **must pay** taxes.
must not can't	something is not permitted	I **must not park** here. I **can't wear** jeans to work.
can	ability	I **can fix** a flat tire.
could would	polite request	**Could** you **answer** the phone? **Would** you **file** these papers?
may might	possibility	I **may get** the job. I **might lose** my job.

Modals change the meaning of a verb.

After a modal, use the base form of the verb. Do not use *-s, -ed,* or *-ing*.

A **Circle** the correct modal.

1. Tony has a job interview. He **should / doesn't have to** arrive on time.

2. At our company all employees **must / might** wear name tags.

3. A nurse **has to / must not** wash her hands after caring for each patient.

4. Work begins at 7:30. You **must not / don't have to** arrive late.

5. **Could you / Should you** please repair the copy machine?

6. You are very good at math. I think you **should / have to** study accounting.

7. Friday is casual dress day. We **have to / don't have to** wear suits.

8. I received a good evaluation, so I **have to / might** get a raise.

9. Employees **must not / don't have to** take home company products.

10. You aren't happy at your job. You **should / have to** look for another opportunity.

11. We **don't have to / can't** make personal phone calls at work.

B **Listen.** (Circle) the letter of the sentence with the same meaning as the sentence you hear.

1. **a.** I should take a break.   **b.** I might take a break.

2. **a.** Could you please look up the   **b.** You should look up the number.
   number?

3. **a.** You don't have to smoke.   **b.** You must not smoke.

4. **a.** You might get a haircut.   **b.** You should get a haircut.

5. **a.** You must renew your license.   **b.** You might renew your license.

6. **a.** We don't have to work.   **b.** We must not work.

C **Complete the conversations.** Stephan is asking questions about his new workplace. Use the correct modal and the verb in parentheses.

1. **A:** What time does work begin?

   B: All employees (sign in) _____ by 8:00.

2. **A:** Which office will I work in?

   B: We're not sure yet. You (be) _____ in Room 245. Or you
   (be) _____ in Room 246. We're going to decide later today.

3. **A:** What papers do I need to fill out?

   B: You (complete) _____ your tax withholding form
   and an employee data form.

4. **A:** What is the dress code here?

   B: It's pretty casual—nice pants and a sweater are fine. You (wear)
   _____ a suit. But don't dress too casually. You (wear)
   _____ jeans and a T-shirt.

D **Talk about your classroom.** Use modals.

> We don't have to stand up when we speak.

1. stand up when we speak   6. have a fire drill this month

2. do our homework   7. turn off our cell phones

3. speak English in class   8. call our teacher by his / her first name

4. bring coffee into our classroom 9. wear jeans to class

5. pay for our books   10. have a test next week

E **Working Together** **Work with a partner.** Write three sentences about your class. Use modals. Then, read your sentences to the class. Your classmates will decide if the sentences are true or false.

A **Discuss.**

1. What kinds of tests does a diagnostic medical lab perform?

2. Who are some of the employees at a diagnostic lab?

3. What kind of paperwork does a medical lab keep?

A diagnostic medical laboratory performs medical tests ordered by a doctor.

  CD2·TR13 **B** **Listen and look at the pictures.** Sharon Taylor is an administrative assistant in a diagnostic lab. She is talking with her co-workers and patients. Write six of her responsibilities.

1. _She schedules the employees._

2. _____

3. _____

4. _____

5. _____

6. _____

C **Complete the sentences.** Use the correct modal and the verb in parentheses. In some sentences, more than one answer is correct.

1. (work) ___Could you please work___ an extra hour today? Carla needs to leave early.

2. If you want a copy of your lab results, you (call) _____ this number.

3. The lab sends the test results to the doctor. The patient (bring) _____ the results to the doctor.

4. (add) _____ two boxes of latex gloves to our order?

5. For a fasting blood test, a patient (eat or drink) _____ anything for twelve hours.

6. (make) _____ a copy of this insurance card?

7. If a patient has insurance, he (bring) _____ his insurance card.

8. If a patient has insurance, he (pay) _____ the full amount.

9. If a patient doesn't have insurance, he (pay) _____ for the test.

D **Word Builder** **Discuss the worker characteristics in the box.** Then, complete the sentences.

> confident
> ~~works well under pressure~~
> good with details
> patient
> team player
> well-organized

1. The office is always busy, but Sharon ___works well under pressure___.

2. Sharon sometimes needs to repeat information, but she is always _____.

3. Everyone knows the responsibilities and schedule, so it is a _____ office.

4. Sharon knows how to run the office. She feels _____ in her abilities.

5. Sharon manages all the supplies and orders. She's _____.

6. Sharon works well with others. She is a good _____.

E **Think about your work style.** Circle *Yes* or *No* for each statement. Then, talk about your answers in a group.

1. I'm always patient with customers or clients.   Yes   No

2. I am a good team player.   Yes   No

3. I work well under pressure.   Yes   No

4. I am organized and good with details.   Yes   No

5. I feel confident at my job.   Yes   No

How to Lose Your Job in Five Easy Steps

A **Discuss.** Then, read.

1. What time does your work begin? What is the policy about arriving late?

2. What is the dress code at your work place?

3. Who speaks to an employee who does not follow a policy?

READING NOTE

A Humorous Article

Sometimes an article is not serious. It looks at a situation from the opposite point of view. For example, this article explains how to *lose* your job, not how to *keep* it.

---

1. Don't worry about time policies.

If you have a half hour for lunch, no one is going to say anything if you take an extra ten minutes. If work begins at 8:30, arrive at 8:45. You can always **blame** the heavy traffic. No one is counting how many breaks you take. If you have two breaks, no one will **notice** if you take three.

2. Blame your co-workers if you miss a deadline or do a poor job on a project.

Be sure that nothing is your **fault**. If the boss complains about your work, explain to him that "Randy gave me the wrong directions." Or say, "I did my part. Nelson didn't do his part."

3. Don't worry about the office dress style.

You should wear what you like to work. Be comfortable. If you are a young woman, you don't need to wear the **traditional** dress style of the older employees. Short dresses and tight pants look good on you. Big earrings are fun.

4. Post your feelings about work on the Internet.

You can **trust** all your friends. No one will share your posts. Your boss and your company don't follow what is happening on the Internet. They will never see the following posts:

My boss always **complains** about everyone. But no one ever sees *him* working.

I lied to my boss today. I told her I had a big exam and needed the day off. Hah! She believes anything!

5. If you like another employee, it's okay to let him / her know.

If there is a woman you like, you can let her know in quiet, personal ways. Send her a birthday card and leave notes on her desk. Stop by her desk two or three times a day. Call her *Honey* or *Babe*. Tell her that she is pretty and that you like the way she dresses and the perfume that she wears. It's fine to touch her on the hand or the arm. She will like the attention.

B **Word Builder** **Discuss the meaning of the words in the box.** Then, write the letter of the correct answer.

1. Jorge often complains about _____.

   a. his schedule   **b.** the Internet

2. The accident was his fault. He _____ at the red light.

   a. stopped   **b.** didn't stop

3. The boss noticed that one of the employees _____.

   a. was wearing a uniform   **b.** was leaving early

4. The boss blamed the secretary for _____ the copy machine.

   a. breaking   **b.** fixing

5. The boss trusted the team to _____.

   a. complete the project   **b.** make a mistake

6. Employees should wear traditional clothes, such as _____.

   a. jeans and a T-shirt   **b.** nice pants and a button-down shirt

blame	traditional
notice	trust
fault	complain

C **Change the suggestion.** How can you *keep* your job?

1. If work begins at 8:30, arrive at 8:45.

   If work begins at 8:30, arrive at 8:20 _____.

2. Blame your co-workers if you do a poor job on a project.

   _____.

3. Wear short dresses to work.

   _____.

4. Post your feelings about work on the Internet.

   _____.

5. If you like someone, stop by his or her desk several times a day.

   _____.

6. Take an extra break.

   _____.

7. It's fine to call a female employee *Honey* or *Babe*.

   _____.

A **Discuss.** Then, read.

1. Where do you work?

2. What do you do there?

3. What do you like about your job? What don't you like?

I work for A1 Carpet Cleaning in Amesville. My company cleans rugs and carpets and strips and waxes floors. I'm a carpet specialist. On most days, I clean carpets in four homes. We work in teams—there are always two people together because there is a lot of equipment and hoses to carry into the house. First, we put small floor protectors under all furniture legs. Next, we remove any stains in the carpet. Then, we lightly shampoo the carpet and remove the water, both with the same machine.

I work the day shift, from 8:00 to 4:00. We have to wear white company shirts, black pants, and black work shoes. Everyone must wear an ID at all times. When I arrive at work, my boss gives me the names, addresses, and phone numbers of the homes I have to visit that day. I drive a small company truck and I have to be very careful. If I have an accident, I might lose my job. When I arrive at a home, I have to call the office. When I finish the job, I have to call the office again.

I like my boss because she is organized and helpful. I also like my hours. I'm home by 5:00, and I don't have to work on the weekends. I get two weeks paid vacation every year. There is one major problem with my job, though. I don't have any health benefits.

Tony

WRITING NOTE

Adding Details

Details make a story more interesting. Give specific examples and information when you write.

B **Read the composition.** What questions can you answer?

> I work for a carpet cleaning company. I'm a carpet specialist. I clean carpets in homes.
>
> I work the day shift. We have to wear a white company shirt. When I arrive at work, my boss tells me the houses I have to visit that day.
>
> I like my boss. I also like my hours. I get two weeks paid vacation every year. I don't have any health benefits.
>
> Martin

1. What is the company's name? What town is it in?

2. Does Martin work alone?

3. What does he do when he gets to a house?

4. What are his hours?

5. What does he wear?

6. What are some of the company policies and procedures?

7. Why does he like the boss?

8. Does this composition have many details?

9. Which composition is more interesting, the one on page 174 or this one?

C **Write a few notes about your job or the job you would like to have.** Then, write a composition about the job. Include a lot of details.

Company and location	
Job title	
Job responsibilities	
Hours	
Uniform or dress code	
Policies	
Things I like	
Things I don't like	

 D **Sharing Our Stories** **Work in a small group.** Read your stories to one another. Ask questions about the jobs.

E **Revise your composition.** Add the information that your classmates asked about.

A **Read the job posting.**

Administrator
Medical Diagnostic Lab
Bay City Hospital

Responsible for daily operation of medical lab, scheduling, patient records, ordering of supplies, and coordination with hospital administration. Two years medical lab administrative experience required.

B **Read the interview tips.**

Interview Tips

1. Research the company.

2. Practice the interview several times.

3. Dress appropriately.

4. Arrive a few minutes early for the interview. Turn off your cell phone!

5. Shake hands with the interviewer.

6. Look at the interviewer. Make eye contact. Smile from time to time.

7. Explain your strengths. Talk about your skills.

8. Answer questions clearly. Give a few details in each answer.

9. Thank the interviewer and shake hands again.

10. Send a handwritten thank-you note two or three days after the interview.

Look at the photo on page 176. Listen to Sharon Taylor's job interview. Then, answer the questions.

CD2·TR14

1. What is Sharon wearing?

2. Describe Sharon's manner at the interview.

3. How do you know that she researched the job before her interview?

4. What skills will she bring to the new job?

5. What positive things does she say about herself?

6. Why does she want the job at Bay City Hospital?

7. How does she end the interview?

 Work in a group. Ask and answer the interview questions about a job you would like.

1. What are your job responsibilities now?

2. What skills do you bring with you?

3. What was your biggest accomplishment at your job?

4. Why do you want to work at [our company]?

5. What are your strong points?

6. What are your weak points?

7. What hours would you like to work?

8. Why should we hire you?

9. What questions do you have for us?

  Working Together **Work with a partner.** Practice an interview for a manager's position at your company. Then, two or three pairs will role-play their interview for the class. Look at the interview tips. What did the job applicant do well? How can the applicant improve his or her interview skills?

  Discuss. Look at the picture. The people are waiting for a job interview. How can they improve their chances of getting a job? Use *should* or *shouldn't*.

Unit 12

Working Parents

 CD2·TR15 **A** **Look at the pictures and listen to Henry's schedule.**

1.

2.

3.

4.

5.

6.

 CD2·TR16 **B** **Pronunciation: Pauses Listen and repeat. Pause at the comma.**

1. After he drops off the children, Henry stops at a coffee shop.

2. As soon as the children get home from school, they call their father.

3. After they eat dinner, Henry helps the children with their homework.

4. When they finish their homework, they can play video games.

5. Before he goes to sleep, Henry watches TV.

Active Grammar

He watches TV **before** he goes to bed.   **Before** he goes to bed, he watches TV.
(main clause)   (time clause)   (time clause)   (main clause)

1. A time clause explains when an action happened. It begins with a time word such as *after, before, when, as soon as, until,* or *if.* A time clause has a subject and a verb.

2. If the time clause is at the beginning of the sentence, use a comma after the time clause. If the time clause is at the end of the sentence, don't use a comma.

The children play games **until** their father comes home.
As soon as Henry gets home**,** he asks the children about school.

A **Circle** *True* or *False.*

1. After Henry gets to work, he drops off the children at school.   True   False

2. Before he drops off the children, Henry gets a cup of coffee.   True   False

3. As soon as the children get home, they call their father.   True   False

4. As soon as the children get home, Henry leaves work.   True   False

5. The family eats dinner before Henry gets home from work.   True   False

6. After the children do their homework, they can play video games.   True   False

7. Henry watches TV after the children go to bed.   True   False

CD2·TR17

B **Listen.** Then, practice the conversation with a partner.

Co-worker: You get a call every day at 3:15, don't you?

Henry: Yes, that's my son. He's 11. My daughter is 10. They walk home together after school. My son has to call me as soon as they walk in the door.

Co-worker: Oh, I see. My boys are still little. They stay at day care until I pick them up at 4:30.

Henry: Big kids, little kids. Childcare is a challenge when you're working.

A Underline the time clauses.

1. Tammy stays in bed until she hears Emma wake up.

2. As soon as Emma wakes up, she wants her bottle.

3. After Emma has her bottle, Tammy feeds her breakfast.

4. Emma has breakfast before she gets dressed.

5. When Emma plays in her crib, Tammy takes a shower and gets dressed.

B Listen. Tammy is talking about Emma's day. Take a few notes.

CD2·TR18

7:00 _bottle, breakfast_   4:00 _____

9:00 _____   5:00 _____

10:30 _____   6:00 _____

12:00 _____   7:00 _____

1:00 _____   8:00 _____

C Complete the sentences. Use *before, after, when, as soon as,* or *until.*

1. Tammy is going to stay home _____ until _____ Emma is two years old.

2. _____ Emma wakes up, she has a bottle.

3. _____ she has her bottle, she eats breakfast.

4. Tammy cleans the house _____ she takes Emma to the park.

5. They stay at the park _____ it is time for lunch.

6. She takes a nap _____ she eats lunch.

7. _____ Tammy takes Emma to the library, she checks out five or six books.

8. Emma plays with her father _____ they eat dinner.

9. Her father reads her a story _____ she goes to bed.

D **Combine the sentences, using the time words.** First, write the sentence with the time clause at the beginning of the sentence. Then, write the sentence with the time clause at the end of the sentence.

1. I turn on my computer. I check my e-mail. (after)

After I turn on my computer, I check my e-mail.

I check my e-mail after I turn on my computer.

2. He gets up. He has a cup of coffee. (as soon as)

_____

_____

3. I leave for school. I make my bed. (before)

_____

_____

4. She gets to school. She talks with her friends. (when)

_____

_____

5. I am busy every moment. I go to sleep at night. (until)

_____

_____

E **Working Together** **Write your daily schedule in the chart.** Then, tell your partner about your day. Add more details as you talk. Use *before*, *after*, *as soon as*, and *when* in your description.

> As soon as I get to school, I buy a cup of coffee in the cafeteria.

Time	Activity
	turn off the alarm
	go to sleep

Some verbs in English are made up of two words.

Some two-word verbs can have other words between the two parts of the verb. These are called separable (S) verbs.

I **put on** my coat.   I **put** my coat **on**.

Some two-word verbs can't have other words between the two parts of the verb.

I **get on** the bus at 7:30 every morning.
NOT   I ~~**get** the bus **on** at 7:30 every morning~~.

drop off (S)	get out of	put on (S)
eat out	get up	take off (S)
get in	hang up (S)	turn off (S)
get off	look at	turn on (S)
get on	pick up (S)	wake up (S)

WORD PARTNERSHIPS

put on	makeup
	a seat belt
	pajamas

A **Match.**

___f___ **1.** hang up   **a.** to leave a car or taxi

_____ **2.** get out of   **b.** to remove a hat, coat, or other clothing

_____ **3.** turn off   **c.** to leave a bus, train, or plane

_____ **4.** get off   **d.** to stop a device or electronic equipment

_____ **5.** eat out   **e.** to leave a person at a place

_____ **6.** drop off   **f.** to put clothing on a hanger or a hook

_____ **7.** get in   **g.** to eat at a restaurant

_____ **8.** turn on   **h.** to start a device or electronic equipment

_____ **9.** pick up   **i.** to enter a car or taxi

_____ **10.** take off   **j.** to go somewhere and get someone

B **Complete the sentences.** Use two-word verbs.

1. It's raining hard this morning. Can you __drop__ the children __off__ at school?

2. It's cold outside. _____ your hat and gloves before you go out.

3. Don't leave your coat on the floor. _____ it _____ in the closet.

4. If you are hot, _____ your sweater.

5. When you _____ the bus, you have to have the exact fare.

6. I wake up my son at 6:30, but he doesn't _____ until 7:00.

7. I can't see very well. Please _____ the light.

8. I always _____ my children after school.

9. I'm too tired to cook tonight. Let's _____.

C **Working Together** **Read each pair of actions.** Explain the order in which you usually do the two actions. Use *before* or *after*.

> I put on my seat belt **after** I start the car.

> Not me. I put on my seat belt **before** I start the car.

put on my seat belt
start the car

wash the dishes
eat dinner

turn off the lights
leave my house

get dressed
eat breakfast

return to my car
the parking meter time expires

eat dinner
do my homework

turn on the computer
check my e-mail

put on my pajamas
go to bed

sharpen my pencil
come to class

turn off the light
get into bed

D **Dictation** **Your teacher will read the paragraph on page 257.** Listen and complete the sentences.

Mimi has a difficult time falling asleep at night. She gets in bed and puts her head on the pillow. But _____,
1
she begins to worry—about her job, her health, and her family. So, she now has a routine to relax herself _____.
2
_____, she drinks a cup of hot herbal tea.
3
Then, she brushes her teeth. _____,
4
she washes her face and puts on her favorite face cream.
_____, she picks up a magazine
5
and reads for a few minutes. Then, she listens to some quiet music.
_____, she falls asleep more easily.
6

A Discuss the words and phrases.

buckle	drop off	jump out of	put on
climb into	get dressed	look at	wake up

CD2·TR19

B Matt and Ava are working parents. Look at the pictures and listen to their morning routine.

1.

2.

3.

4.

5.

6.

7.

8.

9.

C **Complete.** Write the correct form of one of the verbs from the box.

1. Matt ___gets up___ at 5:45 in the morning.

2. He _____ bed when the alarm clock rings.

3. He _____ Ava after he takes a shower.

4. Matt _____ a DVD for the boys.

5. Ava _____ after she eats breakfast.

6. The boys _____ their carseats.

7. Ava _____ the boys into their carseats.

8. She _____ the boys at the day care center.

put on
get dressed
drop off
jump out of
buckle
~~get up~~
wake up
climb into

D **Complete the sentences.** Use *before*, *after*, *when*, or *as soon as*. For some sentences, more than one answer is possible.

1. _____ the alarm rings, Matt gets up.

2. Matt takes a shower _____ Ava gets up.

3. _____ Matt gets out of the shower, he wakes Ava up.

4. _____ the boys wake up, they watch a video.

5. Matt kisses everyone good-bye _____ he leaves for work.

6. _____ everyone is ready, they leave.

7. The kids always climb into their carseats _____ they get into the car.

8. Ava's customers don't get angry _____ she's late for work.

E **Answer the questions with a partner.**

1. Who gets up first?

2. What time does Matt get up?

3. When does he wake Ava up?

4. What does Ava do after she wakes up?

5. When does Ava eat breakfast with the boys?

6. When does Ava get dressed?

7. What does Ava do before she starts the car?

8. Where does Ava take the kids before she goes to work?

9. Why aren't Ava's customers annoyed when she is a little late?

Reading

 A **Discuss.** What is the best way to discipline a child? Give your opinion of each method.

1. Yell at your child.

2. Spank him.

3. Send him to his room.

4. Take away a privilege, like watching TV.

5. Talk to him about his behavior.

6. If he is doing something you don't like, suggest another activity.

7. Give him a "time out." He has to sit by himself for five or ten minutes.

B **Word Builder** **Match.** Then, complete the sentences.

_b__ **1.** aggressive	**a.** wanting something that someone else has
____ **2.** jealous	**b.** unfriendly and angry
____ **3.** praise	**c.** words of respect and approval
____ **4.** behavior	**d.** a special right or benefit
____ **5.** privilege	**e.** a person's actions

1. Parents should _____ their children's good behavior so that the children will repeat the behavior.

2. My son is too _____ with other children and often gets into fights.

3. My son's teacher is very happy with his good _____ at school.

4. When my daughter doesn't clean her room, we take away a _____, like watching TV.

5. My daughter is _____ because her brother gets better grades in school.

C **Dr. Bob is a child psychologist.** He gives parents advice about their children. Read the letters to Dr. Bob and his responses.

Dear Dr. Bob,

My daughter is two years old. I walked into her bedroom and found her coloring on the wall with her crayons. I told her, "No! No! Never color on the wall with your crayons. You can only color on paper." My husband thinks I was too easy on her and that she needed a spanking. What is your opinion?

Debbie

Dear Debbie,

You handled the situation well. Children this age are too little to understand a spanking. It's time to check your home carefully. Put crayons, paints, medicines, and cleaning products in places where she can't reach them.

Dr. Bob

Dear Dr. Bob,

I was visiting my sister, who has two boys, ages seven and five. They were throwing a ball in the living room. She asked them several times to stop, but they didn't listen to her. Finally, one of the boys threw the ball and broke a lamp. She yelled loudly at them for several minutes. Then, she sent them to their room. She looked at me and said, "They never listen to me."

Carmen

Dear Carmen,

Your sister needs to be clear with her children about the **behavior** she expects. She should tell her boys, "Don't throw the ball in the house. If you throw the ball one more time, I'm going to take it away." Then, she needs to do what she says. Her boys will soon learn to listen to her.

Dr. Bob

Dear Dr. Bob,

I have a six-year-old son and a four-year-old daughter. My son hits his sister or pulls her hair several times a day. When my husband sees my son do this, he hits him. The next day, my son does the same thing again.

Joanna

Dear Joanna,

There is always some fighting when children are growing up. Is your son **jealous** of his sister? Do you think he needs more special time or attention from you or your husband?

Try to remain calm. When he hits his sister, take away a **privilege**, like TV, for the evening. At other times, **praise** the good things he does. "I like the rocket you built," or "Thank you for setting the table." Your husband might be angry with your son, but it doesn't help to hit him. Children who are hit learn that it's okay to hit when you are angry. Studies show that children who are hit are often more **aggressive** with other children.

Dr. Bob

READING NOTE

Understanding the Author's Opinion

Sometimes an author states an opinion directly. At other times, the reader can understand or guess the author's opinion from clues in the reading.

D **What is Dr. Bob's opinion on child discipline?** (Circle) *True* or *False*.

1. It's okay to hit your children when you are angry.   True   False

2. When you are angry with your children, yell at them.   True   False

3. Praise your children when they do things well.   True   False

4. Try to remain calm when your children are a problem.   True   False

5. Children learn how to act from their parents.   True   False

6. Try to understand the reasons for behavior problems.   True   False

A **Discuss.**

1. Do you ever write short notes or e-mails? If yes, who do you write to?

2. Do you have any children in school? Do you have to write a note or an e-mail when they are absent from school?

B **Read the notes to a teacher.**

October 10

Dear Mrs. Toma,

Please excuse Melissa's absence from class last week. She had the flu. Melissa missed a lot of classwork and homework. Please give her the assignments, so she can complete the work at home. Thank you,

Paula Romero

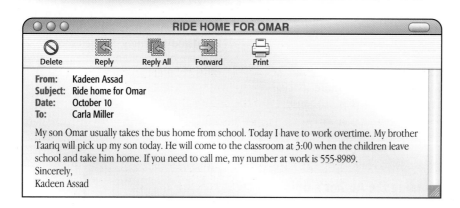

RIDE HOME FOR OMAR

Delete   Reply   Reply All   Forward   Print

From: Kadeen Assad
Subject: Ride home for Omar
Date: October 10
To: Carla Miller

My son Omar usually takes the bus home from school. Today I have to work overtime. My brother Taariq will pick up my son today. He will come to the classroom at 3:00 when the children leave school and take him home. If you need to call me, my number at work is 555-8989.
Sincerely,
Kadeen Assad

October 10

Dear Mr. Evans,

When my daughter came home yesterday, she was crying. When she was playing outside at recess, a girl pushed her. Another girl pulled her hair.

My daughter does not know the names of the girls. She said they are older and in another class. Can you please talk to my daughter and to the older girls?

My daughter is very upset. Thank you.

Julie Lin

C Write the reason for each note on page 188.

1. Her child was absent from school. The child needs the homework assignments .

2. _____
   _____ .

3. _____
   _____ .

WRITING NOTE

Writing a School Note

Notes to teachers should be short and specific.
- Do not include unnecessary information.
- Include the date.
- Spell the teacher's name correctly. Use *Mr.* for a *man* and *Mrs.* or *Ms.* for a *woman*.
- Sign your full name.

D **Edit the note.** Add any missing information. Cross out any unnecessary sentences.

> Dear Teacher,
>
> My son Victor has an appointment at the doctor on Wednesday at 9:00. I will bring him to school immediately after the appointment. This was the only time available. I am sorry that he will be late tomorrow.
> You are a very good teacher, and Victor is very happy in your class.
> Thank you.
> Tamara Lapinsky

E **Write a note to a teacher.** You have a parent-teacher conference on Monday night at 7:00. You work at night. Suggest a different day and time for the conference.

F **Sharing Our Stories** **Work in a small group.** Read your notes. Which note does the group like the best? Why?

A Discuss.

1. When you were a child, how often did you receive a report card?

2. Were you happy with your grades?

3. How often do children in your town receive report cards? Do parents have to sign the report cards?

 ### B Look at the report card and answer the questions.

WASHINGTON MIDDLE SCHOOL
Student Progress Report

Student: *Yolanda Figeroa* Student ID: *123-12-123* Grade: *8*

Attendance	1	2	3	4
Absent	5	3		
Tardy	4	6		

Subject	1	2	3	4	Teacher's Comments
English	B	C			3 6 16 20
Spanish 2	A	B			7 21
Geography	D	C			1 13 14 21
Social Studies	C	D			3 12 13 14
Algebra 1	C	D			2 14 20 22
Physical Education	B	B			
Computer Science	B	B			3 4 15
Art	A	A			15

A = Excellent
B = Good
C = Fair
D = Having Difficulty
E = Failing

1. What grade is Yolanda in?

2. What does *tardy* mean?

3. How many times was Yolanda absent in the second marking period?

4. What is Yolanda's best subject?

5. What subjects are difficult for Yolanda?

6. In which subject is Yolanda improving?

C Read the teacher's comments. Put (+) next to a positive teacher comment. Put (–) next to a negative teacher comment.

__+__	**1.** Improved skills		_____	**12.** More study required
__–__	**2.** Performs poorly on tests		_____	**13.** Work not well-organized
_____	**3.** Always cooperative		_____	**14.** Seldom asks for help
_____	**4.** Excellent effort		_____	**15.** Very good work
_____	**5.** Absent too frequently		_____	**16.** Fails to complete assignments
_____	**6.** Often late for class		_____	**17.** Notebook well-organized
_____	**7.** Follows directions well		_____	**18.** Good writing ability
_____	**8.** Good work habits		_____	**19.** Project not done or incomplete
_____	**9.** Work has improved		_____	**20.** Needs to come in for extra help
_____	**10.** Work well organized		_____	**21.** Good class participation
_____	**11.** Interrupts the class		_____	**22.** Conference needed

D Look at the teacher's comments on Yolanda's report card. What are Yolanda's problems with her classwork?

1. Yolanda does not ask for extra help from the teacher _____ .

2. _____ .

3. _____ .

4. _____ .

5. _____ .

E Talk with a partner. You are Yolanda's parents. How can you help Yolanda with her schoolwork? Should you call any of her teachers?

Unit 13

Crime

A **Discuss each kind of crime.**

1. Crime: shoplifting

Person: shoplifter

Action: shoplift, steal

2. Crime: mugging

Person: mugger

Action: mug, steal

3. Crime: robbery, burglary

Person: robber, burglar

Action: steal (a thing)
     rob (a place, person)

My car is gone!

4. Crime: car theft

Person: car thief

Action: steal

B **Discuss.** Have you ever been the victim of a crime? What happened?

Active Grammar

CD2·TR20

A **Listen.** Jonathan came home and saw that someone had robbed his apartment. A police officer is interviewing Jonathan. Write the things the thief stole.

1. _____   2. _____   3. _____

4. _____   5. _____

B **Complete the sentences.** Use verbs from the box. One of the verbs is negative. Some of the verbs can be used more than once.

find	open
go	realize
leave	thank
lock	try
look	

1. When Jonathan _____left_____ his apartment, it was 8:30.

2. Jonathan _____ his door when he _____ his apartment this morning.

3. Before Jonathan _____ to bed last night, he _____ the windows.

4. Jonathan thinks that he _____ the windows before he _____ to work.

5. Jonathan _____ that something was wrong as soon as he _____ to put his keys on the table.

6. When Jonathan _____ for the TV, he _____ that it was gone.

7. When Jonathan _____ the refrigerator, he _____ his leftover Chinese food.

8. Jonathan _____ the police officer before she _____.

Crime · **193**

I locked my door **before** I went to work.   **Before** I went to work, I locked my door.
(main clause)   (time clause)   (time clause)   (main clause)

1. A time clause explains when an action happened. It usually begins with a time word such as *when, before, after,* or *as soon as.* A time clause has a subject and a verb.

2. A time clause can come at the beginning or the end of a sentence. If the time clause is at the beginning of a sentence, use a comma (,) after the time clause.

CD2·TR21

G **Pronunciation: Word Stress** **Listen and repeat.** Pay attention to the content words in **bold**.

1. Before I **left** my **home**, I **locked** the **door**.

2. When we **went** on **vacation**, we **stopped** the **mail**.

3. She **turned on** the **alarm** before she **left** her **apartment**.

4. They **closed** all the **windows** before they **left**.

5. I **called** the **police** as soon as I **saw** the **broken door**.

6. I **dialed 911** when I **heard** a **noise downstairs**.

7. After **someone robbed** their **house**, they **bought** a **dog**.

CD2·TR22

D **Listen and complete the conversation.**

A: Someone robbed my house!

B: Oh, no! What happened?

A: _____

B: Really? How did they get in?

A: _____

B: Oh. What did they take?

A: _____

B: Did you call the police?

A: _____

WORD PARTNERSHIPS

break into	a house
	an apartment
	a car

E **Working Together** **Work with a partner.** Write a conversation about a robbery. Then, act out your conversation.

F **Combine the sentences.** Yesterday, John and Sue visited their friends. They did not know that a thief was watching their car.

1. John and Sue found a parking space. They parked their car. (when)

   When John and Sue found a parking space, they parked their car.

2. They locked the car. They walked away. (before)

_____

3. The thief looked around carefully. The couple left. (after)

_____

4. He didn't see anyone. He walked to the car. (when)

_____

5. He touched the car. A large dog jumped up and began to bark. (as soon as)

_____

6. The thief ran away. He saw the dog. (when)

_____

 G **Working Together** **Choose eight of the phrases.** Tell your partners about events in your life. Use *before*, *after*, or *when*.

> After I had a baby, I stopped working.

> Before I got my driver's license, I went to a driving school.

came to this country	fell in love	graduated from high school
got a visa	found a job	enrolled in English classes
became a citizen	found an apartment	got my driver's license
bought a house	got divorced	graduated from college
got married	had a baby	got robbed

I		
He	**was**	sleep**ing**.
She		

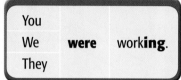

You		
We	**were**	work**ing**.
They		

> The past continuous describes an action that was in progress at a specific time in the past.
>
> Refer to page 250 for past continuous spelling rules.

A **Complete the sentences.** Use the past continuous form of the verbs. What was happening at 4:00 yesterday afternoon?

1. Yesterday at 4:00 P.M. I (drive) _____was driving_____ home from work.

2. I (listen) _____ to the radio.

3. My wife (shop) _____ at the supermarket.

4. My children (study) _____ at the library.

5. You (sleep) _____.

6. My neighbors (watch) _____ TV.

7. Three police officers (investigate) _____ a bank robbery.

8. And yesterday at 4:00 a thief (climb) _____ in my window!

 B **Working Together** **Work in a group of three students.** Ask and answer the questions about your activities last weekend. Take notes.

	Student 1	Student 2
Where were you on Friday night?		
What were you doing?		
Where were you on Saturday morning?		
What were you doing?		
Where were you on Saturday afternoon?		
What were you doing?		
Where were you on Saturday evening?		
What were you doing?		
Where were you on Sunday afternoon?		
What were you doing?		

> **While** I **was driving** to school, I **was listening** to the radio.
> I **was listening** to the radio **while** I **was driving** to school.
> **While** the professor **was talking**, the students **were taking** notes.
> The students **were taking** notes **while** the professor **was talking**.

> Use *while* with the past continuous to show that two actions were happening at the same time.

A **Complete the sentences.** Use your own ideas.

1. While I was walking to school today, I <u>was talking on my cell phone</u> .

2. While the teacher was returning the tests, the students _____ .

3. While the class was listening to the teacher, I _____ .

4. The boss _____ while the employees _____ .

5. While I was taking the bus to school, I _____ .

6. While Mr. Green was vacuuming the living room, Mrs. Green _____ .

7. I _____ while I was studying.

8. My friend _____ while I was watching TV.

B **Work with a partner.** Take turns making sentences with *while* and the past continuous.

> While I was cooking dinner, I was listening to the radio.

1. I / cook dinner   I / listen to the radio

2. neighbors / have a party   I / try to sleep

3. He / watch TV   he / cook dinner

4. She / walk in the park   she / talk to her friend

5. I / do my homework   the baby / cry

6. He / talk on his cell phone   he / drive

7. you / watch TV   I / take a nap

8. I / cook dinner   my daughter / set the table

9. You / work   I / apply for a job

10. I / enter the building   many students / leave

> While I **was sleeping**, I **heard** someone in my living room.
>
> I **was shopping** in the mall when a thief **stole** my car.
>
> The past continuous can describe an action that was interrupted. One action was going on when another action happened.

A **Complete the sentences.** Use the verbs in parentheses.

1. I (watch) <u>was watching</u> TV when a man (look) <u>looked</u> in my window.

2. We (sit) _____ in class when the fire alarm (ring) _____.

3. A shoplifter (steal) _____ a camera when the security guard (see) _____ her.

4. While the security guard (take) _____ a break, two men (rob) _____ the jewelry store.

5. Someone (steal) _____ my car while I (work) _____.

6. While I (drive) _____ to work, I (see) _____ an accident.

B **In your notebook, write two sentences about each set of pictures.** Use *when* or *while*.

While I was reading, I heard a noise.   I was reading when I heard a noise.

1.

I was reading.   I heard a noise.

2.

Natalie was walking her dog.   A man stole her wallet.

3.

Tyler was walking down the street.   He saw a bank robbery.

4.

Grace was talking on her cell phone.   A police officer pulled her over.

C **Read the timeline of the bank robbery.** Then, complete the sentences.

2:55	Several customers were in the bank.
2:58	The security guard went on break.
3:00	A robber entered the building. He told everyone to lie down.
3:01	A teller pressed the alarm.
3:02	The robber took $10,000.
3:03	The robber ran out the door. He jumped in his car and drove away.
3:05	The police arrived at the bank. They questioned everyone.

1. Marco was using the ATM machine when *the robber entered the bank* .

2. When the robber entered the bank, the security guard _____.

3. As soon as the robber entered the bank, _____.

4. A teller pressed the alarm when _____.

5. Before the robber left the bank, _____.

6. The robber ran away before _____.

7. While the police were rushing to the bank, _____.

8. After the police arrived at the bank, _____.

A **Match each word with the correct picture from the story below.** Write the number of the picture.

_____ arrest	_____ block	_____ fist	_____ take off
_____ mask	_____ break into	_____ get out of	_____ climb into
_____ put on	_____ chase	_____ handcuff	_____ pick up

 B **Last night, Spike and Tina tried to rob a jewelry store.** Look at the pictures and listen to the story.

CD2・TR23

1.   2.  3.  4.

5.  6.  7.  8.

9.  10.  11.  12.

13.  14.  15.  16.

 C **Look at the pictures.** Tell a partner what you remember about each picture.

D **Complete the sentences.** Use *before, after, when, while,* or *as soon as.*

1. Spike put on gloves _____ he went into the store.

2. Spike took some jewelry _____ he got into the store.

3. Spike looked around _____ he entered the store.

4. The alarm rang _____ Spike dropped his bag.

5. _____ Tina was sitting in the car, Spike was robbing the store.

6. Tina started the car _____ she heard the alarm.

7. The police officers handcuffed Spike and Tina _____ they put them into the police car.

E **Circle** *True* or *False.*

1. Spike put on gloves after he broke the window.   True   False

2. Spike climbed into the store after he broke the window.   True   False

3. While Spike was looking around the store, the police arrived.   True   False

4. When Spike saw the pizza, the alarm rang.   True   False

5. Before Spike left the store, he took some jewelry.   True   False

6. As soon as Spike saw the police car, he tried to run away.   True   False

7. Spike took off his mask and hat while he was running away.   True   False

F **Answer the questions.**

1. What did Spike put on while he was going to the store?

2. How did Spike break the window?

3. What was Tina doing while Spike was in the store?

4. What did Spike do as soon as he got into the store?

5. What did Spike steal?

6. When did Spike see the pizza?

7. What happened when he picked up a slice of pizza?

8. When did the alarm ring?

9. When did the police officer get out of the car?

10. What did the police officers do after they arrested Spike and Tina?

Reading

A **Discuss.** Then, read.

1. Have you ever seen anyone shoplift? Where were you? What did you do?

2. What is an Internet Forum or Discussion Group?

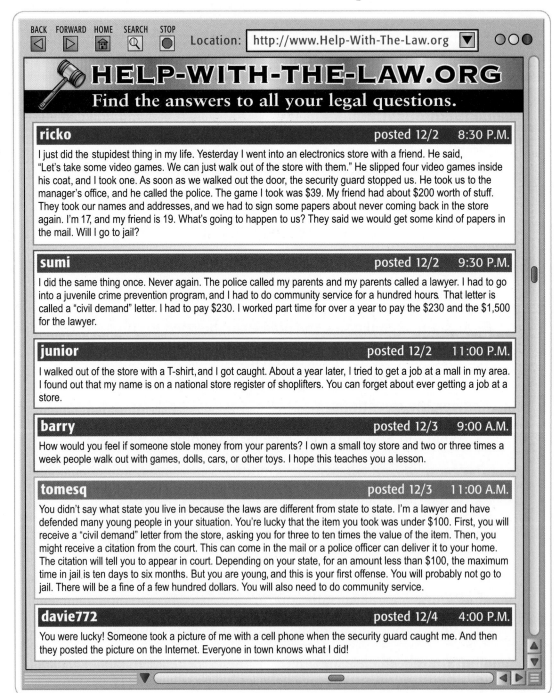

HELP-WITH-THE-LAW.ORG
Find the answers to all your legal questions.

ricko posted 12/2 8:30 P.M.

I just did the stupidest thing in my life. Yesterday I went into an electronics store with a friend. He said, "Let's take some video games. We can just walk out of the store with them." He slipped four video games inside his coat, and I took one. As soon as we walked out the door, the security guard stopped us. He took us to the manager's office, and he called the police. The game I took was $39. My friend had about $200 worth of stuff. They took our names and addresses, and we had to sign some papers about never coming back in the store again. I'm 17, and my friend is 19. What's going to happen to us? They said we would get some kind of papers in the mail. Will I go to jail?

sumi posted 12/2 9:30 P.M.

I did the same thing once. Never again. The police called my parents and my parents called a lawyer. I had to go into a juvenile crime prevention program, and I had to do community service for a hundred hours. That letter is called a "civil demand" letter. I had to pay $230. I worked part time for over a year to pay the $230 and the $1,500 for the lawyer.

junior posted 12/2 11:00 P.M.

I walked out of the store with a T-shirt, and I got caught. About a year later, I tried to get a job at a mall in my area. I found out that my name is on a national store register of shoplifters. You can forget about ever getting a job at a store.

barry posted 12/3 9:00 A.M.

How would you feel if someone stole money from your parents? I own a small toy store and two or three times a week people walk out with games, dolls, cars, or other toys. I hope this teaches you a lesson.

tomesq posted 12/3 11:00 A.M.

You didn't say what state you live in because the laws are different from state to state. I'm a lawyer and have defended many young people in your situation. You're lucky that the item you took was under $100. First, you will receive a "civil demand" letter from the store, asking you for three to ten times the value of the item. Then, you might receive a citation from the court. This can come in the mail or a police officer can deliver it to your home. The citation will tell you to appear in court. Depending on your state, for an amount less than $100, the maximum time in jail is ten days to six months. But you are young, and this is your first offense. You will probably not go to jail. There will be a fine of a few hundred dollars. You will also need to do community service.

davie772 posted 12/4 4:00 P.M.

You were lucky! Someone took a picture of me with a cell phone when the security guard caught me. And then they posted the picture on the Internet. Everyone in town knows what I did!

Reading Internet Forums and Discussions

On the Internet, there are many forums and discussion groups. A person asks a question or tells about an experience. Other users "post" their answers or write comments.

B Complete.

1. What did ricko do? _____

2. What are his questions? _____

3. Five people answered ricko:

   a. These people shoplifted in the past: _____ _____

   _____

   b. This person is a store owner: _____

   c. This person is a lawyer: _____

C What might happen to ricko? In the reading, underline six possible results of shoplifting.

D Word Builder Complete the sentences with a word or phrase from the box.

offense	community service	register
citation	juvenile program	posted

1. In a _____, teenagers who commit a small crime pay a fine and volunteer in the hospital on the weekends.

2. The police have a _____ of criminals in their area.

3. My brother _____ a video of our trip on the Internet.

4. Paul received a _____ to appear in court next Tuesday at 10:00 A.M.

5. For her _____, Sarah worked in a soup kitchen, making dinner for homeless families.

6. Robbery of a home is a serious _____.

A Discuss.

1. Have you or anyone you know ever been robbed?

2. Where did the robbery happen? What did the thief take? Was anyone hurt?

B Read Martin's story about a robbery in his neighborhood.

In July 2010, my grandparents and a neighbor were talking in the living room. It was a Saturday night at about 9:00. My grandfather was looking out the window when he saw a large green truck on the street. Ten minutes later, he saw two men. They were wearing brown uniforms. The men were putting a sofa, two armchairs, and a coffee table in the truck. Then, he saw them putting two TVs, a computer, and a stereo in the truck. He asked my grandmother and the neighbor, "Are Maria and Pablo moving?"

As soon as the neighbor saw the men, he said, "They're thieves!"

My grandfather went out of the house and got into his old car, and the neighbor got in the car, too. My grandmother stayed in the house. My grandfather and the neighbor drove after the thieves, but the thieves' truck was faster than my grandfather's car, so they couldn't catch them.

When the owners of the house, Maria and Pablo, came back from the beach, my grandfather said, "I'm sorry. I saw what happened, but I couldn't stop them. My car is too old."

Maria and Pablo said, "Fortunately, you didn't catch the thieves. Don't worry. The insurance will pay for everything and more."

My grandfather was surprised. He said, "I will never risk my life again for problems that aren't mine."

Martin

WRITING NOTE

Using Quotes

To show the exact words of a speaker, use quotations marks ("). Start the quote with a capital letter. Put quotation marks at the beginning and end of the quote.

The neighbor said, "They're thieves!"

My grandfather said, "I'm sorry. I saw what happened, but I couldn't stop them."

C Write the sentences again. Put the correct punctuation in each sentence. Use quotation marks. Use capital letters where necessary.

1. The robber said give me your wallet

The robber said, "Give me your wallet."

2. The police officer asked did you lock your door this morning

_____

3. I answered yes. I always lock the door in the morning

_____

4. A woman on the street shouted help

_____

5. The store owner said I'm going to call the police

_____

D You are going to write about a crime that happened to you or a crime you heard or read about. Answer the questions.

1. Who did the crime happen to? _____

2. Who committed the crime? _____

3. What was the crime? _____

4. When did the crime happen? _____

5. Where did it happen? _____

E Write about the crime.

• Use the information in Exercise D.

• Include one or two quotations in your story.

F Sharing Our Stories Read your story to a partner. Your partner will ask you more questions about the crime.

A **Read and discuss the process from arrest to trial.**

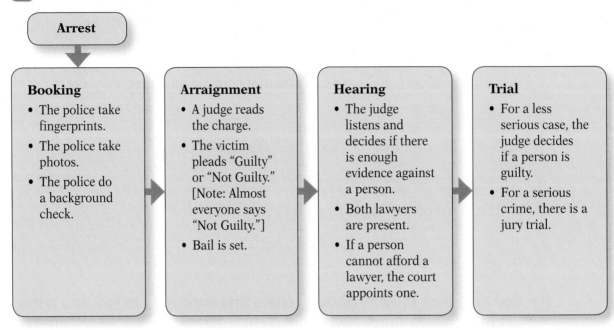

Arrest

Booking
- The police take fingerprints.
- The police take photos.
- The police do a background check.

Arraignment
- A judge reads the charge.
- The victim pleads "Guilty" or "Not Guilty." [Note: Almost everyone says "Not Guilty."]
- Bail is set.

Hearing
- The judge listens and decides if there is enough evidence against a person.
- Both lawyers are present.
- If a person cannot afford a lawyer, the court appoints one.

Trial
- For a less serious case, the judge decides if a person is guilty.
- For a serious crime, there is a jury trial.

B **Look at the chart.** Put the events below in order from 1 to 8.

_____ The judge decided that the police had strong evidence against Spike.

_____ The police took Spike's fingerprints.

_____ At the trial, the jury found Spike guilty. The judge sentenced Spike to one year in jail.

_____ At the arraignment, the judge said, "You are charged with robbing a jewelry store."

__1__ The police arrested Spike and read him his rights.

_____ The judge set bail at $5,000 to be sure Spike would appear for his hearing.

_____ Spike could not afford a lawyer, so the court appointed one for him.

_____ In his background check, the police found that this was Spike's third robbery.

CULTURE NOTE

When the police arrest a person, they must read the person his / her rights:

You have the right to remain silent. Anything you say can and will be used against you in a court of law. You have the right to speak to an attorney and have an attorney present during any questioning. If you cannot afford a lawyer, one will be provided for you at government expense.

A Complete each definition with a word or phrase from the picture.

1. The _____judge_____ is the person in charge of the court.

2. The _____ is the person charged with a crime.

3. The _____ is the lawyer for the defendant. He / She tries to show that the defendant is innocent, that is, not guilty.

4. The _____ is the person who files a legal complaint against another person.

5. The _____ is the lawyer for the plaintiff. He / She tries to prove that the defendant is guilty.

6. A _____ is a person who brings information to the court about a crime.

7. The _____ is the group of people who sits in court and decides if a person is guilty.

B **Steve Jenkins is on trial for robbing Town Bank.** Who is speaking?

1. My client, Steve Jenkins, is innocent. He is a hardworking young man who has a full-time job and is going to school part time.

2. I did not rob the bank. I was sitting in school at that time. I have a math class on Tuesday and Thursday from 3:00 to 4:00.

3. The bank has video of the bank robbery. The man on the video was wearing the clothes that the police found in his house.

4. My name is Tamara Clemens. I am Mr. Jenkins's math teacher. Mr. Jenkins was not in school on the day of the robbery. I cancelled class that day.

5. Your Honor, we find the defendant, Steve Jenkins, guilty of the crime.

Unit
14 Careers

A **Write the name of the job under each picture.**

1. _____

2. _____

3. _____

4. _____

5. _____

6. _____

B **Discuss.**

1. Would you like to have one of the jobs in the photos? Which one?

2. Where would you like to work—in an office or outside?

3. Would you like to supervise other people?

4. What kind of job did you have in your native country?

5. What job would you like to have in the future?

6. What kind of education do you need?

C **Write each occupation under the education it requires.** Some occupations fit in more than one category.

Occupations	Education Required
carpenter	**Professional Degree**
computer engineer	1. _____
cook or chef	2. _____
dental hygienist	3. _____
dentist	**Bachelor's Degree (Four-year college)**
electrician	1. _____
emergency medical technician (EMT)	2. _____
	3. _____
	4. _____
hairstylist	**Associate's Degree (Two-year college)**
home health aide	1. _____
lawyer	2. _____
licensed practical nurse (LPN)	3. _____
machine operator	**Vocational Training**
manicurist	1. _____
physical therapist	2. _____
physician	3. _____
plumber	4. _____
registered nurse (RN)	**Learn on the job / Short-term training**
respiratory therapist	1. _____
secondary school teacher	2. _____
social worker	3. _____
	4. _____
	5. _____
	6. _____

She **will go** to college <u>after she **graduates** from high school</u>.
  (main clause)   **(time clause)**

<u>After she **graduates** from high school</u>, she **will go** to college.
        (time clause)   **(main clause)**

Notes

1. A time clause begins with a time word such as *if, before, after, as soon as,* and *when*. A time clause has a subject and a verb.

2. The verb in the main clause is in the future tense (with *will* or *be going to*). The verb in the time clause is in the present tense.

3. A time clause can be at the beginning or at the end of a sentence.

A **Match.**

___b___ **1.** If I do well in my English course,

_____ **2.** After Julia completes her engineering degree,

_____ **3.** When Frank becomes a nurse,

_____ **4.** Before Rick applies to the police department,

_____ **5.** If I receive a good evaluation,

_____ **6.** After Laura finishes high school,

_____ **7.** Before I go to the job interview,

a. he will need to take a physical exam.

b. I will become an interpreter.

c. she'll enter a community college.

d. I will research the company.

e. she'll design automobiles.

f. I will get a promotion.

g. he will have to give medication.

B **Dictation** **Your teacher will dictate the sentences on page 257.** Listen and complete the sentences.

1. Maria _____ for a job before she _____.

2. Before she _____ for a job, she _____ her resume.

3. She _____ out her resume when she _____ a good job posting.

4. If she _____ of a job opening, she _____ the company.

5. When she _____ on an interview, she _____ a suit.

6. If she _____ a good impression, the company _____ her.

C Complete the sentences about Bernato. He would like to open his own restaurant someday.

1. After Bernato (graduate) _graduates_ from high school, he (go) _will go_ to cooking school.

2. When he (go) _____ to cooking school, he (work) _____ in a restaurant part time.

3. Bernato (take) _____ a few business classes after he (graduate) _____ from cooking school.

4. Bernato (work) _____ in a restaurant for several years after he (finish) _____ his education.

5. When he (decide) _____ to open a restaurant, he (discuss) _____ his plans with his family.

6. If he (have – negative) _____ enough money, he (apply) _____ for a bank loan.

7. He (look) _____ for a good location when he (be) _____ ready to open a restaurant.

D Combine the sentences about Miguel. His company will close next month.

1. When / Miguel's company / close   he / apply for / unemployment benefits
   When Miguel's company closes, he will apply for unemployment benefits.

2. After / he / get laid off   he / register for night classes
   _____

3. When / his friend / have / extra work   Miguel / help him
   _____

4. Miguel's wife / work / full time   when / Miguel / get laid off
   _____

5. When / his wife / be / at work   Miguel / take care of / the children
   _____

A **Read about a career as a bookkeeper.**

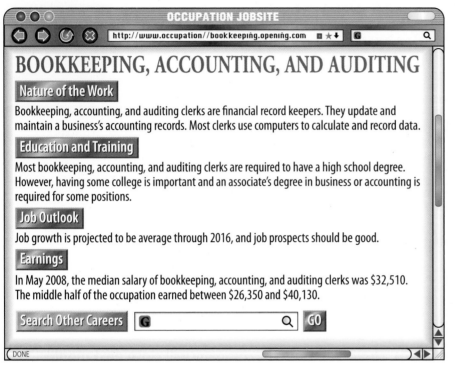

OCCUPATION JOBSITE

http://www.occupation//bookkeeping.opening.com

BOOKKEEPING, ACCOUNTING, AND AUDITING

Nature of the Work

Bookkeeping, accounting, and auditing clerks are financial record keepers. They update and maintain a business's accounting records. Most clerks use computers to calculate and record data.

Education and Training

Most bookkeeping, accounting, and auditing clerks are required to have a high school degree. However, having some college is important and an associate's degree in business or accounting is required for some positions.

Job Outlook

Job growth is projected to be average through 2016, and job prospects should be good.

Earnings

In May 2008, the median salary of bookkeeping, accounting, and auditing clerks was $32,510. The middle half of the occupation earned between $26,350 and $40,130.

Search Other Careers G **GO**

DONE

B **Complete.** Use the correct form of the verbs in parentheses.

Lian wants to be a bookkeeper. At this time, Lian (work) _____1_____ in the shipping department of a company. At night, she (study) _____2_____ English. When she (complete) _____3_____ her English classes, Lian (apply) _____4_____ to the community college near her home. She (take) _____5_____ courses in accounting. She (continue) _____6_____ to work full time while she (study) _____7_____ accounting. After she (take) _____8_____ a few classes, she (look) _____9_____ for an entry-level job in accounting. She (earn) _____10_____ her associate's degree in accounting in three years. After she (complete) _____11_____ her degree, she (apply) _____12_____ for a promotion at work.

212 · Unit 14

C **Read about a career as a physical therapy assistant.**

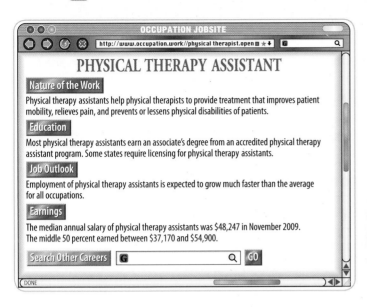

OCCUPATION JOBSITE

http://www.occupation.work//physical therapist.open

PHYSICAL THERAPY ASSISTANT

Nature of the Work

Physical therapy assistants help physical therapists to provide treatment that improves patient mobility, relieves pain, and prevents or lessens physical disabilities of patients.

Education

Most physical therapy assistants earn an associate's degree from an accredited physical therapy assistant program. Some states require licensing for physical therapy assistants.

Job Outlook

Employment of physical therapy assistants is expected to grow much faster than the average for all occupations.

Earnings

The median annual salary of physical therapy assistants was $48,247 in November 2009. The middle 50 percent earned between $37,170 and $54,900.

Search Other Careers **G** **GO**

DONE

 D **Listen to Jessica's career plans.** Take notes. Then, answer the questions.

CD2·TR24

Jessica's career plans:

_____ .

_____ .

_____ .

_____ .

_____ .

1. Where does Jessica live?

2. What is she studying now?

3. What program is she going to begin when she completes these classes?

4. Is she going to work while she attends the program?

5. What is she going to do before she begins the program?

6. How many years is the program?

7. Who is going to help Jessica with expenses?

8. What kind of experience is Jessica going to get before she graduates?

9. When will she apply for a job?

10. How much money will she earn after she graduates?

What **are** you **going to do** after you **graduate**?

Where **is** he **going to live** if his company **transfers** him?

When he **starts** school, **is** he **going to work** full time?

In a question with a future time clause, use the future question form in the main clause.

CD2·TR25

A **Pronunciation: Question Intonation Listen and repeat.**

1. What are you going to do if you win the lottery?

2. What will you do after you finish this class?

3. If she gets a promotion, what is she going to buy?

4. When he finishes college, where will he work?

B **Answer the questions.**

1. What are they going to do if they win the lottery?

_____

_____

2. What is she going to do if she gets laid off?

_____

_____

3. What are they going to do if it starts to rain?

_____

_____

4. What is he going to buy if he gets a promotion?

_____

_____

C **Ask and answer the questions with a partner.**

1. What are you going to do today when you finish this class?
2. What are you going to do if you go back to your native county?
3. What career will you study when you finish your English classes?
4. When you finish your classes, where will you work?
5. What will you do when your friends come to visit?
6. What are you going to do if you win the lottery?

 **D** **Listen to the conversation between two students.** Then, practice the conversation with a partner.

CD2·TR26

A: What are your plans for next year?

B: I'm going to finish my English classes.

A: What are you going to do when you finish your classes?

B: When I finish my English classes, I'm going to enter nursing school.

A: Where are you going to work after you graduate?

B: I'm going to work in the emergency room of a hospital.

E **Complete the chart with your plans for the future.**

Year	My Plans

 F **Working Together** **Tell a partner about your future plans.** Then, write a conversation about your plans. Act out your conversation for the class.

CD2·TR27

A **Ronaldo Silva has to make a career choice.** Will he begin a new job with a large company or start his own business? Listen and take notes about the advantages and disadvantages of each choice.

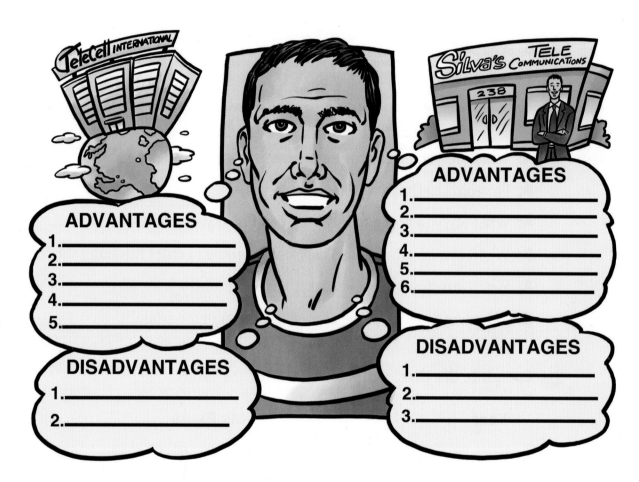

ADVANTAGES
1._____
2._____
3._____
4._____
5._____

DISADVANTAGES
1._____
2._____

ADVANTAGES
1._____
2._____
3._____
4._____
5._____
6._____

DISADVANTAGES
1._____
2._____
3._____

 CD2·TR28

B **Listen.** Circle the job that fits each description.

1. Large company   Own business   Both

2. Large company   Own business   Both

3. Large company   Own business   Both

4. Large company   Own business   Both

5. Large company   Own business   Both

6. Large company   Own business   Both

7. Large company   Own business   Both

8. Large company   Own business   Both

C Match.

h **1.** After Ronaldo works for one year at the company,

2. Ronaldo's wife will handle the bills

3. When Ronaldo goes on a business trip,

4. Ronaldo will receive a promotion

5. Before Ronaldo opens his store,

6. If Ronaldo takes the new job,

7. Ronaldo will apply for a bank loan

8. If Ronaldo starts his own business,

a. he may miss activities with his family.

b. he will have to hire a few employees.

c. if he does not have enough money to rent a store.

d. if he becomes one of the top twenty salespeople.

e. when she has free time.

f. he will have to travel.

g. he will have to pay for his own medical insurance.

h. he may receive a promotion.

D In your notebook, combine each pair of sentences into a longer sentence with a future time clause. Use the time expression in parentheses and change repeated subjects to pronouns.

1. Ronaldo takes the new job. Ronaldo will discuss his decision with his family. (before)

Before Ronaldo takes the new job, he will discuss his decision with his family.

2. Ronaldo takes the new job. Ronaldo will give his employer two weeks' notice. (if)

3. The company hires Ronaldo. The company will give him a company car. (after)

4. The company will pay for Ronaldo's expenses. Ronaldo has to take a trip. (when)

5. Ronaldo will have two weeks of vacation. Ronaldo takes the new job. (if)

6. Ronaldo will fill out a loan application. Ronaldo wants to start a business. (if)

7. Ronaldo's family will have a party. The new store opens. (when)

8. Ronaldo will install an alarm system. Ronaldo opens the store. (before)

9. Ronaldo may open a second store. The first store is very successful. (if)

E What should Ronaldo do? Discuss your opinion with a group of students.

The *Occupational Outlook Handbook* is a career guide that is published every two years by the United States Department of Labor. It gives specific information on hundreds of careers:

- An explanation of what people do at the job (nature of the work)
- Working conditions
- The training and education needed
- Earnings
- The future for the career, that is, the number of jobs in the future

This handbook is available online and in the library.

A **Word Builder** **Read the sentences.** Circle the meaning of words in bold.

1. Automobiles are **complex** machines.

   a. easy to understand   **b.** difficult to understand

2. Automotive service technicians inspect, **maintain**, and repair automobiles.

   a. drive   **b.** take care of

3. Service technicians in large shops often **specialize in certain types of repairs**.

   a. take care of one kind of repair   **b.** take care of all kinds of repairs

4. Almost 16 percent of service technicians were **self-employed**.

   a. They worked for a large shop.   **b.** They had their own business.

B **Scan the article to answer the questions.** Do not write sentences. Just take notes.

> **READING NOTE**
>
> **Scanning for Information**
>
> Sometimes, it is not necessary to read every word. You look at the text quickly to find specific information you need or the answers to specific questions.

1. What skills does an automotive service technician need?

   a. _____   **b.** _____   **c.** _____

2. What education does an automotive service technician need?

   _____

3. What is the job outlook for an automotive service technician?

   _____

4. How much does an automotive service technician make? _____

 C **Talk to a partner.** Is automotive service technician a good job for you? Explain why or why not.

Automotive Service Technicians and Mechanics

Significant Points

- Automobiles are **complex** machines. Automotive service technicians and mechanics need to know about the newest technology and repair techniques.
- Formal automotive technician training is the best preparation for these jobs.
- Opportunities should be very good for automotive service technicians and mechanics.

Nature of the Work

Automotive service technicians inspect, **maintain**, and repair automobiles and light trucks that run on gasoline, electricity, or alternative fuels such as ethanol. Technicians use different tools—power tools, hand tools, and machine tools. Computers are important in repair shops. Today, most automotive systems, such as braking, transmission, and steering systems, are controlled by computers. Automotive technicians in large shops often **specialize in certain types of repairs**. For example, *brake repairers* adjust brakes, replace brake linings and pads, and make other repairs on brake systems.

Education

Automotive technology is becoming more complex, and most people looking for work in automotive service complete a training program in high school or in a vocational school or a community college. However, some service technicians still learn by helping and learning from experienced workers. National Institute for Automotive Service Excellence (ASE) certification is important for those who want to work in large, urban areas. Technicians need good reading, mathematics, and computer skills to study technical manuals. They must also continue to read about new technology and new repair procedures.

Employment

Automotive service technicians and mechanics held about 763,600 jobs in 2008. Automotive repair and maintenance shops and automotive dealers employed about 60 percent of automotive service technicians and mechanics. About 16 percent of service technicians were **self-employed**.

Job Outlook

The number of jobs for automotive service technicians and mechanics will grow more slowly than average for all occupations over the next decade. Many new openings will occur as skilled technicians retire. The job outlook is good for workers who complete automotive technology programs.

Earnings

Median hourly wage-and-salary earnings of automotive service technicians and mechanics, including commission, were $16.88 in May 2008. The middle 50 percent earned between $12.44 and $22.64 per hour.

Source: The information in this article was adapted from the *Occupational Outlook Handbook,* 2010–2011 edition.

Diego Medina

937 Franklin Lane

Red Bank, NJ 07701

Tel: 732-555-6347

e-mail: dmedina@call*me.com

> Put your name, address, telephone number, and e-mail address at the top of the resume.

Career Objective:

To pursue a career as a paralegal in the public or private sector; to use my experience in conducting case research and collecting and analyzing evidence for attorney use.

> Explain the kind of job you are looking for.

Education:

Brookdale Community College, Lincroft, NJ

A.A.S. in Paralegal Studies, GPA 3.6, May 2010

> Write the names of the schools you attended and the date you graduated.

Employment History:

Lord and Robbins, P.C. Personal and Injury Law

2009 to Present

Conduct case research, organize and track files

Paner and Elliot, LLC   Criminal Law

Intern, Summer 2009

Maintained reference files for ongoing cases

County Court

Intake Intern, 2008

Obtained intake information on juveniles

> List the jobs you have had and your responsibilities. Write your resume in reverse chronological order, from the present to the past.

Activities:

Paralegal Club, Brookdale Community College

Speech Alliance, Brookdale Community College

Member, Paralegal Association of New Jersey

> Name activities and organizations you belong to.

Skills:

Computer: MS Office, FileMaker Pro, Adobe Photoshop

Languages: fluent Spanish, advanced Portuguese

> List your computer skills, languages you can speak, and other skills you have.

A **Prepare to write your resume.** Complete the information.

Career Objective:

_____

_____

_____

Education: (Note: Start with the name of your school now.)

_____

_____

Employment History: (Note: Start with your current job.)

_____

_____

_____

Activities:

_____

_____

_____

Skills:

_____

_____

_____

B **Use your notes and write your resume.** Follow the form on page 220.

WRITING NOTE
Editing a Resume
1. Type your resume.
2. Ask a teacher or counselor to proofread your resume.
3. Review all the dates on your resume.

CULTURE NOTE

There are thousands of careers. In the United States, students use many resources to think about their careers. Some of these resources are:

1. Career counselors at high schools and colleges
2. Career books and guides like the *Occupational Outlook Handbook*
3. Interest inventories – Tests in which students choose what they like to do. The results help students see what work they might like to do.
4. Websites about careers
5. Volunteer and part-time work
6. Job fairs – People from many different careers come to a school or other location. People can walk around and talk to people in different careers.
7. Talking to people in the kind of work you are interested in

 A **Working Together Talk about your skills and interests with a partner.** Check (✓) your skills and your partner's skills.

	You	Your Partner
1. I am artistic. I like to draw and design things.		
2. I am good at math. I like to calculate and analyze numbers.		
3. I am good at managing and supervising people.		
4. I like to teach people how to do things.		
5. I like to operate and drive vehicles.		
6. I am persuasive and good at selling things to people.		
7. I like science and solving problems.		
8. I like to read and write and work with information.		
9. I like clerical work like filing and using software programs.		
10. I like to repair and maintain machines.		
11. I like to entertain people. I can sing, dance, or play an instrument.		
12. I like to build things.		
13. I like to help people who are sick.		

B **Complete.**

1. I like to _____.

2. Two possible careers for me are _____ and _____.

3. My partner likes to _____.

4. Two possible careers for him / her are _____ and _____.

C **Go online.** Find the *Occupational Outlook Handbook*. Choose a career from Exercise B or a career that you would like to learn more about. Take notes.

Career: _____

Job Description: _____

_____

_____

Education Required: _____

_____

Job Outlook: _____

Earnings: _____

D **Working Together** **Several students will describe the career they researched to the class.** As you listen, write two careers that you would like to have.

1. _____

2. _____

E **Write the steps you need to take to find a job in the career you researched.**

Year	Steps to Take
	Finish my English classes.

City Life

A **In the picture above and on the next page, write the number next to the correct person or people.**

1. clothing shop owner
2. construction worker
3. doorman
4. server
5. sanitation workers
6. window washer

7. customers
8. parking violations officer
9. hot dog vendor
10. dog walker
11. firefighters

12. delivery person
13. mail carrier
14. travel agent
15. taxi driver
16. businesswoman

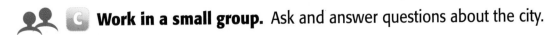

B **Listen and write the answers.** Use the words on page 224.

CD2·TR29

1. The customer is. _____

2. _____

3. _____

4. _____

5. _____

6. _____

7. _____

8. _____

9. _____

10. _____

C **Work in a small group.** Ask and answer questions about the city.

Active Grammar

For and *Since*

For	Since	
for a few minutes	since 8:00	*For* shows an amount of time.
for three weeks	since 2009	*Since* tells when an action
for two years	since Sunday	started.
	since she began her new job	

A **Write the words under *for* or *since*.**

8:00	I came to the U.S.	an hour
ten minutes	a long time	2009
a little while	three days	more than five years
a year	this morning	July
Monday	she lost her job	

For	Since
ten minutes	8:00

B **Circle *for* or *since*.**

1. She has been trying on sunglasses **(for)**/ since an hour.

2. He has been washing windows **for / since** 9:00 this morning.

3. They have been waiting for the bus **for / since** 30 minutes.

4. She has been walking dogs **for / since** early this morning.

5. The travel agent has been helping that customer **for / since** two hours.

6. The mail carrier has been walking the same route **for / since** ten years.

7. The doorman has been working at that building **for / since** 1990.

8. The construction worker has been remodeling that store **for / since** April.

Active Grammar

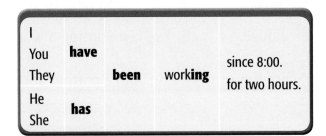

I You They	**have**			since 8:00.
		been	work**ing**	for two hours.
He She	**has**			

> The present perfect continuous talks about an action that started in the past and continues in the present. The action is not yet finished.

A **Complete the sentences about the people on pages 224–225.**

1. Larry (wash) _has been washing_ windows since 8:00 this morning.

2. Janet (try on) _____ sunglasses for an hour.

3. They (waiting) _____ for the bus for a long time.

4. The parking violations officer (write) _____ tickets for two hours.

5. The travel agent (help) _____ Mrs. Johnson since she sat down.

6. The firefighters (wash) _____ the fire truck for 30 minutes.

7. The dog walker (walk) _____ in the park for 20 minutes.

8. The hot dog vendor (work) _____ on that corner for ten years.

9. The couple (sit) _____ in the restaurant since noon.

10. The sanitation workers (collect) _____ trash since 6:00 A.M.

11. These people (be) _____ busy all morning.

B **Write five more sentences about the "picture" on pages 224–225.** Use the present perfect continuous.

1. _____

2. _____

3. _____

4. _____

5. _____

C Pronunciation: 've been, 's been Listen and repeat.

CD2·TR30

1. He's been looking for a job.

2. We've been planning a vacation.

3. They've been painting their house.

4. I've been enjoying my new boat.

5. She's been reading a good book.

6. I've been dating a wonderful guy.

D Listen and repeat. Then, practice the conversation with a partner. Talk about your own life.

CD2·TR31

A: Hi, Raj. How's it going?

B: Pretty boring. I've been putting in a lot of overtime. How about you? What've you been up to?

A: We've been looking at apartments. We might move to the city.

B: Really? Good luck!

WORD PARTNERSHIPS	
put in	overtime
work	

E Look at the list of things next to each person. What do you think each person has been doing?

1. Maria: paint, easel, brushes

2. Omar and Ali: sleeping bags, tents, backpacks

3. Jacob: shovel, watering can, seeds

4. The boys: ball, bat, glove

5. Emily and Mark: vacuum cleaner, mop, dust cloth

6. Aruna and Tom: suitcase, passport, tickets

7. David: batteries, camera, flash

8. Eva: lipstick, mascara, powder

> I think she's been painting a picture.

F Working Together Write three related items that a person is using. Read the list to your classmates. Can the other students guess what the person has been doing?

1. _____ _____ _____

2. _____ _____ _____

3. _____ _____ _____

How long	**have**	you they	**been**	work**ing** at that company?
				talk**ing** on the phone?
	has	he she		watch**ing** TV?
				sleep**ing?**

 A Ask and answer questions about the pictures with a partner.

A: How long have they been looking at apartments?

B: They have been looking at apartments for three hours.

1.

2.

3.

4.

5.

6.

B Complete the sentences about yourself.

1. I live in _____.

2. I work at _____.

3. In my free time, I _____.

4. I like to play _____.

5. I study at _____.

6. To stay healthy, I _____.

C Read the sentences in Exercise B. Your partner will ask *How long* questions.

I live in Minneapolis.

How long have you been living in Minneapolis?

I've been living here for two years.

A Match.

__d__ **1.** I got laid off,

_____ **2.** I broke up with Marie,

_____ **3.** I bought a new house,

_____ **4.** I got engaged last month,

_____ **5.** I bought an RV,

_____ **6.** I started college,

a. so I've been painting and decorating it.

b. so I've been traveling around the country.

c. so I've been using an online dating service.

d. so I've been looking for a job.

e. so I've been studying a lot.

f. so I've been planning the wedding.

B Complete the sentences. Use the present perfect continuous.

1. I joined a health club, so _____.

2. I bought a camera, so _____.

3. I just retired, so _____.

4. I began English classes, so _____.

C Read the sentence. (Circle) the letter of the sentence that has the same meaning.

1. She worked at the travel agency for six years.

   a. She is still working there.

   b. She isn't working there anymore.

2. She's been delivering the mail since 9:00.

   a. She's finally finished work for the day.   **b.** She's still delivering the mail.

3. Janet has been trying on sunglasses for an hour.

   a. She is still trying on sunglasses.   **b.** She left the store.

4. They waited for the bus for 40 minutes.

   a. They have been waiting for 40 minutes.   **b.** The bus finally came.

5. Pablo washed windows from 8:00 to 4:00. It's now 4:30.

   a. He's washing windows.   **b.** He finished washing windows.

6. The couple has been sitting in the restaurant since noon.

   a. They are back at work.   **b.** They are still eating lunch.

D **Read.** Label the people in the picture.

Andre is the owner and the chef at Andre's Café. He's been cooking and managing the restaurant for ten years. The food is delicious, so the restaurant is full for lunch and dinner every day.

Andre opened the restaurant at 11:00 this morning. He has four employees. It's lunchtime and the kitchen is busy. Andre is standing at the stove and grilling sandwiches. Ted is his assistant, and he's been working at the restaurant for six months. When Ted began to work, he was very thin. Ted loves Andre's cooking, so he's always eating. He has been gaining a lot of weight. Victor is a server. He's been working with Andre since the restaurant opened. He's picking up an order.

Cara is Andre's sister. She's been working with her brother for ten years. Cara is very talkative. She's been talking with Anna for an hour. They've been talking about the new beauty salon that is going to open next door. Anna is Andre's girlfriend. She's been going out with Andre for three months. She's only been working at the restaurant for one month. Right now, she's making salads. She had better be careful. She's using a sharp knife and she isn't paying attention to her work.

Andre

E **Working Together** **Student to Student.** Andre's Café.

Student 1: Turn to pages 255–256. Read the questions in **Set A** to Student 2.

Student 2: Listen to Student 1 and write the questions.

Then, Student 2 will turn to pages 255–256 and read the questions in **Set B**. Student 1 will write the questions.

1. _____
2. _____
3. _____
4. _____
5. _____
6. _____

F **With your partner, ask and answer the questions from Exercise E.**

Listen. Harry, the doorman, is talking about the tenants in the apartment building.

CD2·TR32

B **Read Harry's comments.** Who is he talking to?

1. Good morning! Beautiful day for a walk!

   He's talking to Ms. Chan.

2. You're better off without her!

3. Don't worry. I didn't see anything. I didn't hear anything.

4. Good luck today!

5. You have another delivery at the front desk. They're beautiful!

6. Happy birthday!

7. I'm a city person, too. I love all that the city has to offer.

8. Excuse me, sir. The landlord will be in the building at 3:00 and he would like to speak with you.

C **Complete the sentences.** Use the present perfect continuous.

> receive ~~look~~ argue send travel look complain

1. Leena ____has been looking____ for a job.

2. Mr. Wilson _____ letters from credit card agencies.

3. Mr. and Mrs. Shapiro _____ around the world.

4. Some of the neighbors _____ about a dog barking.

5. Silvia's new boyfriend _____ her flowers.

6. Mr. and Mrs. Alvarez _____ about where to live.

7. Many people _____ at the apartment for rent.

D **Listen to Harry again.** Then, answer the questions.

CD2·TR32

1. Why is Manuel depressed?

2. When did Manuel's girlfriend leave him?

3. Why didn't Harry like Manuel's girlfriend?

4. How old is Ms. Chan?

5. How far does Ms. Chan walk every day?

6. What has Leena been doing?

7. What is Leena wearing today?

8. When did Silvia meet her new boyfriend?

9. What has Silvia's boyfriend been sending her?

10. Which apartment have people been looking at?

11. How much is the rent?

E **Listen.** (Circle) the letter of the correct answer.

CD2·TR33

1. a. No, he didn't.　　　　**b.** No, he isn't.

2. a. Yes, he does.　　　　**b.** Yes, he has.

3. a. She got a dog.　　　　**b.** She is getting a dog.

4. a. No, he hasn't.　　　　**b.** No, he doesn't.

5. a. He received an offer in a small town.　　**b.** He will receive an offer in a small town.

6. a. She wants to live in the city.　　**b.** She wanted to live in the city.

7. a. They argued.　　　　**b.** They have been arguing.

8. a. He lived in Apartment 4A.　　**b.** He lives in Apartment 4A.

9. a. He has been receiving cards.　　**b.** He received cards.

10. a. He was a doorman for ten years.　　**b.** He has been a doorman for ten years.

A **Discuss.**

1. What are the advantages of living in a city?

2. What are the advantages of living in a suburb?

Smart Growth Communities

The population of the United States is a little over 300 million people. Eighty percent of the population lives in cities or in the suburbs, that is, towns and areas near the cities. As the population of the United States grows and cities become more **crowded**, people are moving to the **suburbs**. They are looking for friendlier communities, larger homes and yards, and a better quality of life. However, they often find that these communities are far from jobs, transportation, and the city **conveniences** they once enjoyed.

Smart growth offers a different idea—stay in the city. It **encourages** cities to carefully plan and renew city neighborhoods. Instead of leaving the city, it wants people to enjoy living there. A smart growth neighborhood is near transportation, is easy to walk and bike around, is near neighborhood schools, and offers a **mix** of houses, businesses, stores, and services.

Southern Village is a smart growth neighborhood in Chapel Hill, North Carolina. The area has 550 houses, 375 townhouses, and 250 apartments. The area feels like an "old" neighborhood, but the first house was only completed in 1995. This is a community that was planned for people, not for cars. Homes are on small lots, close to the street. They have front **porches**, so people can sit outside and wave and talk to neighbors. All the streets have wide sidewalks on both sides. Market Street is the town center. There are stores, businesses, a movie theater, and a day care center. It's possible to walk everywhere in the neighborhood in ten minutes or less. In the middle is a village green, a large park with a stage in the middle for concerts and other performances. Residents enjoy the bike paths and the neighborhood swim club.

Stapleton, Colorado, is another smart growth community. In 1995, Denver's Stapleton Airport closed. This large area is 4,700 acres and only about fifteen minutes from downtown Denver, the busy capital of Colorado. The area has a mix of single-family homes, apartments, townhouses, and homes for low-income residents and for senior citizens. There are four town centers, and all homes are within a ten-minute walk to one of these. All homes are **energy efficient**. The population of this area is expected to grow to about 30,000 people. Stapleton includes over 1,000 acres for parks, walking and bike trails, and for wildlife. Like many U.S. cities, traffic in Denver is very heavy. Stapleton is on several bus routes. A rail line is planned to connect Stapleton and Denver.

As the population of the United States continues to grow, many cities will use smart growth to **revitalize** their cities.

B **Word Builder** **Complete the sentences.** (Circle) the letter of the correct answer.

1. We moved to the city to be near **conveniences** like _____.

   a. stores and buses   **b.** friends and relatives

2. Planned communities **encourage** people to _____.

   a. stay in the city   **b.** move to the suburbs

3. My class has a **mix** of students from _____.

   a. my country   **b.** many different countries

4. After dinner, we often sit outside on our **porch** and _____.

   a. talk with our neighbors   **b.** watch TV

5. We bought **energy-efficient** appliances to

   a. use less electricity   **b.** use more electricity

6. The _____ **revitalized** the area.

   a. old factory   **b.** new park and theater

C (Circle) the features of a smart growth area.

1. large homes and yards
2. sidewalks for people to walk to the store
3. near transportation
4. heavy traffic area
5. bike trails

6. many apartment buildings together
7. houses close together
8. parks
9. stores near homes
10. neighborhood activities

D (Circle) the pictures that came to your mind as you read this story.

a crowded city street
a home in the suburbs
a home with a porch
streets with wide sidewalks

people walking in a park
a bike trail
a pretty area of a city

READING NOTE

Visualizing the Story

As you read, try to visualize (see a picture in your mind) the people, places, and actions in the story.

A **Read the two paragraphs.** One writer would like to move to New York City. The second writer is thinking about leaving New York City.

I'm thinking about moving to New York City. (First,) there's always something happening in New York. There are concerts, museums, and sport events. I could watch my favorite team, the New York Mets. Next, it's easy to get a job in New York and the salaries are high. My friend is a waiter in a nice restaurant and he makes about $400 a week. Finally, I would feel more at home in New York because there is a Thai community in the city. There are Thai grocery stores, Thai restaurants, and Thai social clubs. I'm going to live with my friend in New York for a month. If I find a job, I'm going to move there.

I live in New York City and I'm thinking about moving to the suburbs. First, the rents in New York are very expensive. My wife and I and our two children live in a one-bedroom apartment. The rent is $1,200 a month. Next, the traffic is impossible. Sometimes it takes me an hour to get to work. And finally, life here is too busy and too fast. The streets and sidewalks are always crowded. People are always in a hurry, too busy to stop and say, "Hello." I'm going to look for a job in a smaller city or town.

B **Look at the paragraphs.**

1. (Circle) the words *first*, *next*, and *finally*.

2. Underline the reasons each person gives for moving or staying.

C **Work in a group.** Discuss the city or town where you live. Give specific examples of your opinions.

> I like the schools. The high school has a great science program.

> I think there's too much crime. Last month, there were three robberies in my area.

traffic
weather
schools
jobs
crime
recreation
entertainment
parks
cost of living

WRITING NOTE

Stating an Opinion

When you state an opinion, give two or three reasons for your ideas. Include an example for each reason.

Finally, I would feel more at home in New York because there is a Thai community in the city. There are Thai grocery stores, Thai restaurants, and Thai social clubs.

D **Choose one of the sentences below and write a paragraph about your plans.** List three reasons for your choice and give an example for each. Use *First, Next*, and *Finally* for your reasons.

☐ I live in _____, and I'm going to stay here.

☐ I live in _____, but I'm thinking about moving.

☐ I live in _____, but I would like to move to _____.

E (Circle) **and correct the eight mistakes.**

    I live in Miami, Florida, and (I)̲ᴵ'ᵐ going to stay here. First, I have a lot of family in this area. My mother, father, and two sister live in Miami. We see them every weekend. Next, I have secure job. I am working at a delivery company since ten years and I'm a manager there. Finally, I am from Cuba and there is a large Cuban community here. I can go to Cuban restaurant, enjoy Cuban music and see my Cubans friends. I'm planning to stay here and enjoy this beautiful city.

 F **Sharing Our Stories** **Read your partner's story.** Answer the questions.

1. Is your partner going to stay in this area?

2. What reasons does your partner give for his / her choice?

A **Complete the information about the city or town where you live.** If you don't know the answer, leave the line blank.

1. Name of city or town: _____

2. Name of mayor: _____

3. Population (approximate): _____

4. Names of two museums in your area: _____ _____

5. Name of a park in your area: _____

6. Location of a community pool: _____

7. Is there a farmer's market in your area? Where? _____

8. Location of a local library: _____

9. Two programs at the library: _____ _____

10. What national park is in your state? _____

11. What activities do you or your family enjoy in your area? _____

_____

12. Your friend has a free Saturday. What place(s) can you recommend to visit?

_____

_____

 B **Work with a small group and share your information.**

Internet Search Tips

1. Be specific: population Dallas Texas

2. Use three keywords or more: Texas state fair

3. Check the date on the website. Some information on the Internet is outdated.

4. Put complete titles and phrases in quotes.

    Example: "Mammoth Cave National Park"

5. For information about community events, museums, parks, and so on, Internet addresses with **.org** are helpful. Internet addresses with **.com** are often advertising businesses and products.

C **Go online.** Find more information about your city or town. Check the information you completed in Exercise A. Add new information to the chart.

Mayor	
Two museums Admission prices	
Area park Location	
Location of community pool Are there swimming lessons?	
Location of farmer's market Days and hours	
Location of next street fair Date	
Location of performing arts center Next event	
Nearest national park	
One of your interests Club in your area for your interest	
One more place or activity of interest	

 D **Discuss your information with a small group.** What new information did you find about your area?

Unit 1

Simple Present Tense

STATEMENTS		
Subject	Verb	
I	work	every day.
You	work	at night.
We	work	in the morning.
They	work	in a restaurant.
He	works	at a hospital.
It	works	each time.

Notes:
1. The simple present tense tells about a repeated or routine action.

2. The present tense tells about facts that are true all the time.
   I live in the city.   *I drive to school.*

3. The verb ends in *-s* for affirmative statements with *he*, *she*, and *it*.

There is / There are

AFFIRMATIVE STATEMENTS
There is a book on the desk.
There are four books on the desk.
There are some books on the desk.

NEGATIVE STATEMENTS
There isn't a book on the desk.
There aren't any books on the desk.

Are there any books on the desk?

YES / NO QUESTIONS
Is there a map in your classroom?
Are there any maps in your classroom?

SHORT ANSWERS	
Yes, **there is**.	No, **there isn't**.
Yes, **there are**.	No, **there aren't**.

Notes:
1. A sentence beginning with *There is* often shows location.
   There is *a book on the desk.*

2. A sentence beginning with *There are* often tells how many.
   There are *twenty students in our class.*

3. Use *some* in a plural statement in the affirmative. Use *any* in a plural statement in the negative. Use *any* in a plural question.

4. Use *there* the first time you talk about a thing. Use *it* or *they* the second time.
   There *is a book on the desk.* ***It*** *is a dictionary.*
   There *are many students in our class.* ***They*** *are from different countries.*

Quantifiers

important !!!

is
are

None	of us	is married.
One	of the students	walks to school.
None A couple Some A few Most All	of us of the students of the children	are married. live in New York.

Note:
None is used in both the singular and the plural form.

{ **None** of us **is** married.
None of us **are** married. }

Unit 2

Simple Present Tense

NEGATIVE STATEMENTS		
Subject	*Do not / Does not*	Verb
I	**don't**	work.
You	**don't**	work.
We	**don't**	work.
They	**don't**	work.
He	**doesn't**	work.
She	**doesn't**	work.
It	**doesn't**	work.

Present Time Expressions

every morning	**once** a week	**on** the weekend	**in** the summer
every day	**twice** a month	**on** Sundays	**in** the winter
every night	**three times** a year		

Adverbs of Frequency

I **always** wear my seat belt.
I **usually** eat breakfast.
I **frequently** eat out.
I **often** eat out.
I **sometimes** work overtime.
I **hardly ever** get up late.
I **rarely** get up late.
I **never** take a taxi.

Notes:
1. Time expressions usually appear at the end of a sentence.

2. Put adverbs of frequency before the verb:
   I **often** <u>walk</u> in the park.
   He **never** <u>takes</u> a taxi.

3. Put adverbs of frequency after the verb *be*.
   I <u>am</u> **never** late for work.
   She <u>is</u> **rarely** sick.

Unit 3

Simple Present Tense

YES / NO QUESTIONS			
Do / Does	Subject	Verb	
Do	I you we they	**bank** **have** **pay**	online? a car loan? rent?
Does	he she		

SHORT ANSWERS	
Affirmative	Negative
Yes, you **do**.	No, you **don't**.
Yes, I **do**.	No, I **don't**.
Yes, we **do**.	No, we **don't**.
Yes, they **do**.	No, they **don't**.
Yes, he **does**.	No, he **doesn't**.
Yes, she **does**.	No, she **doesn't**.

WH- QUESTIONS			
Wh- word	Do / Does	Subject	Verb
When	do	I	work?
Where	do	you	study?
What	do	we	need?
When	do	they	eat?
How much	does	he	save?

ANSWERS		
Subject	Verb	
You	work	at 2:00.
I	study	at the adult school.
We	need	a computer.
They	eat	at 7:00.
He	save**s**	$100 a week.

Who Questions

Who works at City Bank?
Laura does.

Who saves money every month?
Henry and **Ivan** do.

Note:
When *Who* is the subject of a sentence, it is always singular.

Who does he drive to work?
He drives **his brother** to work.

Who do they send money to?
They send money **to their parents**.

Note:
When *Who* is the object of a sentence, it can be singular or plural.

Unit 4

Count Nouns

Singular	Plural
a state	states
every state	all the states
each of the states	many of the states

Notes:

1. Count nouns are people, places, or things that we can count individually (one by one). Count nouns can be singular or plural.

2. Expressions with *one of the*, *every*, and *each* are singular.
   Every state ***has*** a capitol building.

3. Expressions with *a few of the*, *some of the*, *many of the*, *all of the*, etc., are plural.
   All of the states ***have*** capitol buildings.

Quantifiers with Count Nouns

There	is isn't	**a**	seaport desert	on the coast. in the North.
	are	**a few** **several** **many** **a lot of**	seaports mountains rivers forests	in the South. in the East. in the West. in the central part of the country.
	aren't	**any**	farms	

Count and Non-count Nouns

Count Nouns	Non-count Nouns
a river	rain
mountains	pollution
tourists	tourism

Notes:

Non-count nouns cannot be counted. They are always singular.

1. Liquids or gasses: *water, oil, oxygen, rain*

2. Items that are too small or too numerous to count: *sand, corn, rice*

3. General categories: *traffic, scenery, music, tourism*

4. Ideas: *information, beauty, work*

5. Some words can be both count and non-count: *crime—crimes, industry—industries*

Quantifiers with Non-count Nouns

| There | is | **no**
a little
a lot of | traffic
rain
crime
industry | in this city.
in my country.
in the United
States. |
| | isn't | **any**
much | | |

How much / How many

How many	museums parks	are	there	in your city?
How much	snow traffic	is		in your country?

Too much / Too many / Not enough

There	is	**too much**	rain.
		not enough	industry.
	are	**too many**	fast-food restaurants.
		not enough	parks.

> Note:
> We often use *not enough* and *too many / too much* to talk about problems or to complain.
>
> *not enough* = less than you want or need
> > There are**n't enough** farms in that country. There is**n't enough** food.
>
> *too many, too much* = more than you want or need
> > There are **too many** cars on the road. There is **too much** traffic.

Unit 5

Present Continuous Tense

STATEMENTS			
Subject	*Be*	(not)	*-ing* Form
I	**am**		send**ing** an e-mail.
You	**are**	**(not)**	order**ing** a movie.
He	**is**		mak**ing** reservations.
They	**are**		work**ing**.

> Notes:
> 1. The present continuous talks about an action that is happening now.
> *He **is using** his computer.*
> 2. The present continuous talks about an action that is temporary.
> *He **is living** with his brother.* (He expects to move soon.)
> 3. The present continuous can talk about specific future plans.
> *I**'m leaving** at 2:00.*

YES / NO QUESTIONS		
Be	Subject	*-ing* Form
Am	I	tak**ing** a picture?
Are	you	send**ing** an e-mail?
Is	she	listen**ing** to music?
Is	it	work**ing**?
Are	they	mak**ing** reservations?

SHORT ANSWERS	
Affirmative	Negative
Yes, you **are**.	No, you **aren't**.
Yes, I **am**.	No, I**'m not**.
Yes, she **is**.	No, she **isn't**.
Yes, it **is**.	No, it **isn't**.
Yes, they **are**.	No, they **aren't**.

WH- QUESTIONS			
Wh- word	*Be*	Subject	*-ing* Form
What	am	I	do**ing**?
Which movie	are	you	order**ing**?
How	is	it	work**ing**?
Where	are	they	go**ing**?

ANSWERS
Subject + Verb
You're check**ing** prices.
I'm order**ing** *Space Age*.
It's work**ing** well.
They are go**ing** to the lab.

WHO QUESTIONS		
Who	Verb	
Who	is buying	a camera?
Who	is fixing	the computer?

> Notes:
> 1. When *Who* is the subject of a sentence, it is always singular.
> > ***Who is buying*** a camera?   *Laura **is**.*
> > ***Who is working*** today?   *Sarah and Ali **are**.*
> 2. When *Who* is the object of a sentence, it can be singular or plural.
> > ***Who is*** Max calling?   *He **is calling** his sister.*
> > ***Who are*** they speaking with?   *They **are speaking** with the customers.*

Non-action Verbs

hate	feel	agree	belong
like	hear	believe	cost
love	look	forget	have
prefer	see	know	need
	seem	remember	own
	smell	think	
	sound	understand	
	taste		

> **Notes:**
> 1. Some verbs in English do not usually take the present continuous tense. They are called non-action verbs. These verbs often show feelings, senses, beliefs, and possession.
> 2. Some verbs can show both non-action and action.
>   I **have** a computer.   I**'m having** a good time.
>   She**'s having** a party.
>   I **think** he's a good teacher.   I**'m thinking** about my vacation.

Unit 6

Future with *Be Going to*

STATEMENTS				
Subject	*Be*	*(not)*	*Going to*	Verb
I	**am**			**exercise**.
You	**are**	**(not)**	**going to**	**make** an appointment.
He	**is**			**call** the doctor.
They	**are**			**take** medication.

YES / NO QUESTIONS			
Be	Subject	*Going to*	Verb
Are	you		**see** the doctor?
Is	she	**going to**	**stay** home from work?
Are	they		**get** a flu vaccine?

ANSWERS	
Affirmative	Negative
Yes, I **am**.	No, I**'m not**.
Yes, she **is**.	No, she **isn't**.
Yes, they **are**.	No, they **aren't**.

WH- QUESTIONS				
Wh- word	*Be*	Subject	*Going to*	Verb
When	**am**	I		
	are	you		
Where	**is**	he	**going to**	**exercise**?
Why	**are**	they		

Future with *Will*

STATEMENTS		
Subject	*Will / Won't*	Verb
I		**walk** every day.
She	**will**	**join** a health club.
They	**won't**	**change** jobs.

> **Notes:**
> 1. Use *will* to express an offer to help.
>   I**'ll drive** you to school.
> 2. Use *will* to make predictions.
>   You**'ll get** the job.

Comparative Adjectives

> New York is **larger than** Atlanta.
> Chicago is **busier than** Denver.
> Houston is **more populated than** Boston.

Notes:
1. Comparative adjectives compare two people, places, or things.

2. For one-syllable adjectives, add -er + than.
   tall – taller than   long – longer than

3. For two-syllable adjectives ending in y, change the y to i, and add -er + than.
   busy – busier than   happy – happier than

4. For other adjectives with two or more syllables, use more + adjective + than.
   beautiful – more beautiful than   populated – more populated than

5. These comparative adjectives are irregular.
   good – better than   bad – worse than   far – farther than

More / Less / Fewer + Noun

New York Los Angeles	has	**more** **fewer**	universities jobs	than	Los Angeles. New York.
		more **less**	traffic noise		

Notes:
1. Use *more* and *less* with non-count nouns.

2. Use *more* and *fewer* with count nouns.

Superlative Adjectives

> Russia is **the largest** country in the world.
> Atlanta Airport is **the busiest** airport in the world.
> New York is **the most populated** city in the United States.

Notes:
1. Superlative adjectives compare three or more people, places, or things.

2. For one-syllable adjectives, add *the* + -est.
   tall – the tallest   long – the longest

3. For two-syllable adjectives ending in y, change the y to i, and add *the* + est.
   busy – the busiest   happy – the happiest

4. For other adjectives with two or more syllables, use *the most* + adjective.
   beautiful – the most beautiful   populated – the most populated

5. These superlative adjectives are irregular.
   good – the best   bad – the worst   far – the farthest

as . . . as,   not as . . . as

| China | is | as interesting as | India. |
| France | | as beautiful as | Italy. |

| Colombia | isn't | as populated as | Brazil. |
| Ecuador | | as large as | Mexico. |

Notes:

1. Use *as . . . as* to show that two people, places, or things are the same.

2. Use *not as . . . as* to show that two people, places, or things are not the same.
   Florida is **not as large as** Texas. = Texas is **larger than** Florida.
   Silver is **not as expensive as** gold. = Gold is **more expensive than** silver.

Unit 8

Past Tense of Regular Verbs

I **lived** in Taiwan.
He **moved** to the United States.
They **signed** a lease.

Notes:

1. Regular past tense verbs end in *-d* or *-ed*.
   (See Spelling Rules Appendix, page 252)

2. The past tense form is the same for singular and plural subjects.

Past Time Expressions

Yesterday	Last	Ago
yesterday morning	last night	a few minutes ago
yesterday afternoon	last week	an hour ago
yesterday evening	last weekend	a week ago
	last Saturday	two years ago
	last month	
	last year	

Note:
Use a past time expression at the beginning or the end of a sentence.

Past Tense—Negative Statements

I **didn't paint** the bedroom.
We **didn't live** in an apartment.
He **didn't study** English.

Note:
Use *didn't* and the simple form of the verb to form the negative past tense.

Past Tense—*Be*

Present Tense—*Be*	Past Tense—*Be*
I **am** busy.	I **was** busy.
You **are** lonely.	You **were** lonely.
He **is** friendly.	He **was** friendly.
It **is** safe.	It **was** safe.
They **are** noisy.	They **were** noisy.

Notes:

1. *Was* and *were* are the past tense of *be*.

2. The negative form of *was* is *wasn't*. The negative form of *were* is *weren't*.
   I **wasn't** busy.
   You **weren't** lonely.

Unit 9

Simple Past Tense

	YES / NO QUESTIONS	
Did	Subject	Verb
	you	**evacuate**?
Did	he	**go** to work?
	it	**rain** all week?
	they	**lose** power?

SHORT ANSWERS	
Affirmative	Negative
Yes, I **did**.	No, I **didn't**.
Yes, he **did**.	No, he **didn't**.
Yes, it **did**.	No, it **didn't**.
Yes, they **did**.	No, they **didn't**.

WH- QUESTIONS			
Wh- word	*Did*	Subject	Verb
When	**did**	the storm	**begin**?
Where	**did**	you	**stay**?
How many days	**did**	it	**rain**?
How much damage	**did**	you	**have**?

WHO QUESTIONS		
Who	Verb	
Who	**helped**	their neighbors after the storm?
Who	**saw**	the tornado?

Note:
In these questions, *Who* is the subject.

Unit 10

Have to / Has to

I		
You	**have to**	**order** the invitations.
They		**plan** the guest list.
She	**has to**	

Note:
Have to and *has to* are modals. They show necessity or obligation.

Don't have to / Doesn't have to

I			
You	**don't**		**order** the invitations.
They		**have to**	**work** today.
She	**doesn't**		

Note:
Don't have to and *doesn't have to* are modals. They show that an action is not necessary.

Had to / Didn't have to

I		
You	**had to**	**work**.
He	**didn't have to**	**send** a gift.
They		

Notes:
1. *Had to* and *didn't have to* are modals.
2. *Had to* is the past of *have to* and *has to*.
3. *Didn't have to* is the past of *don't have to* and *doesn't have to*.

> *Should / Shouldn't*
> You **should wear** your blue dress.
> She **shouldn't get** married now.
> She **should finish** college first.

> Notes:
> 1. *Should* is a modal. *Should* gives advice or an opinion.
> 2. *Should* has the same form for all persons.

Unit 11

> *Can*
> I **can install** Internet service in your home.
> He **can change** the lights in your home.

> Notes:
> 1. *Can* is a modal. It shows ability.
> 2. *Can* has the same form for all persons.

> Polite requests
> **Could you** please call Mr. Smith?
> **Would you** please help this customer?

> Notes:
> 1. *Could you* and *Would you* are modals. Use these expressions to make polite requests.
> 2. *Could you* and *Would you* have the same form for all persons.

> *Must / Must not / Can't*
> I **must** wear a name tag.
> We **must** sign in.
> You **must not** make personal calls at work.
> You **can't** use your cell phone.

> Notes:
> 1. *Must, must not*, and *can't* are modals. They explain rules, policies, and regulations.
> 2. *Must* and *have to* are similar in meaning.
>   I **must wear** a uniform.   I **have to wear** a uniform.
> 3. *Must not* and *can't* show that an action is not allowed or permitted.
> 4. Be careful! *Must not* and *(not) have to* do not have the same meaning.
>   I **must not bring** my children to work. ≠ I **don't have to** bring my children to work.
> 5. *Must, must not*, and *can't* have the same form for all persons.

> *May* and *Might*
> I **may** quit my job.
> The company **might** close.

> Notes:
> 1. *May* and *might* are modals. They show possibility.
> 2. *May* and *might* have the same form for all persons.

Unit 12

Present Time Clauses

> He watches TV **before** he goes to bed.   **Before** he goes to bed, he watches TV.
> (main clause)   **(time clause)**   **(time clause)**   (main clause)

> Notes:
> 1. A time clause explains when an action happens. A time clause begins with a time word such as *after*, *before*, *when*, *as soon as*, *until*, or *if*. A time clause has a subject and a verb.
>
> 2. If the time clause is at the beginning of the sentence, use a comma after the time clause. If the time clause is at the end of the sentence, don't use a comma.
> ***When*** *Henry gets home, he makes dinner.*
> *The children watch TV* ***until*** *their father comes home.*

Two-Word Verbs

> Some verbs in English are made up of two words.
> Some two-word verbs can have other words between the two parts of the verb. These are called separable (S) verbs.
>   *I **put on** my coat.*   *I **put** my coat **on**.*
> Some two-word verbs can't have other words between the two parts of the verb.
>   *I **get on** the bus at 7:30 every morning.*   NOT   ~~*I **get** the bus **on** at 7:30 every morning.*~~

Unit 13

Past Time Clauses

> I locked my door **before** I went to work.   **Before** I went to work, I locked my door.
>   (main clause)   **(time clause)**   **(time clause)**   (main clause)

Past Continuous Tense

I	**was**	read**ing**.
He	**was**	sleep**ing**.
You	**were**	work**ing**.
We	**were**	watch**ing** TV.
They	**were**	driv**ing**.

> Note:
> The past continuous describes an action that was in progress at a specific time in the past.

Past Continuous with *While*

> **While** I **was driving** to school, I **was listening** to the radio.
> I **was listening** to the radio **while** I **was driving** to school.

> Note:
> Use *while* with the past continuous to show that two actions were happening at the same time.

The Past Continuous and the Simple Past

> I **heard** someone in my living room while I **was sleeping**.
> Boris **was eating** dinner when someone **knocked** at his door.

> Note:
> The past continuous can describe an action that was interrupted. One action was going on when another action happened.

Unit 14

Future Time Clauses: Statements

She **will get** a good job <u>after she **graduates** from college</u>.
   (main clause)   **(time clause)**

<u>After she **graduates** from college</u>, she **will get** a good job.
     (time clause)   (main clause)

Note:
The verb in the main clause is in the future tense (with *will* or *going to*). The verb in the time clause is in the present tense.

Future Time Clauses: Questions

What are you going to do after you graduate?
Where is he going to live if his company transfers him?
When he starts school, **is he going to work full time**?

Note:
In a question with a future time clause, use the future question form in the main clause.

Unit 15

Present Perfect Continuous Tense

FOR AND SINCE	
For	*Since*
for a few minutes	since 8:00
for three weeks	since 2009
for two years	since Sunday
	since she began her new job

Notes:
1. *For* shows an amount of time.
2. *Since* tells when an action started.

STATEMENTS				
Subject	*Have / Has*	*Been*	Verb	
I You They	**have (not)**	**been**	work**ing**	since 8:00.
He It	**has (not)**			for two hours.

Note:
The present perfect continuous talks about an action that started in the past and continues in the present. The action is not yet finished.

HOW LONG QUESTIONS				
How long	*Have / Has*	Subject	*Been*	Verb
How long	**have**	you they	**been**	work**ing** at that company? talk**ing** on the phone? watch**ing** TV? sleep**ing**?
	has	he she		

Plural Nouns

1. For most nouns, add an -s.
   boy – boys   store – stores   student – students

2. If a noun ends with a consonant and a *y*, change the *y* to *i*, and add -es.
   city – cities   dictionary – dictionaries   baby – babies

3. If a noun ends with *sh, ch, x,* or *z,* add -es.
   box – boxes   dress – dresses   watch – watches

Present Continuous Verbs

1. For most verbs, add -ing.
   walk – walking   play – playing   eat – eating

2. If a verb ends in *e,* drop the *e* and add -ing.
   write – writing   come – coming   drive – driving

3. If a verb ends in a consonant + vowel + consonant, double the final consonant and add -ing.
   sit – sitting   run – running   put – putting

4. If a verb ends in *w, x,* or *y,* do not double the consonant. Add -ing.
   play – playing   relax – relaxing   snow – snowing

Present Tense Verbs: Third Person

1. For most verbs, add -s.
   make – makes   call – calls   sleep – sleeps

2. If a verb ends with a consonant and a *y*, change the *y* to *i*, and add -es.
   try – tries   cry – cries   apply – applies

3. If a verb ends with *sh, ch, x,* or *z,* add -es.
   wash – washes   watch – watches   fix – fixes

4. These verbs are irregular in the third person.
   have – has   do – does

Past Tense Verbs

1. For most verbs, add -d or -ed.
   rent – rented   save – saved

2. If a verb ends in a consonant + y, change the y to i and add -ed.
   try – tried   study – studied

3. If a verb ends in a consonant + vowel + consonant, double the final consonant and add -ed.
   stop – stopped   rob – robbed

4. If a verb ends in w, x, or y, do not double the consonant. Add -ed.
   play – played   relax – relaxed   snow – snowed

Comparative Adjectives: -er

1. For most adjectives, add -r or -er.
   large – larger   short – shorter   tall – taller

2. If a one-syllable adjective ends in a consonant + vowel + consonant, double the final consonant and add -er.
   big – bigger   thin – thinner   sad – sadder

3. If an adjective ends in a consonant + y, change the y to i and add -er.
   happy – happier   heavy – heavier   friendly – friendlier

Superlative Adjectives: -est

1. For most adjectives, add -st or -est.
   large – largest   short – shortest   tall – tallest

2. If a one-syllable adjective ends in a consonant + vowel + consonant, double the final consonant and add -est.
   big – biggest   thin – thinnest   sad – saddest

3. If an adjective ends in a consonant + y, change the y to i and add -est.
   busy – busiest   noisy – noisiest   friendly – friendliest

Student to Student

Unit 2

For Page 21, Exercise E

Student 1: Read the sentences in Set A to Student 2.

Student 2: Read the sentences in Set B to Student 1.

Set A

a. He gets up late.
b. He plays tennis.
c. He studies in the morning.
d. He doesn't pick up his clothes.
e. He makes his bed.
f. He gets up early.

Set B

a. He doesn't get up early.
b. He keeps his things neat.
c. He takes morning classes.
d. He studies at night.
e. He plays basketball.
f. He doesn't make his bed.

Unit 4

For Page 56, Exercise B

Student 1: Look at the chart below. Complete the chart about Canada.

Student 2: Look at the chart on page 56. Complete the information about Mexico.

How much tourism is there in Canada?

There is a lot of tourism in Canada.

	Mexico	Canada
Tourism	a lot	
Deserts	nine	
Mountains	many	
National parks	64	
Snow	very little	
Ski resorts	one	
Official languages	one	

Unit 6

For Page 87, Exercise C

Student 1: Read the questions in Set A to Student 2.

Student 2: Read the questions in Set B to Student 1.

Set A

1. How are you feeling?
2. Are you going to need an operation?
3. How long are you going to stay in the hospital?
4. When are you going home?
5. What other tests are you going to need?

Set B

1. What's the problem?
2. When is the doctor going to talk to you?
3. When are they going to take X-rays?
4. When are you going to know the test results?
5. When are you going to return to school?

Unit 7

For Page 107, Exercise D

Student 1: Read the questions in Set A to Student 2.

Student 2: Read the questions in Set B to Student 1.

Set A

1. Which city is the most populated?
2. Which city has the highest percentage of Hispanics?
3. Which city has the highest household income?
4. Which city has the least expensive houses?
5. In which city do workers have the longest commute?
6. Which is the sunniest city?
7. Which city has the fewest sunny days?

Set B

1. Which city has the lowest population?
2. Which city has the lowest unemployment?
3. Which city has the most expensive houses?
4. In which city do workers have the shortest commute?
5. Which city has the most museums?
6. Which city has the least rain?
7. Which city receives the most snow?

Unit 15

For Page 231, Exercise E

Student 1: Read the questions in Set A to Student 2.

Student 2: Read the questions in Set B to Student 1.

Set A

1. How long has Andre been managing the restaurant?
2. Why is the restaurant always busy?
3. What is Andre doing?
4. How long has Ted been working at the restaurant?
5. Why is he always eating?
6. Has Ted been gaining weight?

Set B

1. What is Victor doing?
2. How long has he been working with Andre?
3. Who is Cara?
4. Who has she been talking to?
5. How long has Anna been working at the restaurant?
6. How long has she been going out with Andre?

Dictation

Unit 2: Page 22

B **Dictation** **Listen and write the sentences you hear.**

1. The average person lives in a house.
2. Sixty-six percent (66%) of Americans own their homes.
3. Many people rent their homes.
4. The average person drinks a cup of coffee a day.
5. Sixty-three percent (63%) of people put sugar in their coffee.
6. Thirty-seven percent (37%) of people drink their coffee black.

Unit 6: Page 91

G **Dictation** **Listen and write the sentences that your teacher dictates.** Refer to the words in the box for spelling.

1. Luis was in an accident.
2. Another driver hit his car.
3. Luis stayed in the hospital overnight.
4. He's going to call his insurance company today.
5. He's going to report the accident.
6. Luis is also going to call his lawyer.
7. He's going to sue the other driver.
8. The accident was the woman's fault.
9. She was talking on her cell phone at the time of the accident.

Unit 7: Page 104

A **Dictation** **Listen and write the sentences that your teacher dictates.**

1. India is as interesting as China.
2. India isn't as large as China.

3. India is almost as populated as China.
4. The people in India are as hardworking as the people in China.
5. India is as diverse as China.
6. Chinese food isn't as spicy as Indian food.

Unit 8: Page 123

D **Dictation Listen and write the sentences you hear.** The verb in each sentence is negative.

1. Yolanda and Diego weren't happy with their first apartment.
2. The landlord didn't fix things.
3. They didn't like the location of the second apartment.
4. The apartment wasn't near Diego's job.
5. Their neighbors weren't friendly.
6. After they had a baby, their apartment wasn't big enough.
7. When they moved to Atlanta, they didn't know anything about the area.

Unit 12: Page 183

D **Dictation Listen and complete the sentences.**

Mimi has a difficult time falling asleep at night. She gets in bed and puts her head on the pillow. But as soon as she closes her eyes, she begins to worry— about her job, her health, and her family. So, she now has a routine to relax herself before she goes to sleep. Before she goes into her bedroom, she drinks a cup of hot herbal tea. Then, she brushes her teeth. After she brushes her teeth, she washes her face and puts on her favorite face cream. When she gets into bed, she picks up a magazine and reads for a few minutes. Then, she listens to some quiet music. When she finally turns off her light, she falls asleep more easily.

Unit 14: Page 210

B **Listen and complete the sentences about Maria.**

1. Maria is going to look for a job before she graduates.
2. Before she looks for a job, she will write her resume.
3. She will send out her resume when she sees a good job posting.
4. If she hears of a job opening, she will call the company.
5. When she goes on an interview, she is going to wear a suit.
6. If she makes a good impression, the company will hire her.

Audio Scripts

CD 1

Unit 1

CD 1, Track 1, Page 3

C. Listen. Gloria is interviewing Kenji about his life in the United States. Take notes. Then, compare your notes with a partner.

Gloria: Hi, Kenji.
Kenji: Hi, Gloria.
Gloria: I'd like to interview you for class.
Kenji: Sure. Go ahead.
Gloria: Kenji, what country are you from?
Kenji: I'm from Japan.
Gloria: How long have you been here in the United States?
Kenji: For six months.
Gloria: Is your family here in the United States?
Kenji: No, my family is in Japan. I came here alone to study English. In Japan, I have my mother and father and one sister.
Gloria: Where do you live?
Kenji: In the student dorms, right here on campus.
Gloria: Are you a new student?
Kenji: Yes, this is my first semester here at school.
Gloria: Do you work?
Kenji: No, I don't.
Gloria: Are you married?
Kenji: No, I'm not. I'm only 21 years old. That's too early to get married.
Gloria: What are your interests?
Kenji: I'm a swimmer. I was on the swim team in high school in my country. They have a great pool here on campus, and I swim four or five times a week. And I like photography. I have a digital camera and I'm sending lots of pictures of California back to my family in Japan.
Gloria: What kind of music do you like?
Kenji: I like rock.
Gloria: Do you have a computer?
Kenji: Yes, I have a laptop.
Gloria: Thank you, Kenji.

CD 1, Track 2, Page 7

E. Pronunciation: Sentence Stress Listen and repeat. Then, listen again and underline the stressed words.

1. The **cafeteria** is on the **first floor**.
2. The **nurse's office** is across from the **elevator**.
3. The **bookstore** is in the **student center**.
4. The **computer lab** is on the **third floor**.
5. There is a **copy machine** in the **library**.
6. The **restrooms** are next to the **stairs**.

CD 1, Track 3, Page 10

The Big Picture: Class Expectations

1. In my country, we can come to school a few minutes late.
2. Only the teacher can talk. We can speak if the teacher calls our name.
3. We call the teacher "Teacher," not his or her name.
4. We don't buy our books. The school gives us our books, notebooks, and pencils.
5. In my country, we cannot bring food to class. But, it's OK to bring a cup of coffee into the classroom.
6. We work quietly by ourselves or listen to the teacher.
7. We have to turn off our cell phones before class.
8. We have many hours of homework every night.

Unit 2

CD 1, Track 4, Page 19

C. Listen. Charlie is talking about himself. Complete the chart. Then, compare Charlie to the average American male.

Hi. My name's Charlie Johnson, and I'm supposed to tell you a little about myself. I'm 32 years old, and I'm single. That's right, I'm not married yet. I'm 6'2" tall, and I weigh about 210 pounds. I guess I could lose a little weight. I'm a computer programmer at a large company. I like my job a lot. It's interesting, and I can be creative. My hours are long—about ten hours a day. Sometimes, I have to come in on the weekends. But, the best part is the salary—$60,000 a year. Yeah, it's good. I live in the city in a one-bedroom apartment. I like it because it's in a good location. It's near public transportation, and that's good for me. I don't have a car, but that's OK. I can walk or take a bus to work. And I have a roommate. He spends most of his time sleeping and lying on the couch. He's my cat, Floppy.

CD 1, Track 5, Page 21

C. Pronunciation: Final s Listen and repeat.

/s/	/z/	/əs/
likes	owns	watches
wants	drives	uses
takes	studies	dances

CD 1, Track 6, Page 21

D. Circle the sound you hear.

1. lives   2. walks   3. drinks
4. washes   5. buys   6. eats
7. misses   8. goes   9. loves

CD 1, Track 7, Page 26

B. Listen. On the pictures, write the missing information about the Shaw family.

1. This is the Shaw family. Mike Shaw is 42 years old. He is a high school math teacher. Like other public school teachers, he works nine months a year. His hours are 7:30 to 3:00. He earns $55,000 a year and gets excellent benefits. His wife, Maria Shaw, is 39 years old. She is a software engineer. She works at a bank from 9:00 to 5:00. She earns $65,000 a year, and she has good benefits, too. She's expecting her second child in about a month. She had her first child when she was 31.
2. Mike Shaw drives to work. It only takes him 20 minutes to get to work. Mrs. Shaw commutes to work. It takes her 40 minutes by train to get to work. At home, she drives a minivan.
3. The Shaws live in a house with their son, Andy. He's eight years old. Mike's parents also live with them. They're retired. Andy likes living with his grandparents. The Shaws have two pets—a cat and a dog. Their house cost $175,000, and it's old. It has three

bedrooms, a living room, a kitchen, a family room, and a small yard.

4. The family eats out every Friday night. They usually eat Chinese or Italian food. After a long, busy week, they like to take a break from cooking.

5. Every summer, they take a vacation for two weeks. They always go to the beach.

6. Like many American families, they spend most evenings at home. Maria, Grandma Shaw, and Andy usually sit in the family room and watch TV or rent a movie. There's another TV upstairs, but everyone likes to sit together in the family room. Grandpa Shaw usually falls asleep in the chair. It's a relaxing evening for everyone except Mike. Mike sits at his desk and corrects his students' homework.

Unit 3

CD 1, Track 8, Page 38
C. Listen and take notes about how Laura spends money each day. Add up the total.

A: I don't know where all my money goes.
B: Do you have a budget?
A: No, I don't.
B: Well, have you ever tried to figure out where you spend money?
A: Umm . . . no.
B: Ok. Get a piece of paper. Let's go through your day.
A: Let's see . . . the first thing I do every morning is stop at the coffee shop. I buy a cup of coffee and a donut there.
B: Alright, how much do you spend there?
A: About four dollars.
B: And how do you get to work? You only live about a mile from work, right?
A: Well, I usually don't get up in time to walk, so I take the bus. That's $2.00.
B: Then, what about lunch?
A: I buy my lunch in the cafeteria. It's about $8.00 for a sandwich and iced tea.
B: Do you spend any more money for food?
A: Hmm . . . just, just a soda from the vending machine. That's $1.00.
B: Do you walk home?
A: No, I'm too tired. I pay another $2.00 for the bus. Oh, and when I get off the bus, I stop and buy a lottery ticket on my way home. That's a dollar.

B: Well, it's easy to see where all *your* money goes!

CD 1, Track 9, Page 42
The Big Picture: Buying a Car

A: Hi, I'm Dion Williams.
B: Hi, Dion. I'm Oscar. Oscar Bravo.
A: Welcome to AutoLand. I see you're checking out different models. This one's a hybrid. Are you looking for a hybrid?
B: Well, I'm thinking about it.
A: You're looking at the best-selling hybrid in the country.
B: How does the engine work?
A: It's a four-cylinder engine. The engine is a regular gas engine, but it also has an electric motor assist. They work together to give you great gas mileage. How many miles do you drive a day?
B: I drive about 80 miles a day. The money I spend on gas is killing me. How many miles does it get a gallon?
A: In city driving, it gets 40 miles a gallon. On the highway, it gets 45.
B: That's really good. I'm getting about 15 miles a gallon on my car now. Let's see, that would save me nine, maybe ten dollars a day on gas. How long is the warranty on the car?
A: Eight years. It has an eight-year warranty.
B: What options does it have? Does it have power steering, air-conditioning, all the standard features?
A: Yes, that's all standard. It also has power brakes, front and side air bags, and an audio system. Why don't I get the key? We can go for a test drive.

CD 1, Track 10, Page 43
D. Listen to the conversation between Oscar Bravo, a new car buyer, and Gloria Grayson, a loan officer at First City Bank. Complete the car loan application.

A: Good afternoon, Mr. Bravo. I'm Gloria Grayson. I'm the loan officer at the bank. I see you started to fill out this form. Let me ask you a few questions. How long have you been working at Park Industries?
B: For three years.
A: And your salary is . . .
B: I make $1,000 a week. That's $4,000 a month.
A: Do you own or rent your home?
B: I rent an apartment.

A: And what is your monthly rent?
B: $800 a month.
A: Now, are you buying a used car or a new car?
B: A new car.
A: And what loan amount do you need?
B: I need a loan for $12,000.
A: For how many years?
B: Three years.
A: Ok. And how much is your down payment on the car?
B: $8,000 dollars.
A: Do you have a checking account with us now?
B: Yes, I do.
A: Do you have your account number with you?
B: Yes.
A: Ok, let me look at your checking account history, and then we'll talk . . .

Unit 4

CD 1, Track 11, Page 52
A. Pronunciation: Syllables and Stress Listen and repeat.
1. the At·**lan**·tic **O**·cean
2. the Ap·pa·**la**·chian **Moun**·tains
3. the Mis·sis·**sip**·pi **Ri**·ver

CD 1, Track 12, Page 52
B. Listen and mark the stress.
1. **Ca**·na·da
2. **Mex**·i·co
3. the U·**ni**·ted **States**
4. the **Rock**·y **Moun**·tains
5. the **Grand Can**·yon
6. A·**las**·ka
7. Ha·**wai**·i
8. the Pa·**ci**·fic **O**·cean
9. Death **Val**·ley

CD 1, Track 13, Page 52
C. Listen. Point to each location on the map.
The United States

This is a map of the United States. The United States is a large country on the continent of North America. There are three countries in North America: Canada, the United States, and Mexico. The United States is in the middle. Canada is to the north, and Mexico is to the south.

The United States reaches from the Atlantic Ocean on the east to the Pacific Ocean on the west. To the south is the Gulf of Mexico.

There are 50 states. Forty-eight states are called the continental United States. Two states, Hawaii and Alaska, are separate. Hawaii is a group of islands in the Pacific Ocean, and Alaska, the largest state, is far to the northwest.

When you look at the map of the United States, you see that many of the major cities are on the coast. These cities all have excellent seaports. On the east coast, you can see Boston, New York, and Miami. New Orleans is on the Gulf of Mexico. On the Pacific Ocean, you can find San Diego, San Francisco, and Seattle.

There are two major mountain ranges in the United States; both run from north to south. In the east, the Appalachian Mountains are an older, lower mountain range. In the west, the Rocky Mountains are a younger and much higher mountain range. Snow covers the tops of the Rocky Mountains most of the year.

This map of the United States shows the east, the central area, and the west.

The east is light green. This is an area of coastal plains and low mountains. From Boston to Washington, D.C., is a line of large cities and towns.

The central area is blue. In the northern part are the five Great Lakes, lying on the border between Canada and the United States. The Mississippi River begins in the north and flows south to New Orleans and into the Gulf of Mexico. There are many farms and ranches in the central and southern areas.

The west is yellow. The geography of the west is very dramatic with high mountains, valleys, and deserts. There are many beautiful national parks in this part of the country such as the Grand Canyon in Arizona and Death Valley in California. Millions of tourists visit the national parks every year.

CD 1, Track 14, Page 57
A. Listen to the complaints about world problems.
Complete the sentences. Use the words in the box.
1. When is it going to rain? It hasn't rained here for two months!
2. Many people are out of work. Stores and factories are closing.
3. Many people don't have a place to live. They are living on the street.
4. That country is very poor. Many people are hungry.
5. It snows and snows. It's snowing again today. When is the snow going to stop?
6. I live in the city. It takes me 30 minutes to drive five miles.

7. I live in the city. It takes me 30 minutes to drive five miles. There aren't any buses in my area.
8. People drink water from plastic bottles. Then, they just throw out the bottles. Most people don't recycle them.

CD 1, Track 15, Page 58
The Big Picture: Montana
Montana is the fourth largest state in the United States. It is located in the northwestern part of the country. On the north, it shares a border with Canada. Montana is divided into two geographic areas. The Rocky Mountains are in the western part of the state. The Great Plains cover the eastern part. Several important rivers run through Montana. The Missouri River, the second longest river in the United States, begins in Montana.

The western part of Montana receives a lot of rain and snow. Because Montana is so far north, it has very cold winters. There are often heavy snowstorms. In the other seasons, there is a lot of rain. Because the Rocky Mountains are so high, they stop the rain clouds, and the eastern part of the state is dry.

With fewer than 800,000 people, Montana has one of the lowest populations in the United States. There are about 50,000 Native Americans living in Montana. Many of the Native Americans live in the state's seven Indian reservations, while others live in small towns and cities throughout the state. Towns and cities are small and far apart.

Thousands of tourists visit Montana every summer and fall to enjoy the beautiful scenery, to hike in the mountains, and to fish in the rivers and lakes. Some tourists stay at the many large horse ranches in the Great Plains. In the winter, skiing is popular.

CD 1, Track 16, Page 59
E. Listen and write the questions you hear. Then, ask and answer the questions with a partner.
1. How many rivers are there in Montana?
2. How many Indian reservations are there?
3. How much snow is there in the Rocky Mountains?
4. How much industry is there in Montana?
5. How much tourism is there?
6. How much traffic is there in Montana?

CD 1, Track 17, Page 65
B. Listen to one student's report. Discuss the questions.
I'm going to talk about Tennessee. You spell Tennessee T-E-N-N-E-S-S-E-E. Tennessee is in the southeastern United States. It borders eight states. On the north, there is Kentucky and Virginia. On the east is North Carolina. On the south, there are three states: Georgia, and Alabama, and Mississippi. The Mississippi River is on the west. The two states on the west are Arkansas and Missouri. The capital of Tennessee is Nashville. You spell Nashville N-A-S-H-V-I-L-L-E. The population of Tennessee is 6,300,000. That's 6,300,000 people. Tennessee is a beautiful state to visit, and there are many things to do there. If you love music, visit Nashville. Nashville is the capital, but people also call it "Music City, USA." Nashville is the center of the country music industry. You can listen to famous country singers at the Grand Ole Opry House. If you like the outdoors, visit Great Smoky Mountains National Park. More people visit Great Smoky Mountains National Park than any other park in the United States. It's in the eastern part of the state and most of the park is a forest. You can go hiking, or fishing, or biking, or camping. There are several historic areas in the park, also. Be careful, there are a lot of bears in the park.

Unit 5

CD 1, Track 18, Page 68
B. Listen to each speaker. Ask questions and guess what he or she is doing. Then, listen again and compare your questions.
1. Ok, everyone . . . smile! Say "pizza"!
2. You are approaching your turn. At the traffic light, turn right on Main Street.
3. The rain will end this afternoon. We're expecting sunny skies tomorrow with temperatures in the upper 60s . . .
4. Yes. I'd like a room for three nights. We're arriving on the 14th . . .
5. I'd like a large order of pork fried rice . . . and the sweet and sour chicken . . . and two egg rolls.
6. Please tell her that Jake called. That's Jake Parker. My number is 555-7172.
7. I'd like the car for the weekend . . . March 15th to the 17th. Do you have a weekend rate? . . . A standard size is fine.

CD 1, Track 19, Page 69
B. Listen to the conversation. Then, practice it with a partner.
A: What are you doing?
B: I'm writing a report.
A: What software are you using?
B: I'm using Write Now.
A: How's it coming?
B: Very slowly. And it's due tomorrow.

CD 1, Track 20, Page 70
C. Pronunciation: Wh-Questions Listen and repeat.
1. Where is he going?
2. Who are you texting?
3. What is she studying?
4. Who is she calling?
5. What're you listening to?
6. Which game is she playing?
7. What are you ordering?
8. Which site are you using?

CD 1, Track 21, Page 74
The Big Picture: Cruiseaway.com
Part 1
Cruiseaway.com is a travel site for cruises. People go on the site and plan their cruise vacations. They can find information on over one hundred cruise companies that offer cruises worldwide. They can look at photos of the ships, they can see the maps of different routes, they can check prices and dates, and they can make cruise reservations, all online. Cruiseaway.com designed, organized, and programmed the website. They update the site with new information every day. But, the employees do not work with customers directly. If people need more information, they call the specific cruise line directly.

CD 1, Track 22, Page 75
Part 2
Today is a typical day at Cruiseaway.com. Megan and Samip are programmers. Megan is updating information for one of the cruise lines. She's adding a new 10-day cruise in the Caribbean. She's playing with a stress ball. Samip is drinking a can of soda. He's debugging the site; in other words, he's checking for errors and fixing them. Michael is the manager. He's on the phone, talking to one of the cruise companies about adding a new ship and several new vacations. Antonio, another programmer, is taking a break. He's drinking a cup of coffee and playing with a remote control car. Lee is just arriving at work. He usually doesn't

arrive until 10:00, but he works until 8:00 in the evening. Most of the employees work nine or ten hours a day. When they are working on a big project, they work 11 or 12 hours a day. When the programmers are not at work, one is always on call. If the site goes down, even in the middle of the night, that person has to get the site up and running again.

Unit 6

CD 1, Track 23, Page 83
C. Pronunciation: Medical Specialists Listen. Mark the stressed syllable. Then, listen again and repeat.

sur-geon
car-di-**ol**-o-gist
oph-thal-**mol**-o-gist
pe-di-a-**tri**-cian
fam-i-ly **doc**-tor
ob-ste-**tri**-cian
der-ma-**tol**-o-gist
gy-ne-**col**-o-gist
al-ler-gist
psy-**chi**-a-trist

CD 1, Track 24, Page 86
A. Discuss the new vocabulary. Then, listen to the conversation between Mr. West and the doctor. Answer the questions.
D: These are the x rays, Mr. West. Jimmy has a broken leg. It's a bad break. The nurse is putting ice packs on his leg now because it's swollen quite a lot. We need to wait for the swelling to go down, so we're going to keep him in the hospital for two days, and then we'll put the cast on.
M: How long is he going to need the cast?
D: For children, it's usually six to eight weeks.
M: He's in a lot of pain.
D: We're going to give him something for the pain in a few minutes. Is he allergic to anything?
M: No, he isn't.
D: He's going to need painkillers for a few days.
M: Can he go to school?
D: Don't worry. He will be back in school next week. But he's going to need crutches.

CD 1, Track 25, Page 88
A. Pronunciation: I'll Listen and repeat.
1. I'll help you.
2. I'll call her.

3. I'll drive you.
4. I'll make dinner.
5. I'll visit you.
6. I'll take you to the doctor.
7. I'll pick up your prescription.
8. I'll see you tomorrow.

CD 1, Track 26, Pages 90 and 91
The Big Picture: The Accident
There was a bad accident at the intersection of Maple and Central Avenue about 10 minutes ago. A woman went past the stop sign and hit another car. A witness who saw the accident immediately called 911. The police and two ambulances were at the scene of the accident a few minutes later.

Luis is lying by the side of the road. His arm is cut very badly. One emergency medical worker is applying a pressure bandage to stop the bleeding. The other technician is talking to him and taking his blood pressure. She's telling Luis that the bleeding is under control. Soon they are going to take him to the hospital. Luis is going to need 30 or more stitches in his arm.

Two other emergency workers are helping the woman on the stretcher. She is pale and confused. She doesn't know her name, and she can't answer any questions. One worker is covering her with a blanket. Because the front windshield of her car is broken, the workers think that she might have a concussion.

A police officer is directing traffic at the scene. Traffic is moving very slowly because everyone wants to look at the accident.

CD 1, Track 27, Page 97
D. Listen to the conversation between a caller and a 911 dispatcher. Answer the questions.
A: 911. What is the emergency?
B: My daughter ate some of my medication. She's lying on the floor of the bedroom.
A: What is your location?
B: 521 Chestnut Street. In Garfield.
A: Please stay calm. Repeat that address.
B: 521 Chestnut Street. Garfield.
A: Stay on the line. Help is on the way. How old is your daughter?
B: She's four. Oh, my baby.
A: Where is your daughter now?
B: She's on the floor. In my bedroom.

A: Is she breathing?
B: Yes, she's breathing. But, she isn't moving.
A: What kind of medicine did she take?
B: It was medication for high blood pressure.
A: How many did she take?
B: I don't know. I don't know.
A: Ma'am, the ambulance is on the way. Is your door unlocked?
B: No. No. It's locked.
A: Unlock the door. Do that right now. Unlock the door.
B: Yes, I unlocked it.
A: When the medics arrive, give them the bottle of medication.
B: Yes. Yes. I will. Oh, the police are here.
A: Ok. The ambulance is right behind them. You can hang up now.

Unit 7

CD 1, Track 28, Page 99
C. Pronunciation: Comparative Adjectives Listen and repeat.
1. busier
2. taller
3. larger
4. noisier
5. friendlier
6. farther
7. rainier
8. higher
9. sunnier

CD 1, Track 29, Page 102
C. Pronunciation: Superlative Adjectives Listen and repeat.
1. the busiest
2. the tallest
3. the largest
4. the noisiest
5. the friendliest
6. the farthest
7. the rainiest
8. the highest
9. the sunniest

CD 1, Track 30, Page 106
The Big Picture: Three Cities
Chicago, Illinois; Los Angeles, California; and New York, New York, are the three largest cities in the United States. New York is the largest of these three cities, with a population of more than 8,325,000 residents. New York includes the five boroughs: Manhattan, Brooklyn, Queens, the Bronx, and Staten Island. New York is

one of the most diverse cities in the world. Approximately 28 percent of the residents are of Hispanic origin. Of the three cities, New York had the lowest unemployment in 2010, with an unemployment rate of ten percent. Household income is the income of all the people living in the same house. The average household income in New York is $43,500. Homes in New York are expensive; if you are looking for a home in New York, plan to spend about $458,000. Commuting to work takes more than 30 minutes in all three cities. Traveling to work takes the average person 44 minutes in New York. Only 25 percent of workers in New York drive to work. It is very expensive to drive into the city and parking is difficult to find, so more than half of the workers in New York use public transportation. There is always something to do in New York City. There are more than 115 museums. The Metropolitan Museum of Art is one of the most visited museums in the world. Another popular tourist destination is the Statue of Liberty. The weather in these three cities is very different. New York receives about 46 inches of rain a year and about 23 inches of snow. It has a lot fewer days of sunshine than Los Angeles. Los Angeles receives about 284 days of sun a year; New York receives about 224 days of sun.

Unit 8

CD 1, Track 31, Page 116
B. Pronunciation: Final -ed Listen. Write the number of syllables you hear. Then, listen again and repeat.
1. changed
2. rented
3. looked
4. needed
5. liked
6. wanted
7. helped
8. called
9. lived
10. painted
11. signed
12. waited

CD 1, Track 32, Page 116
C. Pronunciation: Linking -ed + vowel sound Listen and repeat.
1. He lived in a small apartment.
2. He looked at many apartments.
3. He filled out a rental application.
4. He signed a lease.
5. He packed all his things.
6. He borrowed a van.

CD 1, Track 33, Page 117
A. Listen and repeat.

Simple Form	Past	Simple Form	Past
be	was / were	buy	bought
become	became	come	came
begin	began	cost	cost
bite	bit	do	did
break	broke	drink	drank
bring	brought	drive	drove
eat	ate	read	read
fall	fell	ring	rang
feel	felt	run	ran
fight	fought	say	said
find	found	see	saw
fly	flew	sell	sold
forget	forgot	send	sent
get	got	sit	sat
give	gave	sleep	slept
go	went	speak	spoke
grow	grew	spend	spent
have	had	steal	stole
hear	heard	take	took
know	knew	teach	taught
leave	left	tell	told
lose	lost	think	thought
make	made	wake	woke
meet	met	wear	wore
pay	paid	write	wrote
put	put		

CD 1, Track 34, Page 120
E. Jarek is talking about some important events in his life. Listen and complete the time line.
Ok. This is my time line. The first date I put is 2003 because in 2003 I graduated from high school. And, a few months after that, I found my first job. And I worked and I saved money and in 2005 I bought a car. I already had my license, but I didn't have a car. The next year, that's 2006, I went back to Poland to visit my family and my friends. My grandparents live in Poland, and it was my grandmother's 75th birthday, so everyone went back to Poland to celebrate. Then in 2008, I found another job, a better job, as a store manager. I met Eva . . . she's now my wife . . . in 2008, too, and we got married in 2009. After we got married,

the next year, in 2010, we moved to Chicago and that's where we still live today, in Chicago.

CD 1, Track 35, Page 122
The Big Picture: We moved . . . again!
A: We just moved . . . again! When I was in my country, I lived in the same house for 22 years. We got married five years ago . . . and I've moved five times.
B: Five times?
A: The first time was the move here, to the United States. I married Diego and we moved to Easton. We had a small one-bedroom apartment in Easton. Our neighbors were really nice.
B: So, why did you move?
A: We liked our neighbors, but the apartment building was old and we had a lot of problems. The landlord wasn't helpful, and he didn't fix things. The elevator was always broken. The air-conditioning was always broken. One time in the winter, we didn't have heat for three days! So, we moved to an apartment in Dover, but we missed our friends and it was too far from Diego's job.
B: Is that why you moved?
A: No. We had a baby and the apartment was too small, so we moved to a two-bedroom apartment. It was back in Easton, but in a nicer building. I was really happy to be near our friends again.
B: But you only lived there for a year.
A: Right. Diego changed jobs. Well, he didn't change jobs. His company promoted him and transferred him here, to Atlanta. But, we didn't know anything about the area, so we rented an apartment. We signed a lease for a year to give us time to look around and get to know the area.
B: That was last year, right?
A: Yes, and we just bought this house last month. There's lots of room for us and for our little girl . . . and now we're expecting another baby. But, yesterday we got a phone call from Diego's sister. She just got a visa, and she wants to come and live with us.
B: Uh-oh!

CD 1, Track 36, Page 128
B. Listen to the conversations. Write the problem and the apartment owner's response.

Conversation 1
Owner: Hello, Mike Paulis speaking.
Tenant: Hi, Mr. Paulis. This is Sam Jenkins, from Apartment 205. Our air conditioning isn't working.
Owner: Oh, no. . . . What's your thermostat set at?
Tenant: 75 degrees. It's 82 in here now.
Owner: I see . . . will you be home this morning?
Tenant: No, I'm working today.
Owner: Well, tomorrow is Saturday. Will you be home?
Tenant: Yes, I'll be home all day.
Owner: Great. I can come tomorrow morning around 10:00.
Tenant: Ok, thanks. See you tomorrow morning.

Conversation 2
Owner: Nora Colwell.
Tenant: Hello, Ms. Colwell. This is Sara Darmon, from Apartment 4. I called you yesterday—about the freezer. It isn't working. All the food in the freezer went bad.
Owner: Really? That's almost a new refrigerator.
Tenant: Actually, I looked at the date on the side of the door. The refrigerator is 15 years old.
Owner: Huh. Well, will you be home this morning?
Tenant: Yes, I'll be home.
Owner: I'll come up this morning, then.
Tenant: Ms. Colwell, you told me that yesterday, and you never came. I had to throw out all the food in the freezer.
Owner: Well, that is a problem. I'll be there today at 9:00.
Tenant: Ok. I'll be waiting.

CD 2

Unit 9

CD 2, Track 1, Page 130
A. Listen and repeat the natural disaster or event. Then, write the correct word under each picture.

hurricane
flood
earthquake
heat wave
drought
volcanic eruption
forest fire
snowstorm / blizzard
tornado

CD 2, Track 2, Page 132
A. Complete the questions and answers. Then, listen and check your work.
1. How deep was the water?
   It was six feet deep.
2. How strong was the wind?
   It was a hundred miles per hour.
3. Were you in Texas during the drought?
   Yes, I was.
4. How long was the drought?
   It was five months long.
5. Was there any rain?
   No, there wasn't.
6. Where were the tornadoes?
   They were in Nebraska.
7. Were you at home?
   No, I wasn't. I was in my car.
8. How many tornadoes were there?
   There were four.
9. When was the earthquake?
   It was last year.
10. How strong was the earthquake?
    Thankfully, it wasn't strong.
11. Were the children in school?
    Yes, they were.
12. Were any children hurt?
    No, they weren't.

CD 2, Track 3, Page 133
A. Pronunciation: _Did you_ Listen and repeat.
1. Did you see the tornado?
2. Did you watch the storm on TV?
3. Did you evacuate?
4. Did you have any damage?
5. Did you feel the earthquake?

CD 2, Track 4, Page 138
The Big Picture: The Hurricane
A: That was a really bad hurricane you had last month!
B: I know. It was our first hurricane since we moved here to North Carolina. We thought it was terrible, but the old-time residents told us it was just an average one.
A: How much warning did you have?
B: Warning? That's all we got. Twenty-four hours a day, all day. For about a week. The radio, the TV, the newspapers. The news was nonstop.
A: So, what did you do to get ready?
B: Well, we had to get everything out of the yard. We put the yard furniture,

the barbecue grill, the garbage cans, everything, into the garage. If we didn't, they could fly through a window during the hurricane. And we bought lots of food—canned food—in case we didn't have power for cooking. We had to buy batteries for flashlights and radios. And they told us to buy water, lots and lots of water. And we filled the bathtub with water, too. We also bought a power saw.

A: A power saw?

B: Hmm, hmm. Hurricanes knock down trees. And in a bad hurricane, two or three trees might fall in your yard. Everyone around here has power saws to cut them up.

A: How bad was the hurricane?

B: I thought it was terrible. The rain was so heavy we couldn't see out the windows. The wind was about 80 miles an hour, and it reached 100 miles an hour at times. It knocked down the power lines, and we didn't have electricity for two days. We were lucky—only one tree came down in the backyard. But our neighbor had a tree come down right through his roof into one of the bedrooms upstairs. He had water all over, in all the rooms.

A: So, did you evacuate?

B: No, we stayed in the house. For this storm, most people stayed in their homes.

A: Were you scared?

B: I was so scared! Most of the time, I stayed in the bathroom. I thought, any minute, something was going to come flying through a window or that a tree was going to fall on our house. My husband was more relaxed. He lit candles and listened to the news on a battery-operated radio.

A: So, are you glad you moved to North Carolina?

B: Well, we really like it here, but these hurricanes . . . I don't know. Maybe we'll get used to them.

Unit 10

CD 2, Track 5, Page 147
C. Jennifer and Brian are engaged. It's October, and they're getting married in late August. Listen. Match the month and the task.

First, Jennifer and Brian have to announce their engagement. They want to tell their family and closest friends. In November, they have to reserve the ceremony site and a place for the reception. It's important to reserve early. In December, Jennifer has to order the dresses for herself and for the bridesmaids. Selecting the right dress sometimes takes a long time. Jennifer and Brian have to book the band in January because they have a favorite band, but it's very popular. In February, they have to start planning the honeymoon. They'll get a good price if they reserve early. Planning the guest list will take time. They have to start planning in March. In April, they have to order the invitations. Jennifer and Brian want to visit different florists, and they plan to reserve the florist in May. In June, they are going to mail the invitations because they want to make sure all of their friends can attend. In July, Brian and Jennifer will go to City Hall to apply for the marriage license. Now, all that's left is the wedding.

CD 2, Track 6, Page 148
B. Pronunciation: *Have to / has to* Listen and circle the correct modal.
1. I have to take my children to school.
2. She has to wear a uniform.
3. They have to start work at 8:00.
4. I have to study for the test.
5. He has to make plane reservations.
6. She has to renew her license.

CD 2, Track 7, Page 148
C. Listen and repeat.
1. I have to go to the Laundromat.
2. She has to work overtime tomorrow.
3. They have to do their homework.
4. I have to pay my telephone bill.
5. He has to get gas on the way home.
6. She has to make a doctor's appointment.

CD 2, Track 8, Page 149
A. Listen. Hannah is talking to an older co-worker. Who does each chore? Write *D* for *Dad*, *M* for *Mom*, or *H* for *Hannah*.

Sofia: Hannah, your life is really going to change after you get married.

Hannah: Change? Of course it's going to change. It's going to be perfect.

Sofia: You have stars in your eyes.

Hannah: What do you mean?

Sofia: Hannah, how old are you?

Hannah: I'm 19.

Sofia: And you live with your mom and dad, right?

Hannah: Until June 15th, our wedding date.

Sofia: Hannah, who cleans the house now?

Hannah: My mom does. And I clean my room.

Sofia: And what about dinner?

Hannah: Well, my dad cooks and my mom washes the dishes.

Sofia: Ok. Who does the food shopping?

Hannah: Usually . . . my mom does.

Sofia: And who pays the bills?

Hannah: I'm not sure. I guess both my parents pay the bills. I pay my cell phone bill.

Sofia: And who does the laundry?

Hannah: My mom.

Sofia: Does Randy live with his parents, too?

Hannah: Yes.

Sofia: And how old is Randy?

Hannah: He's 20.

Sofia: Do you and Randy ever talk about your life after you get married? Who is going to cook, clean, and do the laundry?

Hannah: No. I'm sure we'll do everything together.

Sofia: Oh, boy. Are you sure you're ready to get married?

Hannah: Of course, we are. We're in love.

CD 2, Track 9, Pages 154 and 155
The Big Picture: Where's My Dress?

Interviewer: Ok, Freddy, I hear that you have an interesting wedding story.

Freddy: Oh, that was a long time ago.

Interviewer: I don't care. Tell me about your wedding. Where did you get married?

Freddy: Well, the ceremony was at my wife's church. It was in August. August 4th.

Interviewer: How many attendants did you have in your ceremony?

Freddy: Let's see. In the ceremony, we had 21 attendants, and there were about 500 people in the church.

Interviewer: Five hundred people in the church? That is a big wedding. So, who was in your wedding party?

Freddy:	My wife, Louise, is an only child, but her father has 15 brothers and sisters. I have a pretty big family, too. Most of the people in the wedding party were our relatives.
Interviewer:	Fifteen brothers and sisters? Wow! So, who was your best man?
Freddy:	My best man was my friend Carl. We grew up together.
Interviewer:	Who was Louise's maid of honor?
Freddy:	She had both a matron of honor and a maid of honor. They were both close friends.
Interviewer:	I see. What did Louise wear?
Freddy:	Well, it's kind of an interesting story. She had a dressmaker. He told her how much the wedding gown would cost, and she gave him the money, but she never saw him again. He left with all the money. When she told me, I said, "Where is he?" I was going to go with her father to get the money. But she wouldn't tell me the address. This was one week before the wedding.
Interviewer:	One week before the wedding? What did she do? Did she call the police?
Freddy:	No, she didn't want to. Oh, and he took all of the bridesmaids' money, too, so we had to do everything again. You know that Louise's a singer, right?
Interviewer:	Right.
Freddy:	Well, Louise was working in a Broadway show at the time. One of the guys who was in the show said, "I'll make your dress for you." This was only one week before the wedding, and he made the dress. It was absolutely beautiful.
Interviewer:	And what about the bridesmaids' dresses?
Freddy:	He made them, too!

Interviewer:	Wow! That's an amazing story. So, did her family pay for this?
Freddy:	Yes, they had to pay for the wedding dress twice and for the bridesmaids' dresses. The first time, the bridesmaids paid for their own dresses, but after the dressmaker ran off with the money, Louise felt bad, so she paid for them as well.
Interviewer:	That is an incredible story. How long have you been married now?
Freddy:	We've been married for 25 wonderful years.

Unit 11

CD 2, Track 10, Page 163
B. Listen. Write the request for each item.
1. Could you please answer the telephone?
2. Would you please bring this to the mail department?
3. Would you please make five copies of this form?
4. Could you please repair the printer?

CD 2, Track 11, Page 163
C. Pronunciation: *Would you* and *Could you* Listen and repeat each request in Exercise B.
1. Could you please answer the telephone?
2. Would you bring this to the mail department?
3. Would you please make five copies of this form?
4. Could you please repair the printer?

CD 2, Track 12, Page 169
B. Listen. Circle the letter of the sentence with the same meaning as the sentence you hear.
1. Maybe I'll take a break.
2. I need the number of the technology department. Please look up the number.
3. There's no smoking in this building.
4. Your interview is tomorrow, and your hair is too long. You need a haircut.
5. Your license is expired. You need to renew it.
6. Tomorrow is Labor Day. The company is closed.

CD 2, Track 13, Page 170
The Big Picture: A Confident Employee
1. Good morning, Carla, Tommy. Carla, how's your mother? Is she still in the hospital? Tommy, could you please work an extra hour today? Carla needs to leave an hour early. Good. Thank you.
2. Mr. Samuels, we send the lab results to your doctor. . . . No, we don't send you a copy. . . . Let me give you a card. If you would like a copy of your results, you have to call the number on the card. . . . The doctor will have the test results in three days. If the doctor doesn't call you, you should call her.
3. Randy, this is Sharon Taylor at County General. We sent you our weekly order, but I'd like to add two boxes of latex gloves. . . . Yes, 500 count. . . . Yes, could you please add two boxes to the order? Thanks.
4. Good morning, Ms. Parks. You are having a blood test this morning. Did you eat anything this morning? . . . Oh, you had coffee and a donut. . . . Ms. Parks, this is a fasting blood test. You can't eat or drink anything for twelve hours before the test. . . . The doctor didn't tell you? . . . Don't worry. We can do the test tomorrow. You have to come back tomorrow morning at 8:00. And you can't eat or drink anything after 8:00 tonight.
5. Ms. Chavan, we have to make a copy of your insurance card. You have Red Lion Insurance, so you only have to make a $10 co-pay. We will file your insurance claim for you. Sam, could you please make a copy of this insurance card? Please put it in Ms. Chavan's file. Thank you.
6. Doug, you were good with that little boy. He was really scared about having a blood test, but he came out of your lab smiling.

CD 2, Track 14, Page 177
C. Look at the photo on page 176. Listen to Sharon Taylor's job interview. Then, answer the questions.
Mr. Parker:	Good afternoon, Ms. Taylor. Please, have a seat.
Ms. Taylor:	Thank you.
Mr. Parker:	So, Ms. Taylor, your experience is good. You work at County General Hospital. Could you tell me more about your job there?

Audio Scripts · **265**

Ms. Taylor: Yes, I am the administrative assistant in the diagnostic labs department.

Mr. Parker: And how long have you had that position?

Ms. Taylor: I received the promotion two years ago to administrative assistant. Before that, I was a receptionist in the department. Then, I attended community college and took courses in administration and computers— word processing . . . spreadsheets.

Mr. Parker: What are your responsibilities in your position?

Ms. Taylor: Well, I make appointments, file patients' records, and schedule meetings. I'm responsible for ordering supplies and scheduling the staff. And I prepare all of the lab letters and forms. I also help with the spreadsheets.

Mr. Parker: That's good. Do you have any experience supervising employees?

Ms. Taylor: I trained the new full-time receptionist, and I trained the weekend receptionist. I introduced them to our procedures and answered their questions about our computer system. We are using the MedStar system, which is the same system you use here at Bay City.

Mr. Parker: Why are you interested in a position here?

Ms. Taylor: Well, County General is a small office. We have 12 employees. Your diagnostic lab division is growing. You have an excellent reputation here at Bay City. I would like to be part of your team. I can bring energy and experience.

Mr. Parker: Well, Ms. Taylor, you have the kind of experience we're looking for. We will be interviewing three more applicants this week. We'll probably have an answer for you next week.

Ms. Taylor: Thank you, Mr. Parker. It was nice meeting with you. I look forward to hearing from you.

Unit 12

CD 2, Track 15, Page 178
A. Look at the pictures and listen to Henry's schedule.

Henry is a single father with two children. His son, Diego, is 11 and his daughter, Jessica, is 10. He drops his children off at school at 8:00. After he drops off the children, Henry stops at a coffee shop for a large cup of coffee. Then, he drives to work at the bank. His children get home from school at 3:15, but Henry doesn't get out of work until 4:00. As soon as the children get home from school, they call their father. Henry gets home from work at 4:30. The family eats dinner at 6:00. After they eat dinner, Henry helps the children with their homework. They can watch TV or play video games when they finish their homework. Before they go to sleep, the kids have to get their backpacks ready for the next day. Henry relaxes or watches sports on TV after the kids go to bed. He goes to sleep at 11:30.

CD 2, Track 16, Page 178
B. Pronunciation: Pauses Listen and repeat. Pause at the comma.

1. After he drops off the children, Henry stops at a coffee shop.
2. As soon as the children get home from school, they call their father.
3. After they eat dinner, Henry helps the children with their homework.
4. When they finish their homework, they can play video games.
5. Before he goes to sleep, Henry watches TV.

CD 2, Track 17, Page 179
B. Listen. Then, practice the conversation with a partner.

Co-worker: You get a call every day at 3:15, don't you?

Henry: Yes, that's my son. He's 11. My daughter is 10. They walk home together after school. My son has to call me as soon as they walk in the door.

Co-worker: Oh, I see. My boys are still little. They stay at day care until I pick them up at 4:30.

Henry: Big kids, little kids. Childcare is a challenge when you're working.

CD 2, Track 18, Page 180
B. Listen. Tammy is talking about Emma's day. Take a few notes.

I am a stay-at-home mom. My little girl, Emma, is one and a half years old, and she keeps me busy all day. I'm planning to stay home until she is two years old. Emma wakes up at 7:00. As soon as she wakes up, she wants a bottle. After her bottle, I give her breakfast. Then, I get her dressed. From 9:00 to 10:30, I clean the house and do laundry. She plays and follows me around the house. At 10:30, we walk to the park. There are lots of other mothers and fathers with their children at the playground. I have a chance to relax and talk to other parents. We are home by 12:00. I give Emma lunch and a bottle. Then, she's ready for her nap. She sleeps from 1:00 to 3:00. At 4:00, I put her in her car seat. We go shopping, or I take her to the library. She loves books, and I check out five or six books a week. We are home by 5:00. When we get home, I start dinner. Emma plays on the kitchen floor with the pots and pans. My husband walks in the door at 6:00, and Emma can't wait to see him. He plays with her until dinner. We have dinner at 7:00. After dinner, I give Emma a bath. Then, my husband reads her a bedtime story. She's in bed by 8:00.

CD 2, Track 19, Page 184
The Big Picture: Working Parents

Ava and her husband, Matt, have two children, Timmy and David. Timmy is three years old, and David is five. The mornings are always busy because Ava and Matt are working parents. At 5:45 the alarm clock rings, and Matt jumps out of bed. He uses the bathroom first and takes a shower. When he goes back into the bedroom, he wakes up Ava. After Ava gets up, she wakes up the children, then starts to make breakfast. Matt puts on a DVD for the boys because they're sleepy, and the DVD gives them a chance to wake up slowly. Matt gets dressed and eats breakfast. Before he leaves for work, he kisses the children and Ava good-bye. After Matt leaves, Ava eats breakfast with Timmy and David. After breakfast, she gets dressed and gets the boys ready for the day. Then she takes them out to the car, and the boys climb into their car seats. Ava buckles the boys into their car seats, then drives to the day care center, which is about 15 minutes from the house. As soon as she drops off the boys, Ava drives to work. She's a hairstylist. She's often a little late for work, but her customers understand because they are mothers, too.

Unit 13

CD 2, Track 20, Page 193
A. Listen. Jonathan came home and saw that someone had robbed his apartment. A police officer is interviewing Jonathan. Write the things the thief stole.

Police officer: Wow! The robber really made a mess.

Jonathan: Uh, Officer . . . my apartment always looks like this.

Police officer: Oh, excuse me. Now, where were we? What time did you leave this morning?

Jonathan: I left at 8:30.

Police officer: Did you lock the door?

Jonathan: Yes, I'm sure I locked the door when I left. I was in a hurry, but I know that I locked the door.

Police officer: Did you lock the windows, too? The windows are open now.

Jonathan: Of course, I did. Well, maybe I didn't. I don't remember. I was late for work, and it was very hot when I went to bed last night. I opened the windows before I went to bed, but I overslept. Maybe I forgot.

Police officer: OK, sir. What time did you come home?

Jonathan: I came home at 6 P.M.

Police officer: When did you notice that something was wrong?

Jonathan: Well, as soon as I walk in the door, I usually put my keys on a table by the door. Well, the table was gone, and the keys fell on the floor!

Police officer: What else?

Jonathan: I went to turn on the TV, but it was gone. And so was my stereo, my DVD player, and all of my CDs! That was a great collection! I can't believe someone stole all of my CDs!

Police officer: Now, we'll have to dust for fingerprints. Did you touch anything else besides the door when you came in?

Jonathan: I opened the refrigerator, and my leftover Chinese food was gone, too.

Police officer: Are you sure that you didn't eat it?

Jonathan: I'm positive! I was saving that food for dinner tonight!

Police officer: I'll call the detectives, and they will check for fingerprints. Then, you'll have to fill out a report.

Jonathan: Thank you, Officer.

CD 2, Track 21, Page 194
C. Pronunciation: Word Stress Listen and repeat. Pay attention to the content words in **bold**.
1. Before I **left** my **home**, I **locked** the **door**.
2. When we **went** on **vacation**, we **stopped** the **mail**.
3. She **turned on** the **alarm** before she **left** her **apartment**.
4. They **closed** all the **windows** before they **left**.
5. I **called** the **police** as soon as I **saw** the **broken door**.
6. I **dialed 911** when I **heard** a **noise downstairs**.
7. After **someone robbed** their **house**, they **bought** a **dog**.

CD 2, Track 22, Page 194
D. Listen and complete the conversation.
A: Someone robbed my house!
B: Oh, no! What happened?
A: When I was at work, someone broke into my house.
B: Really? How did they get in?
A: I forgot to lock the windows before I went to work.
B: Oh. What did they take?
A: They took my computer, the TV, and my camera.

B: Did you call the police?
A: I called the police as soon as I walked in the door.

CD 2, Track 23, Page 200
The Big Picture: A Robbery at the Jewelry Store
1. This is Spike, and he's a burglar. Last night, he tried to rob a jewelry store, but the police caught and arrested him. Spike likes to break into homes, jewelry stores, and cars, but he is not good at his profession.
2. Late last night, Spike and his girlfriend, Tina, drove downtown. While Tina was driving, Spike put on a mask, a black hat, and a pair of gloves.
3. When they arrived at a jewelry store, Tina parked on the side of the store, where it was dark. Spike got out of the car.
4. Spike broke a window with a towel and his fist. He didn't make a lot of noise.
5. As soon as he broke the window, he climbed into the store.
6. After he got into the store, he looked around at the jewelry. He decided to take some expensive watches, necklaces, and rings. He put the jewelry into his bag.
7. While he was robbing the store, Tina was waiting in the car. She was watching for the police.
8. Spike was getting ready to leave when he saw some leftover pizza on a table. "I'm a little hungry," he thought. When Spike picked up the pizza, he dropped his bag of jewelry.
9. As soon as the bag fell on the floor, an alarm rang.
10. When Spike heard the alarm, he grabbed the bag and left the store. When Tina heard the alarm, she started the car and tried to drive away.
11. When Spike got out of the store, he saw a police car coming down the street, and he began to run.
12. As soon as the police saw Spike, one officer got out of the car and chased him. The other officer stayed in the car.
13. The other officer blocked Tina's car before she could drive away.
14. While Spike was running, he took off his mask and hat, but he forgot to take off his gloves.

15. Spike stood on a corner with a group of other men, but as soon as the police officer saw his gloves and the necklace in his pocket, he arrested Spike.
16. The police officers then arrested Tina. They handcuffed both of them and put them in the back of the police car.

Unit 14

CD 2, Track 24, Page 213
D. Listen to Jessica's career plans. Take notes. Then, answer the questions.

Jessica is a student at a community college. She is 20 years old, and she lives at home. Right now, she is taking the last level of English classes. She's also taking a math class and a biology class. When she completes these classes, she is going to begin the physical therapy assistant program. School is expensive. Before she begins the program, Jessica is going to apply for financial aid. When she attends classes, Jessica is not going to work. She is going to go to school full time. Her parents are going to help her with her expenses. Jessica plans to complete the program in two years. Before she graduates, Jessica is going to get a lot of experience because all students work in physical therapy clinics two afternoons a week. Jessica will apply for a job before she graduates. The college helps all the students find jobs. After she graduates, Jessica will earn about $30,000 a year.

CD 2, Track 25, Page 214
A. Pronunciation: Question Intonation Listen and repeat.
1. What are you going to do if you win the lottery?
2. What will you do after you finish this class?
3. If she gets a promotion, what is she going to buy?
4. When he finishes college, where will he work?

CD 2, Track 26, Page 215
D. Listen to the conversation between two students. Then, practice the conversation with a partner.
A: What are your plans for next year?
B: I'm going to finish my English classes.
A: What are you going to do when you finish your classes?
B: When I finish my English classes, I'm going to enter nursing school.
A: Where are you going to work after you graduate?
B: I'm going to work in the emergency room of a hospital.

CD 2, Track 27, Page 216
The Big Picture: Career Choices

I have a decision to make. Right now, I'm a salesman at a small telephone company. I sell cell phone plans and, to tell you the truth, I'm pretty good at it. I have had the job for five years, and this year, I'll make $40,000. But I'm bored, and I'm thinking about making a change. I'm not sure what to do. I had a job interview last week at TeleCell International, a large telecommunications company. The company is looking for someone with my experience. The job sounds interesting because it offers more variety than my current job. If I get the job, I will sell both national and international cell phone plans. The company offers good benefits, including medical and dental insurance. The salary is higher, too. I will make $5,000 more than I do now. I will also receive a promotion after one year if I become one of the top 20 salespeople. The company is located only 30 minutes from my home, so I won't have to move. But there are disadvantages to the new job. At this company, I will have to take frequent business trips to other states to visit customers. Also, I will have to go overseas seven or eight times a year to visit our international customers. That's a lot of travel.

I have another idea. I'm thinking about opening my own business. There's a small store available downtown. I'm thinking about renting it. It's right in our neighborhood. If I'm my own boss, I'll be more independent. I can select my own employees. My wife, who is an accountant, will take care of the bills and the payroll on the weekend. I won't have to travel unless I want to, and I can set my own working hours. In my store, I would like to sell telephone cards, cell phones, and all the accessories, like headsets. I'm really excited about the idea of having my own place.

But, you know, there's a lot of risk in opening my own business. I'll need a bank loan, and I'll have to pay for my own medical insurance. There's a lot of paperwork, too. I like working with customers, not paperwork. This is a very important decision for me and for my family, but I need to make a decision this week. I just received a job offer from TeleCell International.

CD 2, Track 28, Page 216
B. Listen. Circle the job that fits each description.
1. He'll have good benefits.
2. He'll sell cell phone plans.
3. He may receive a promotion after one year.
4. He'll be more independent.
5. He'll have to travel often.
6. He'll sell telephone cards.
7. He won't have to move.
8. He'll set his own working hours.

Unit 15

CD 2, Track 29, Page 225
B. Listen and write the answers. Use the words on page 224.
1. Who's trying on sunglasses?
2. Who's collecting garbage?
3. Who's delivering a package?
4. Who's washing the windows in the apartment building?
5. Who's making plane reservations?
6. Who's walking the dogs?
7. Who's delivering mail?
8. Who's selling hot dogs?
9. Who's writing parking tickets?
10. Who's remodeling the hair salon?

CD 2, Track 30, Page 228
C. Pronunciation: 've been, 's been Listen and repeat.
1. He's been looking for a job.
2. We've been planning a vacation.
3. They've been painting their house.
4. I've been enjoying my new boat.
5. She's been reading a good book.
6. I've been dating a wonderful guy.

CD 2, Track 31, Page 228
D. Listen and repeat. Then, practice the conversation with a partner. Talk about your own life.
A: Hi, Raj. How's it going?
B: Pretty boring. I've been putting in a lot of overtime. How about you? What've you been up to?
A: We've been looking at apartments. We might move to the city.
B: Really? Good luck!

The Big Picture: Harry, the Doorman

Hello. My name is Harry and I'm the doorman at the Plaza, an expensive apartment building downtown, across from the park. I've been opening and closing the door at the Plaza for ten years. I stand here at the door all day, watching people come and go, talking to everyone. I know a lot about the people who live in the building.

Manuel is the young man in Apartment 1A. He's very depressed because his girlfriend moved out a few days ago. Manuel has been sitting in his apartment looking out the window. I didn't like his girlfriend very much. She never talked, never even said "Hello."

This is Ms. Chan, Apartment 1B, walking into her apartment. She's in great shape. She's 82 years old, but she walks two miles every day. She's been walking every day since she retired 17 years ago.

Denise lives in Apartment 2A and just got a dog. She brought it into the building late at night. No pets are allowed in the building. Some of the neighbors have been complaining to the landlord and saying that they hear a dog barking at night. But me, I say, "Dog? Barking? No, I don't know anything about a dog."

Leena is the tenant in Apartment 2B. She lost her job last month, and she's been looking for a new one. That's her right now. She's walking out of the apartment building. She has a job interview at 12:00.

There has been a lot of arguing in Apartment 3A for the past few months. Mr. Alvarez is tired of city life. He has a job offer in a small town. Mrs. Alvarez loves the excitement of the city with the restaurants, and shows, and museums. She wants to stay in the city.

Silvia lives in Apartment 3B. A few weeks ago, she met a nice young man at a party. He's been sending her flowers twice a week.

It's Danny birthday today. Danny lives in Apartment 4A, and he has lots of family and friends. He's been receiving cards and packages all week.

Mr. Wilson, in Apartment 4B, has been having financial problems. He didn't pay his rent last month or the month before. He's been receiving letters from different credit agencies, too.

There isn't much happening on the fifth floor. Apartment 5A is empty. Lots of people have been looking at the apartment, but rents in the city are very high. That apartment is renting for $3,000 a month. The apartment has been empty for three months.

Apartment 5B is quiet, but it's not empty. Mr. and Mrs. Shapiro have been traveling. They're on a cruise around the world, and they'll return at the end of the month.

E. Listen. Circle the letter of the correct answer.

1. Did Mr. Wilson pay his rent last month?
2. Has Mr. Wilson been having financial problems?
3. What did Denise get?
4. Does the landlord know that Denise has a dog?
5. Where did Mr. Alvarez receive a job offer?
6. Where does Mrs. Alvarez want to live?
7. What have Mr. and Mrs. Alvarez been doing?
8. Where does Danny live?
9. What has Danny been receiving?
10. How long has Harry been a doorman at the Plaza?

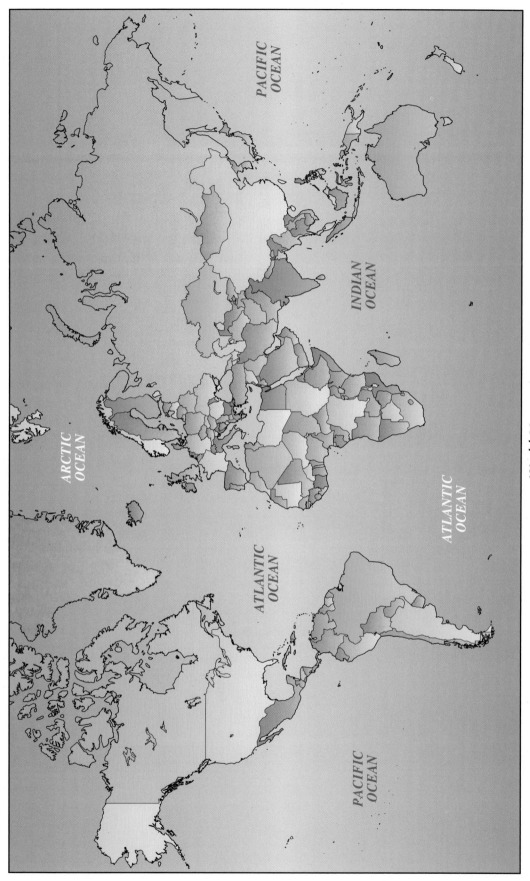

World Map

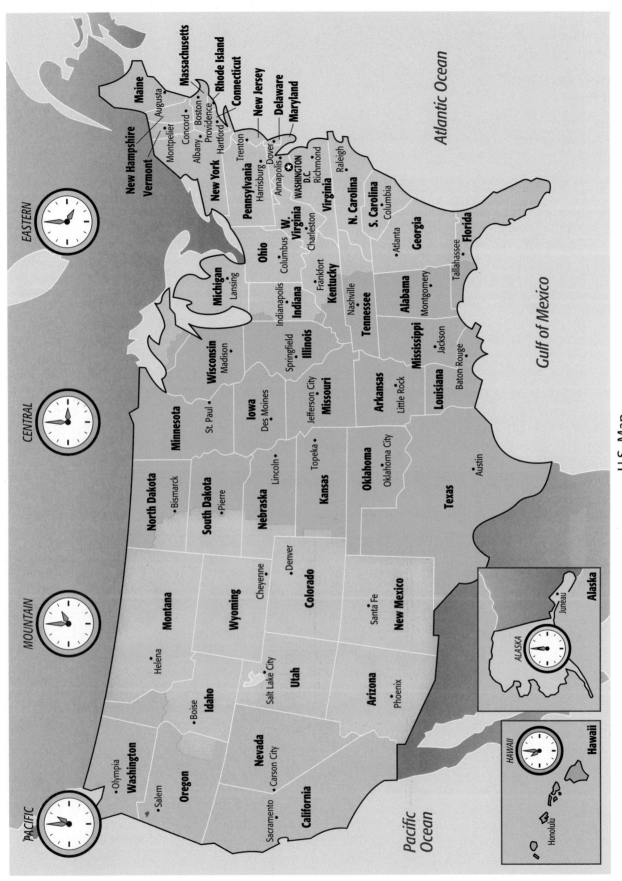

U.S. Map